Folk Songs of the World

Gathered from more than one hundred countries,
selected and edited, with commentary on their musical cultures
and descriptive notes on each song; in the
original languages with English translations, and with
chord suggestions for instrumental accompaniment.

CHARLES HAYWOOD

Drawings by Carl Smith

THE JOHN DAY COMPANY

New York

AMSCO MUSIC PUBLISHING COMPANY
Exclusive Distributor to the Music Trade

"Book designed by Carl Smith"

PRINTED IN THE UNITED STATES OF AMERICA

To Margaret Axtell Crane

Great teacher, musician, and pioneer
in bringing the riches of the world's folk music
to the children of America

"All songs of current lands come sounding round me."
—WALT WHITMAN

Preface

The major problem facing an anthologist is selecting the material and not the collecting, although the search may often be difficult and frustrating. Out of the thousands of folksongs (from published sources and oral transcriptions) carefully scrutinized for melodic contour, rhythmic elements, harmonic quality, textual content, and ethnic characteristics, the choice had to be made. Even then, more doubts and new questions rose up, and further evaluation was necessary. At last, the final "agonizing reappraisal," knowing full well that for every item selected voices would rise up, in friendly advice or critical disagreement, demanding to know why this or that song was excluded. What is finally presented must indeed be a reflection of personal taste, and, whatever the shortcomings, one can humbly declare, "mea culpa."

How much relatively easier it would be to compile a collection of songs for each country represented in this volume; one could be liberal and extensive in the selection. The songs would then reflect *every* facet of the peoples' lives. In this anthology, alas, stern considerations of space and expense obliged one to choose only a few songs—often not more than one or two!—for each country.

The chords are merely a suggestion for accompaniment of the piano, guitar, or any other suitable instrument. Any competent musician can easily offer other harmonic possibilities. The chords are, in most instances, quite simple, and mindful of the modal or tonal character of the melodies.

In dealing with the songs of cultures that do not employ the Western tempered tonal system—where the intervals between notes are smaller (microtonal) than our half-steps; where, consequently, Western concepts of harmony are in complete variance with the character of their melodies; where the methods of performance dif-

5

fer from Western practices—the suggested chords will hardly convey the true character of the melody. They are, at best, approximations. Indeed, the tunes themselves, as transcribed into Western notation, are approximations of the original performance. It might be advisable that those tunes be sung unaccompanied. Where the drumbeat or the handclap is available, that should suffice for background. Even in those instances where the melodies "appear" to offer Western harmonic possibilities and chords are given, they may be considered tentative, and their use be left entirely to the discretion of the performer.

To recapture the idiomatic folk expressions of one people into the language of another is well-nigh impossible. English does not often lend itself or yield easily to translation of inflectional languages, where a single word often conveys rich imagery and subtle nuance. I have tried to convey the general spirit and mood of the original poetic text, and wherever possible, I have maintained its rhyme and meter. Above all, I have sought to make the English versions singable.

In folk singing there is frequently great freedom and flexibility of text in the various verses in relation to the notes of the melody. It is, therefore, important that the singer become fully acquainted with the tune, its rhythm and structure. He will then find no difficulty in making the adjustment: prolonging a note, or subdividing it to admit more than one syllable of the text.

Adhering to the international character of this collection, Italian terminology has been used throughout to indicate tempi, dynamics, and occasional interpretive aspects.

Although the order in the Table of Contents and the classification of the various countries and peoples have been largely based on culture area similarities and affiliations, rather than on purely geographic location, this was not always possible. Due to the mobility, overlapping, and the intermingling of various peoples and their cultures, all classification involves elements of uncertainty. Although Madagascar, to cite but one example—and there are others—was placed among the countries *South of the Sahara,* because of its geographic position, it might, with equal justification, be placed with the *Indonesian Culture Area.* For a discussion of this matter, see the brief essay preceding "Madagascar." Indeed, all descriptive commentary is brief and general. I have tried to avoid overly detailed and highly technical discussion. It is hoped that the suggested selective Bibliography will encourage further research.

Charles Haywood
Queens College of the City University of New York

Acknowledgments

Grateful acknowledgments are extended to the following authors, publishers, editors and journals for their kind permission to use the material in this book. If any required acknowledgments have been omitted it is entirely by accident; it is deeply regretted and forgiveness humbly desired.

African Music Society, Hugh Tracey's comments in article "Short Survey of African Folk Music . . ." in *African Music Society Newsletter* No. 6 (Sept. 1953); Alma Book Co., London, Songs No. 67 and 89 in *The Golden Book of Polish Songs* by Adam Harasowski (1955); American Folklore Society, "Yo te amo idolatro," and "La Guajira" in *Spanish American Folksongs* (MFS 10) by Eleanor Hague, "Open de do" in *Folk Tales of the Antilles*, French and English by Elsie Clews Parsons (MFS 26), and "Isabella" in *Jamaican Folklore* by Martha W. Beckwith (MFS 21); Ernest Benn, Ltd., "Ho ro 'yo," in *The Celtic Song Book* by Perceval Graves (1928); Bishop Museum Press, "Mereu" in *Native Music of the Taumotus*, Bull. 109; Bruns, F. Bokhandel, "Karusellen" in *Sanglekene Våre* by Onkel George (1946); Paul Burlin, "Ockaya" in *The Indians' Book* by Natalie Curtis (1907); Clarendon Press, "Yadua" in F. E. Williams, *Papuans of the Trans-Fly* (1936); Columbia University Press, "Leba Gado" in *Suriname Folklore* by Melville and Frances Herskovits (1936); Community Publishers, Manila, Philippines, "Lulay" in *Filipino Folk Songs* by Emilia S. Reyso-Cruz (1950); Cooperative Recreation Service, "Keel Row" in *Informal Notes* (1960), "Mfoni" and "I'm Goin' Chop Crab," in *Africa Sings* (1958); Harold Courlander, "Danse Juba" in *Haiti Singing*, University of North Carolina Press (1939); Helen Creighton, "Crocodile Song" in *Songs and Ballads of Nova Scotia*, Dent & Sons (1933); A. B. Creyghton, "Khoe li" in *Inter. Gesell. f. Musik.* (1952) by Arend Koole; Crowell & Co., quotation from *Music of Latin America* by N. Slonimsky (1945); J. Curwen & Sons, Ltd., "Llinwgwyn Rhosyn Yr Haf," in *Old Welsh Songs* by S. Gwynn Williams (1927); John Day Co., "Hu a ku-ko," No. 2 in *The Flower Drum and Other Chinese Songs* by C. H. Chen and S. H. Chen (1943); Drei Masken Verlag, "Bucura t'e tintirim," in *Volksmusik der Rumänen von Maramures* by Béla Bartók (1923); L'Éclair (Montreal), "Gbodi," in *Aux Rythmes des Tambours* by Frère Basile (1951); Elias' Modern Press, Cairo, "Bintil Shalabeya," "Ah Ya Zane," and "Bafta

Hindi" in *Egyptian Folk Songs* by Baheega Sidky Rasheed (1958); A. P. Elkin (Australian Research Council), "Kaduguwai," in *Songs of the Trobriand Isles* by B. Baldwin, *Oceania* (1950); L'Eroica, "Shellila shek," in *Canti sacri e Profane degli Arabi dei Somali e dei Suahillie* by Gustavo Pesenti; *Ethnomusicology*, "Ngai i tanga i," by Edwin Grant Burrows, II (1958), "Nan Soboy," by Joseph Maceda, II (1958), "Seba Alaso," by Walter Kaufmann, VI (1962); Farrar, Straus & Young, "Barney and Katey," *Ballad Migrant in New England* by Helen Hartness Flanders and Marguerite Olney (1953); Foetisch Frères S. A., "Mir Senne heil's lustig," "Calme du Soir," and "E mi son chi in barchetta," in *Unsere Schweitzerlieder* by Paul Keller; Funk & Wagnalls Co., comments from Jonas Balys's articles on Estonia, Latvia and Lithuania in *Dictionary of Folklore* (1950); Harvard University Press, "Nuri," in *A Solomon Island Society* by Douglas L. Oliver (1955), "The Maid of Newfoundland," in *Ballads and Sea Songs of Newfoundland* by Elisabeth Bristol Greenleaf (1933); W. Heffer & Sons, "Sein kyu kya nyang," in *Six Songs of Burma* (1937); Hispanic Institute, Columbia University, "Las Chaparreras," in *Canciones Mexicanas* by Vincent T. Mendoza (1948); Instituto Español de Musicología, "Wou liang," in *Anuario Musical* 5 (1950), by Marius Schneider; International Folk Music Council, *Journal*, comments from A. L. Lloyd's review of Ramadan Sokoli's "Polifonia jöne populare" 13 (1961); Walter Kaufmann, "The Folksongs of Nepal ('Kana ma laune')," *Ethnomusicol.* 6 (May 1962); Alfred A. Knopf, "Night Herding Song," and "Great Grand-Dad," in *Singing Cowboy* by Margaret Larkin (1931); Henry Lemoine & Cie., "Debwangue," "Ka tam ma wui," "Tou oua," in *Choeurs de L'Afrique Equatoriale* by Elaine Barat-Pepper (1950); John McIndoe, Ltd., "Waita Aroha," in *Songs of the Maori* by Alfred Hill (1926); Macmillan & Co., "E! E! E!," in *The Mafalu Mountain People of British New Guinea* by Robert W. Williamson (1912); Edward B. Marks Music Corp., "Bailando el Gato," in *Recuerdo Latino Americano* by Irma Labastille (1943), "U Starej Breclavy," in *Memories of Czechoslovakia* by H. A. Schimmerling (1945); National Museum of Canada, Ottawa, "En roulant ma boule roulant" in *Come A Singing*, by M. Barbeau, A. Bourinot and A. Lismer (1947); Martinus Nijhoff, "Man paman goejang djaran," in *Music in Java* by Jaap Kunst, Vol. II (1949); The Nippon Times Ltd., "Yoneyama Jinku," in *Thirty-One Japanese Folk Songs* by Ryutaro Hattori (1954); Nordiska Musikförlaget, "Nu ar det jul igen," in *Sweden Sings* by Josef Jonsson (1955); Oesterreichischer Bundesverlag, "Der blaue Montag," in *Von der Eisenstrasse, Volksleider* . . . by Hans Commenda (1926); Ongaku-No-Tomo Sha Co., "Kochaé-Bushi," in *Japanese Folk*

Songs by Schuichi Tsugawa (1949); Oxford University Press, "Sovu Dance," in *Studies in African Music* by A. M. Jones (1959), "Thola li na mulandu," in *The Bavenda* by Hugh A. Stayt (1931), comments from Henry Farmer's article on "Arabian Music," in *New Oxford History of Music*, Vol. I (1957); Pan American Union, "Por un beso de tu boca," "Nací el la Cumbre," "Cancion del Marinero Hondureño," and "Estilo," in *Cancionero Popular Americano* (1950); Payot, Paris, "Mfene sandhleni," in *Moeurs et Coutumes des Bantous* by Henri A. Junod, Vol. II (1936); Frederick A. Praeger, "Balobere Nkere," and "Ssemusota," in *African Music from the Source of the Nile* by John Kyagambiddwa (1955); Routledge & Kegan Paul Ltd., "Gille Beag O," in *Folksongs and Folklore of South Uist* by Margaret Fay Shaw (1955); St. Martin's Press, Comments from the article on "Folk Songs," in *Grove's Dictionary of Music and Musicians*, Vol. III (1953); G. Schirmer, "Manth'ki," and "Iganda lo Ta'ndo," in *Songs and Tales from the Dark Continent* by Natalie Curtis (1920), "En Avant Grénadiers," in *Bayou Ballads* by Mina Monroe (1921); Silver Burdett Co., "La Tejedora de Ñandutí," in *Canciones Tipicas* by Irma Labastille; Barbara B. Smith, "Folk Music in Hawaii," *Journ. Inter. Folk Music Council*, 11 (1959); Société des Missions Évangéliques de Paris, "E, ie mo, tulene," in *Chants Zambéziens* by Théophile Burnier (1927); T. G. H. Strehlow, "Makereben," in *Jour. Inter. Folk Music Council* 7 (1955); Charles E. Tuttle Co., "Tuhl Tahryung," in *Folk Songs Hawaii Sings* by John M. Kelly, Jr. (1962); U. S. Government Printing Office, "Gonige Tagina," in *Chippewa Music* (II) by Frances Densmore (1913); "Aheru Tekis," in *Pawnee Music* by Frances Densmore (1929); University of Alabama Press, "Dese Bones Gwine Rise Ag'in," in *Folksongs of Alabama* by Byron Arnold (1950); Waterloo Music Co., Ontario, Canada, comments from Edith F. Fowke's Introduction to her *Folk Songs of Canada* (1954).

I am also very grateful to the Fulbright Commission for the grant as Research Professor in Austria, 1961–62. This gave me the rare opportunity to make extensive use in Vienna of the superb research material on the folk music of all peoples contained in the *Volkskunde Museum* (Dr. Leopold Schmidt), *Volkslied Archiv* (Prof. Karl M. Klier), *Phonogramm Archiv* (Dr. Walter Graf), and the *Musiksammlung* of the National Bibliothek (Dr. Leopold Nowak). These gracious scholars and their assistants were most helpful and cooperative. For Mr. Phil Rappaport's expert advice, I am very thankful. To the many libraries where I have worked, and to the librarians, who were always ready with helpful suggestions and wise counsel, my profound gratitude.

Contents

Latin America

13

Europe   105

15

Asia

17

Africa

Oceania

Australia 307

Folk Songs of the World

Greenland

Eskimo Music

Although various cultural levels and physical differences are present in this vast Arctic area, one may safely state that the main stylistic musical characteristics of the Eskimos inhabiting Greenland are generally similar to the other Eskimo tribal groups of the circumpolar Arctic culture area extending from Alaska to Greenland. With rare and notable exceptions, the majority of commentary before 1900 by travelers, explorers, social scientists, and in some instances, even musicians on "primitive music" have been steeped in cultural bias and aesthetic prejudice.

Based on the scholarly studies of Franz Boas, Zygmunt Estreicher, Diamond Jenness, Helen H. Roberts, William Thalbitzer, Hjalmar Thuren, to mention but a few, and, more recently, Bruno Nettl's perceptive and critical observations in his *North American Indian Musical Styles,* Eskimo music emerges as a highly integrated and, often, complex folk art expression. What appeared to Murdoch as "a monotonous chant" is really an undulating melody, usually lying within the range of fifth or major sixth, with the majority of the intervals consisting of major seconds and minor thirds, but often varied with alternating minor seconds and major thirds, with a general downward direction at the end of the tune. The melodic patterns fall within a three (tritonic), four (tetratonic), or five (pentatonic) tone scale. The songs are usually performed in a recitative-declamatory style, with frequent vocal tension, producing uncertain pitches (according to the Western notational system). Each melody consists of the repetition and variation of short motifs. However, the recurrence of the variations, at different points, produce startlingly refreshing effects, and convey a feeling of improvisation. In Greenland the melodic and structural variation is effected through the alternation of solo and chorus response.

Perhaps the most exciting aspect of Eskimo music is the rhythmic complexity; the interplay of a variety of durational note values, producing a pulsing activity of contrasting accents and meters. And yet, within this heterometric organization, there is rhythmic unity and control. Indeed, a remarkable example of consummate folk art. The musical performance is further heightened by rhythmic drumbeats, and enlivened by appropriately expressive bodily movements. The frame drum with handle is common in Greenland.

There is a great variety of dances, reflecting the social culture of the group. They range from the solo dances of the Caribou Eskimo, with very little bodily movement, with only a few steps forward and backward, to wild round dances with torches by the Eskimos of Alaska, or the orgiastic dances observed in Greenland.

Canada

The mainstreams of Canadian folk music have been well summarized (with allowance for a few breezy oversimplifications) by Edith Fulton Fowke: "Canadian songs spring from varied and colorful sources: from the French-Canadian *habitants* [the rural peasantry] who sang as they cleared their farms along the St. Lawrence, and from the *coureurs de bois* who sang as they paddled across Canada's many waterways; from the pioneer settlers who brought to the new world the traditional ballads of England, Scotland, and Ireland; from the sailors and fishermen of our maritime provinces who sang as they ran up the sails or pulled in their nets; from the prospectors of the far north, the sod-busters of the prairies, and the roving lumberjacks who sang around the shanty stoves when their day's work was done. Even before the white man came to Canada, our plains and forests resounded to the songs of the Indians invoking their gods, and the Eskimos sang in their igloos to while away the long Arctic nights."

A fuller discussion of North American Indian music can be

26

found in the introductory essay dealing with the folksongs of the United States; and for a more correct estimate of the place of music in Eskimo society, see the comments under Greenland.

Although considerable research has been done in Anglo-Canadian folksong traditions, particularly in the Maritime Provinces, it does not compare with the wealth of material collected and studied among the French-Canadians. The pioneering work was begun by F. A. H. LaRue and Ernest Gagnon in the 1860's, and continued by a number of highly gifted and enthusiastic researchers and scholars; the most prominent among them has been Marius Barbeau. Their studies and collections contain a rich variety of old ballads, lyric songs, work songs, carols, children's songs and games that have their roots in France.

The early French settlers in the seventeenth century came from the provinces of Normandy and the Loire River, which had been strongly influenced by the music and poetry of the *jongleurs* (medieval wandering minstrels, whose accomplishments also included juggling). Their songs were more deeply rooted in the folk traditions than those of the *troubadours* of southern France, where the strict forms of courtly poetry and their related and dependent vocal compositions evolved. In contrast, as Marius Barbeau lucidly stated, "the *jongleurs* had not come under the influence of medieval Latinity; these northern poets had never given their allegiance to a foreign language since the birth, before the fifth century of Christianity, of the Low Latin vernaculars, in France, Spain, Portugal, and Italy. They had inherited and conserved the older traditions of the land. Presumably they were the heirs of the ancient Druids and the Celtic culture that had undergone a mutation without altogether going out of existence." However, southern cultural influences later did affect northern areas, particularly in the Loire. These contrasting aspects in the folk music can be found in the French settlements in Canada. Those who migrated to the eastern districts of Quebec, Charlevoix and Gaspé, came from Normandy. Here one finds more ballads and *complaintes* (similar to the British and Anglo-American "Come All-Ye's"). Those who

27

settled around Three Rivers and Montreal came mainly from the Loire area; they brought with them a greater number of lyric songs, *pastourelles*, and strongly rhythmic tunes and dances.

The United States

Numerous factors have shaped American civilization and have given it its uniqueness. To mention but a few: the people, of different ethnic, social and cultural backgrounds, flocking to its shores from all corners of the earth; the abundance of land for exploration, settlement and exploitation, and where "democratic vistas" were beckoning and could be turned to reality. The saga of this dramatic adventure, from the Colonial days to the present, is vividly reflected in its folk music. It was this stirring music on the land that fired Walt Whitman's poetic imagination and prompted him to announce, "I hear America singing, her varied carols I hear."

Here one can only touch upon a few of the highlights, and briefly mention the various types and chief characteristics of the American folksong heritage. But first, a few comments on the music of the American Indian, frequently neglected in popular anthologies. To the untutored ear all Indian music (and this may also be said of all "primitive" music) sounds alike. Yet careful scrutiny reveals a variety of musical styles among the various culture areas, and often among the tribes within the same area. This diversity, observed in the structure, and configuration of the melodies, the rhythmic patterns, and the manner of percussion accompaniment, and style of performance, is a reflection of the total culture: the physical environment, manner of gaining a livelihood, the social organization, religious beliefs, and all other aspects that affected and shaped their lives. Thus, in some areas, the music is relatively simple (the desert tribes of Nevada and the Yumans), while the songs of the Northwest area Indians are of great rhythmic complexity. Similar stylistic diversities may be observed in the music of other culture areas.

Nevertheless, certain traits persist to a great extent in the majority of Indian songs. The most noticeable are: The pentatonic mode is prevalent; the tunes are largely monophonic, and are sung solo

28

or in unison, harmony or part-singing is rare (and this occurs only in the more complex culture areas); the frequent downward motion of the melodies, where the final note, on the tonic, is usually the lowest note of the song; the most frequent intervals are major seconds and minor thirds, with the range of the melodies usually extending between a perfect fifth and a perfect twelfth; the rhythms are often quite complicated and are constructed heterometrically; most Indian songs are strophic, the same melody repeated for each verse; the song texts often consist of meaningful words and meaningless syllables, and the latter remain unchanged in a particular or related series of songs from one performance to another (these sounds evidently possess definite poetic significance to the Indian); there is a metrical independence between the singing voice, and the accompanying drum; the latter usually in a rapid unaccented beat, and the voice, according to Frances Densmore, having a rhythm which bears relation to the mental concept of the song; independent drumming, the kind one encounters in Africa, never developed among the North American Indians; and the same may be said of purely instrumental music, the exception being the flute love songs of the Plains Indians. Indian music is functional and encompasses every aspect of the Indian's life.

Since the English colonists succeeded in establishing permanent settlements on the North American continent, their cultural heritage is the dominant factor in American life. Theirs is the language of the land, and their folk music the strongest influence. Indigenous factors—ethnic, geographic, historical, and social—have deeply affected the Old World music, and have endowed it with special characteristics peculiar to the American scene. These distinctive features are evidenced in the textual, melodic, and rhythmic American variants of old English ballads, lyric songs, nursery songs and dances performed in the various states and regions in the country.

The westward movement and frontier life created a large body of folk music reflecting every aspect of this mighty epic. These songs not only depict the hardships and privations, but their rollicking gaiety and inherent humor as well. This hardy folk also knew how to release their energies in lively dances, social games, play parties, spirited fiddle tunes, twanging banjo rhythms, or sing sentimental songs to the droning accompaniment of the dulcimer.

The various wars, from '76 to World War II, and, particularly, the Civil War, have contributed a large repertory of folksongs. The various ethnic groups that make up the essential uniqueness of the United States have furnished their share of folk music and dance. And, *above all,* the Negroes have contributed to this country the richest vein of musical tradition. Indeed, they have given to the United States (through a long agonizing history of despair, blood and tears) the peculiar flavor and idiom, through its melody and rhythm, the most distinguishing characteristics of American music in general.

America at work: lumberjacks, miners ('49ers, bituminous and anthracite), the cowboy, the railroaders, the sailormen and river boatmen, the industrial workers—all have produced a body of folksongs reflecting their toil and economic struggles. The overwhelming problems of America's growth have brought forth a group of characters, historical and legendary—"good, bad, and awful"—who dramatized through their deeds the birth pangs of a growing country, and with appropriate songs to recount their bold careers. The multifarious religions practiced by these heterogeneous peoples—the American folk—are reflected in their spiritual and devotional folksongs.

As a consequence of the profound social, political, and economic changes brought into American life in the twentieth century, we have witnessed a gradual shifting of the population from the rural areas to urban centers. This has had a marked effect on folksong tradition, continuity, and creation. The rural area is gradually giving way to the urban center, not only as a repository of old traditions, but where a new folksong is being created.

Greenland

Eskimo songs are usually performed in a declamatory (or *recitative*) manner, demanding strong initial attack, and aspirate accent at the end of the tune is quite common. The rhythms are quite complex, the melodies are of limited range, and are predominantly pentatonic, tetratonic and tritonic. This song is a violent expression of anger and derision.

English version by
Charles Haywood

Ajaaj—Drum Song
(Ammasalik Eskimo)

Moderato(♩=96)

A^wn^waa jaaa ha - jee   an - o aa   kee - a - gi - a -
Ah, ah, you've come back; You were once filled with fu - rious

nee nü aa - ni ta - taa - ja ja-aj - jaa - jaa
rage, You   were once coward and a-fraid to fight.

a - ja - ay__ oo__ jaa__   jaa - jee a^wn^waa ja-aa ha - jee
Have you ____ come back__ at last To__ seek__ ven - geance?

a^wn - o - aa   taa wa aa   te - nu - ät taa____
Wretch - ed fool! ride__ your bro - ken pu - ny sled

ja ja aj - jaa   jaa   a - ja - aj ___ oo.
For the fight; beat drums!   I am read-y, oh!

(♩=112) DRUM BEAT

etc.

31

Canada

A Huron war dance, depicting in strong rhythmic movement, vivid gesture, special costume, and sharply accented melody the discovery of the enemy, slow advance, sudden attack, and violent cry of victory.

Aniô—On to War

English version by
Charles Haywood

(Huron)

Allegro barbaro (♩=108)

A - ni - ô! A - ni - ô! A - ni - ô! A - ni - ô! A - ni - ô!
On to war! On to war! On to war! On to war! On to war!

A - ni - ô! A - ni - ô! A - ni - ô! *Jou oua___ ta - ni - a.*
On to war! On to war! On to war! My en'-my lurk-ing there.

Jou oua___ ta - ni - a. A - ni - ô! A - ni - ô!
My en'- my lurk- ing there. On to war! On to war!

A - ni - ô! A - ni - ô! A - ni - ô!
On to war! On to war! On to war!

You ken non oua ké - rin, You kin - cha can- non ouak... Oua!
Rea - dy am I for fight, Strik- ing with all my might...Oua!

(♪=92)   DRUM BEAT

etc.

Exaggeration in folksong, as in the tall tale, is characteristic of a people's growing-up; a kind of adolescent boasting in overcoming insurmountable odds.

Crocodile Song

1. When I was ship - wrecked and driv - en from the shore And all I had to go a - round the coun - try to ex - plore, was my Right val - ar - i - ty, whack val - ar - i - ty, chook val - ar - i - ty dey.

2. And steering up the other side I found the crocodile,
   From the tip of his nose to the end of his tail he was 10,000 miles,
   with a
   Right valarity, whack valarity, chook valarity dey.

3. The crocodile, you see, was not of the common race,
   For I had to get up a very tall pine for to look into his face,
   with a Right valarity, etc.

4. I bore away from his head one day with every stitch of sail,
   And going nine knots by the log in ten months reached his tail,
   with a Right valarity, etc.

5. The crocodile he set his mouth and thought he had his victim,
   But I went down his throat you see, and that is how I tricked him,
   with a Right valarity, etc.

One of the most popular and most widespread of French-Canadian folksongs. The *voyageurs* sang it lustily; the strong duple rhythm accentuating their paddling motion. In the words of Marius Barbeau: "For three centuries it has escorted as paddling song with its alternating solo and chorus the pioneer canoemen, *coureurs-de-bois*, and discoverers on their rambles up and down the rivers and across the prairie, the waste land, and the mountain."

En Roulant Ma Boule Roulant

English version by
J. Murray Gibbon

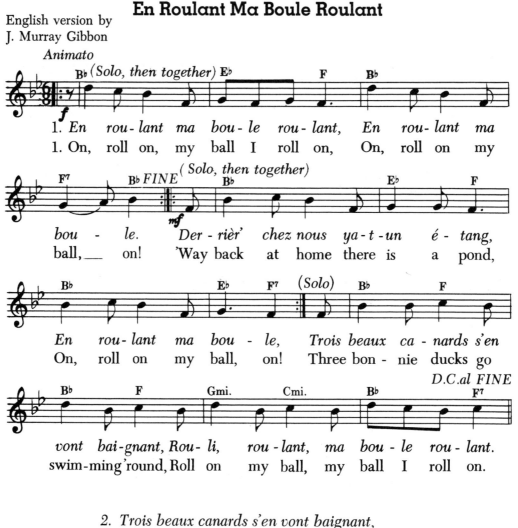

2. Trois beaux canards s'en vont baignant,
   En roulant ma boule.
   Le fils du roi s'en va chassant,
   Rouli, roulant, ma boule roulant, etc. etc.

3. Le fils du roi s'en va chassant,
   Avec son grand fusil d'argent.

34

4. *Avec son grand fusil d'argent,*
   Visa le noir, tua le blanc.

5. *Visa le noir, tua le blanc,*
   O fils du roi! tu es méchant!

6. *O fils du roi, tu es méchant!*
   D'avoir tué mon canard blanc.

7. *D'avoir tué mon canard blanc,*
   Par dessous l'aile il perd son sang.

8. *Par dessous l'aile il perd son sang,*
   Par les yeux lui sort' des diamants.

9. *Par les yeux lui sort' des diamants,*
   Et par le bec l'or et l'argent.

10. *Et par le bec l'or et l'argent,*
    Toutes ses plum' s'en vont au vent.

2. Three bonnie ducks go swimming round,
   On, roll on my ball, on!
   The prince goes off a-hunting bound,
   Roll on my ball, my ball I roll on, etc. etc.

3. The prince goes off a-hunting bound,
   His gun so big with silver crown'd.

4. His gun so big with silver crown'd,
   The black he saw, the white he down'd.

5. The black he saw, the white he down'd,
   O prince that was a wicked wound.

6. O prince, that was a wicked wound,
   To kill the white duck that I own'd.

7. To kill the white duck that I own'd,
   Each eye becomes a diamond.

8. Each eye become a diamond,
   Silver and gold her beak surround.

9. Silver and gold her beak surround,
   Beneath her wings a bloody wound.

10. Beneath her wings a bloody wound,
    The feathers in the wind fly round.

A favorite sentimental love song of the "old-timers" of Newfoundland.

The Maid of Newfoundland

1. Ye __ mu - ses mine, with me com - bine; Your aid __ I __ do in -
vite To sing in praise __ of her I love, My __
own sweet - heart's de - light; To sing in praise __ of
her I love Your __ aid I do de - mand. She's a
maid - en fair, I do de - clare, And __ she dwells in New-found-land.

2.

The diamond sparkles bright and clear
In many a queenly crown;
The virgin pearl beneath the sea
Lies many a fathom down;
The diamond, pearl, and peerless gem
Of Africa's sunny strand
Cannot compare, I do declare,
With the maid of Newfoundland.

3.

I've seen the maids of many lands
On many a foreign shore,
The French, the Greek, the Portuguese,
Likewise the swarthy Moor,
Chinese, Malay, and Austrian maids,
And the girls of Hindustan,—
But for beauty rare, they can't compare
With the maid of Newfoundland.

36

The United States

Song of a victorious Chippewa war party. The women led the procession, the scalp bearers in advance, singing and waving the scalps of the Sioux. After feasting and dancing, gifts were distributed. The following derisive and taunting song, consisting of a short, incisive rhythmic unit, repeated (with slight variation) five times, is then sung with great vigor. This pentatonic melody is made up of the intervals of fourths, minor thirds and major seconds, in downward motion ending on the dominant (the fifth of the scale).

Gonigétaginá—I Wonder

English version by
Helen Densmore

(Chippewa)

Allegro molto (♩=160)

Go - ni - gé - ta - gi - ná   a - ga - děn - da - mo -
Oh, I won - der at   her,   is she real - ly dis -

dog   O - ma - mi - k ▪ we (we)   gi - kic - ki - gwe-
graced, This wo - man of the Sioux,   I   cut   her head

jûg.   gi - kic - ki - gwe - jûg.   Ah!_____
off,   I   cut   her head off,   Ah!_____

(♩=104) DRUM RHYTHM

etc.

37

The Zuñi (Pueblo) women grind the corn in stone grinding troughs, or "metates." They do this work in a kneeling position, singing and swaying rhythmically back and forth.

English version by
Charles Haywood

Ockaya—Corn-Grinding Song

(Zuñi)

Allegro (♩=132)

E - lu hon- kwa lo - nan __ i - ya - ne! __
See the clouds are gath' - ring up in the sky. __

E - lu hon- kwa hli - ton __ i - ya - ne! Le - - kwa
See the rain will come _____ by __ and by. List - en __ well,

ke - la __ ai - yan - to - wa Pe - ne __ ai - ya -
lit - tle corn ear __ speak - ing, On the __ stalk gent - ly

ye _____ Ma - i - ho - ma an - tu - na, _____
sway - ing. Hear what __ she __ says, whisp' - ring soft - ly: __

Ai - yan __ tu - na Ho - lon - el - le - te Lilth - no
Clouds gath - er quick - ly, Bring down heav - y rains; Come, move

ke - la Kia - we __ kwai - i nu - wa - ne! _____
this way, Flood our __ gard - ens This ve - ry day! _____

> DRUM BEAT >

etc.

A variant of "Lord Randal" (Child, 12), one of the most widespread English traditional ballads. It appears under many different titles. Compare with Italian and Swedish versions, p. 156 and p. 169.

Henry, My Son

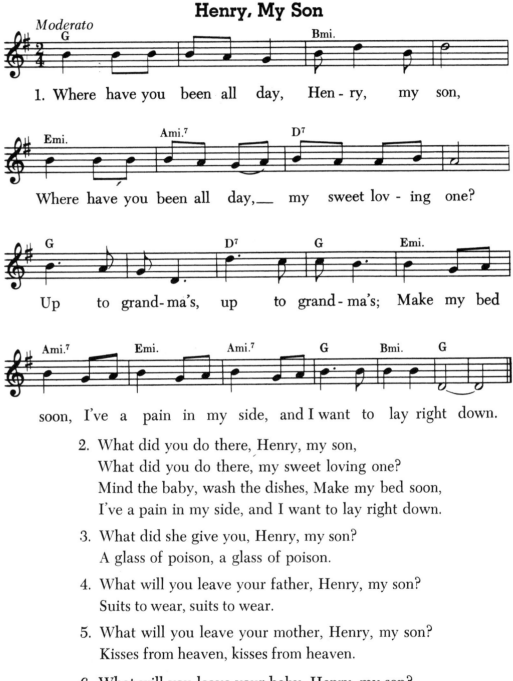

1. Where have you been all day, Hen-ry, my son,
Where have you been all day,— my sweet lov-ing one?
Up to grand-ma's, up to grand-ma's; Make my bed
soon, I've a pain in my side, and I want to lay right down.

2. What did you do there, Henry, my son,
What did you do there, my sweet loving one?
Mind the baby, wash the dishes, Make my bed soon,
I've a pain in my side, and I want to lay right down.

3. What did she give you, Henry, my son?
A glass of poison, a glass of poison.

4. What will you leave your father, Henry, my son?
Suits to wear, suits to wear.

5. What will you leave your mother, Henry, my son?
Kisses from heaven, kisses from heaven.

6. What will you leave your baby, Henry, my son?
Toys to play with, toys to play with.

7. What will you leave your Grandma, Henry, my son?
Ropes to hang her, knives to kill her.

39

This is truly one of the great American ballads celebrating the exploits of the mightiest steel-driving man in the country. A hero's legend has grown around John Henry, who, during the construction of the Big Bend Tunnel on the C. & O. railroad about 1873, dared stand up against the steam drill, and "died with his hammer in his hand." This unique version was sung by a student at the University of Minnesota.

John Henry

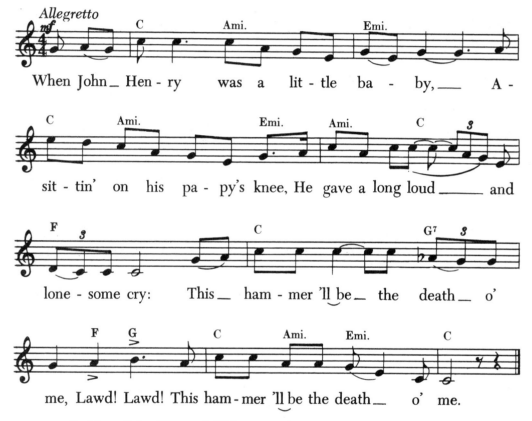

When John— Hen - ry was a lit - tle ba - by, ___ A -
sit - tin' on his pa - py's knee, He gave a long loud ___ and
lone - some cry: This ___ ham - mer 'll be ___ the death ___ o'
me, Lawd! Lawd! This ham - mer 'll be the death ___ o' me.

2. Now John Henry told his Capt'n one day,
   A man ain't nothin' but a man;
   But befo' I'll let this steam drill beat me down
   I'll die wi' dis hammer in mah hand, Lawd! Lawd!
   I'll die wi' dis hammer in mah hand.

3. When John Henry swung de hammer wid his mighty arm,
   An' brought it down deep in de groun',
   De people down in Mobile, a hundred miles away,
   Heard an awful rumblin' soun', Lawd! Lawd!
   Heard an awful rumblin' soun'.

40

4. John Henry had a pretty little woman,
   An' her name was Polly Anne;
   When John Henry took sick an' was layin' in bed,
   Polly drove steel like a man, Lawd! Lawd!
   Polly drove steel like a man.

5. When John Henry laid down an' died,
   Dere wasn't no grave big enough to hold his bones,
   So dey buried him in a box-car deep in de groun'
   An' de two tallest mountains are his grave stones, Lawd! Lawd!
   An' de two tallest mountains are his grave stones.

A glimpse at frontier life, its hardship and humor.

Great-Granddad

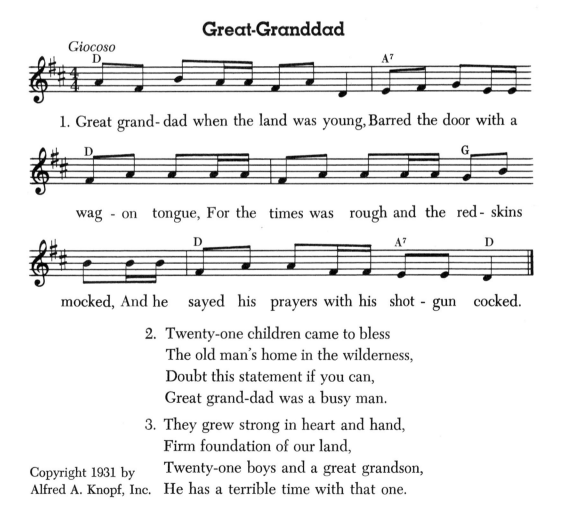

Giocoso

1. Great grand-dad when the land was young, Barred the door with a

wag - on tongue, For the times was rough and the red-skins

mocked, And he sayed his prayers with his shot-gun cocked.

2. Twenty-one children came to bless
   The old man's home in the wilderness,
   Doubt this statement if you can,
   Great grand-dad was a busy man.

3. They grew strong in heart and hand,
   Firm foundation of our land,
   Twenty-one boys and a great grandson,
   He has a terrible time with that one.

41

In the spirituals and blues the Negro has expressed his deepest feelings: the agonizing oppression, the profound outcry for freedom and redemption, as well as bitter and angry protest against human injustice. The Bible heroes became his leaders who would lead him to the "promised land." The African roots of Negro folk music are apparent in the leader-chorus pattern, in the importance of syncopation, and in the frequent downward motion of the melody.

Dese Bones Gwine Rise Ag'in

1. De Lawd he thought he'd make a man, Dese bones gwine rise a - g'in.

Made I'm out - a mud an' a han' full o' san',

Dese bones gwine rise a - g'in. I know'd it,

in - deed I know'd it brud - der.

I know'd it, dese bones gwine rise a - g'in.

2. *Solo:* He thought he'd make a woman too,
   Chor.: Dese bones gwine rise ag'in.
   Solo: Didn't know 'xactly what to do.
   Chor.: Dese bones gwine rise ag'in.
   Solo: I know'd it, indeed I know'd it brudder.
   Chor.: I know'd it, dese bones gwine rise ag'in.

3. He took a rib from Adam's side,
   Made Miz Eve for to be his bride.

4. He put 'em in a garden rich an' fair,
   Tole 'em dey could eat whatever wuz dere.

5. But of one tree you mus' not eat,
   Caize ef you do youse got to skeet.

6. De sarpint wrap him roun' a chunk,
   An' at Miz Eve his eye he wunk.

7. De Lawd he come wid a monstrous voice,
   Shook his ole earth to its joints.

8. Adam, Adam where art thou?
   Yes, good Lawd, I'se comin' now.

9. You stole my apples, I believe,
   No, Mas Lawd, I spec twas Eve.

10. From dis garden you mus' get,
    An' earn yo' livin' by yo' sweat.

11. Now of dis tale der am no mo',
    Caize Eve et de apple an' give Adam de core.

43

The cowboy's life—not the novelist's exaggerated hero nor Hollywood's tintype—more often a hard-working and weary cowpuncher.

Night Herding Song

2. I've cross-herded, and trail-herded, and circle-herded, too,
   But to keep you together, that's what I can't do.
   My horse is leg weary, and I'm awful tired,
   But if I let you get away, I'm sure to get fired.
   Bunch up, little dogies, bunch up!
   Hi-up! Hi-up!

3. Oh say, little dogies, when you going to lay down,
   And quit this forever a-sifting around?
   My back is weary, my seat is sore,
   Oh, lay down, little dogies, like you laid down before.
   Lay down, little dogies, lay down!
   Hi-up! Hi-up!

44

The influence of the French settlements in Louisiana is still vividly alive in the customs, songs and dances performed in New Orleans today. The Creole Negroes expressed their feelings in a curious admixture of French patois ("gumbo") and rhythmic melodies displaying African and French salon origins.

En Avant, Grénadiers—Forward March, Grenadiers

English version by
Charles Haywood

45

Latin America

The Caribbean Islands

These islands comprise four major divisions: the Bahamas, closely resembling Florida; the Greater Antilles, consisting of Cuba, Jamaica, Hispaniola (Haiti and the Dominican Republic) and Puerto Rico; the Lesser Antilles (extending from Curaçao to the Virgin Islands, consisting of the Windward and Leeward Islands); and the three islands of Trinidad, Tobago and Barbados. The Indian population of the West Indies was almost completely destroyed by 1600, with the exception of Cuba. However, by 1900 all Indian elements had disappeared there too. Nevertheless, traces of their musical heritage are still in evidence. Within the highly organized society in which they used to live, through the accounts left by the early chroniclers, and observation of the life and habitat of the present-day Circum-Caribbean tribes, one fully realizes the important role music played in their daily activities and in their religious and social festivals. Panpipes, flutes, conch shells, shell trumpets and a variety of drums, whistles, ocarines, calabash rattles, gourd rattles and musical bows were their chief instruments. The Arawaks and Caribs performed elaborate dances and songs (*areitos*).

The importation of Negroes from West Africa, the seizure and colonization of these islands, and the division of this imperial booty among France, England, Spain, the Netherlands, and, more recently, the United States, have profoundly affected the folk music of this heterogeneous population. Although the official language of these islanders has been determined by the colonial power in possession, the African culture and musical tradition have left their distinctive characteristics on their dialects, songs and dances.

Thus, in the folksongs of the various islands comprising this vast area, the dominant factor is the music of the African Negro fused with the cultural traits of the settlers. In Cuba one finds African traits blended with Spanish elements; in Haiti the influence of the French predominates; in Jamaica the Afro-English (or American) characteristics are apparent; in Trinidad, in the calypso, the acculturative effects of the French, Spanish and the English are displayed. All these varieties of African hyphenated musical patterns are found in the folk music of the islanders.

The Bahamas

The mainspring of Bahaman folk music comes from the Negro inhabitants of these many islands. Their songs and dances bear strong kinship with those of their "brethren" in the American Southern states. In their spirituals they too sing of their poverty, sorrows, and hopes; in "Egypt Lan'," exhorting "the sinners to "git on board" to the "Promised Lan'." In their evening gatherings, the "settin' up," they participate in communal song and dance.

African musical tradition has left its effects, in melody, rhythm and style of performance. One can readily recognize three distinct styles in their music: religious anthems, survivals of Anglican polyphonic hymn singing of the eighteenth century; spirituals, variants of those heard in the United States; and a popular folksong style used for dancing and parties. The guitar accompaniments often display remarkable virtuosity, but the technique is subsidiary to the absorbing group of rhythmic devices by which often-repeated simple figures are woven and interwoven into a colorful fabric. Other instrumental accompaniments are provided by the harmonica, fife and brass band music.

Cuba

Africa and Spain have shaped the music of Cuba. Thanks to the meticulous zeal and proselytizing fervor of the early *conquistadores* and settlers, the native Indian inhabitants were thoroughly exterminated, and there is little trace of their traditions in the folk culture of Cuba today. Acculturative factors in the last four centuries have created a distinct indigenous Afro-Cuban folk music. African cult life—with its myths, rituals, ceremonies and music—is still a formidable force in certain areas of Cuba. The four main cults that are found in western Cuba, according to Harold Courlander, are the *Lucumí* (Yoruba), the *Arará* (Dahomey), *Abakwá* (probably the Abakpa of Niger), and the *Kimbísa* (Congo). Each of these secret societies with its hierarchy of deities has its "own special constellation of musical instruments, and, to some extent, [its] own peculiar musical idiom." The African cultural traits are apparent in the character and quality of the melodies, the manner of performance, and in the richness and variety of drum rhythms and accompaniment: the solo-refrain pattern, and choral devices involving aspects of harmonic and contrapuntal character. Hispanic folk music has added its color and rhythm to the African melody. However, these subtleties are not always appreciated by those accepting cheap and exaggerated popularizations and stereotypes. Emilio Grenet, who has devoted many years to the study and collection of Cuban folksongs, is justly indignant at those who would corrupt or misrepresent his country's songs: "To our neighbors in the north, all Cuban music is reduced to the *Rumba*. But even the *Rumba*, that creature of our robust virility, is diluted and emasculated. . . . The Spanish are a step ahead in their comprehension of our music. They interpret it as a tropical siesta, in a slow cadence of the *Habañera* and the *Danzon*, no doubt because these dances are so ostentatiously Hispanic. . . ." Among other song-dances of Spanish origin may be mentioned the *guajira*, the *punto*, the *guaracha*, and the *comparsa* (pre-Easter procession). The *conga* and the *rumba* display the strongest characteristics of their African origin.

Dominican Republic

The island of Santo Domingo, of which the Dominican Republic occupies the eastern two thirds and Haiti the western third, was originally named Hispaniola by Columbus. The island has had a long, rich and varied musical tradition. Numerous early *comen-*

tarios (chronicles) give detailed description of the elaborate native Indian rituals and festivals in which singing, dancing, and numerous percussion and wind instruments played an integral part. The *areítos* (dance-songs), musical narratives recounting the heroic deeds of their gods and great leaders, were performed in resplendent costumes, intricate dance patterns, in which the whole community participated, singing loudly or softly as indicated by the leader, accompanied by drums of various sizes and sonorities. Little is left today of this heritage. Las Casas, who arrived at Santo Domingo in 1502, reports that "during the eight years when Don Nicholas de Ovando was Governor, nine-tenths of the native Indian population had perished at the hands of the Spanish colonists."

Although the Spanish influence is the dominant element in Dominican folk music today, the Negroes left their distinctive features. The latter are particularly discernible in many rhythms, dances and songs. One can still hear many old *romances* (ballads), *villancicos* (Christmas songs), and lyric songs of Spanish origin, as well as the more contemporary topical *corridos*. The most popular and representative dance-song of the country is the *merengue*. It is a spirited, syncopated tune in duple meter, consisting of two symmetrically constructed periods of sixteen bars each. The first section is usually in the major key, and the second is in the dominant or relative minor, with a cadential return to the original key. The *merengue* also includes a short introduction, called the *paseo*, and interludes known as *jaleo*. A national favorite is also the *bolero*, in two-four time, differing from the Spanish *bolero*, which is in three-four time.

Haiti

The population of the western third of the island of Santo Domingo, descendants of African slaves who were brought from the western coast of Africa, employs French as the official language of the country. Although historically influenced by the democratic principles of the French Revolution, it has maintained an unbroken cultural link with African traditions. Whatever "Latin" elements are present, they are, in the words of a native writer, Arthur C. Holly, "on the surface, while the primeval African strain dominates our souls. . . . Our senses respond naturally to the syncopated rhythms of the sacred dances of the Voodoo ritual, which inspire us with passion." Harold Courlander, long a keen and perceptive student of Haitian musical idiom, has clearly noted the roots of its distinctive qualities. "Some ballads and love songs in the more common Latin-American idiom are also heard in the towns but the full impact of *rumbas, congas, sones* and other so-called Afro-Cuban or Afro-Latin forms has never been felt because there has never been a musical vacuum in Haiti, and because the social sense of its own tradition was so deeply rooted."

As in most African music, the variety and complexity of the drumbeat dominate native Haitian musical expression. The drum patterns (often involving complex polyrhythms), the vocal inflections, and the expressive bodily movements of the dance are largely determined by religious beliefs and ritual ceremonies. The two chief African cults that still play a significant role in Haitian spiritual and musical life are the *Congo-Guinée* and the *Arado-Nago* groups, each with its own songs, dances, drum rhythms, deities, and rituals.

The national dance-song of Haiti is the *meringue,* similar to the *merengue* of the Dominican Republic. However, the former shows greater influence of African elements, and, more recently, jazz idiom. The Haitian composer Ludovic Lamothe has graphically described the manner in which this dance is performed: "The *meringue* is danced in the salons in a more dignified manner than the populace in the streets. There it is a veritable earthquake of hips and thighs, as in Africa."

Puerto Rico

Puerto Rico, more than any other island of the Caribbean, has maintained the closest cultural ties with its mother country. "Even today," declares Richard A. Waterman, "after two generations of American control, the roots of Puerto Rican art and literature are in Spanish soil." The same dominating tradition persists in its folk music—in the melodic contour and rhythmic accentuation. African musical influences have been minimal, with the exception of instrumentation or rhythmic patterning of some songs, such as the *plena*.

The *décima*, an old ballad song, popular in seventeenth-century Spain, consisting of ten octosyllabic lines rhyming *abbaaccddc*, is still heard in Puerto Rico today. It not only challenges the singers to display their skill in improvisation upon a given quatrain, but also to exploit the subject matter of current events. The *aguinaldo*, frequently in *décima* form and sung by masked strolling country folk, is heard during the *Pascuas* and Christmas time. Other favorite religious songs are the baptismal *Seis Villaran*, consisting of a quatrain followed by six lines; the *baquiné*, a wake for a young child, performed as a festive game-song; and the *Rosarios Canta'os*, sung rosaries. The *plena*, "sprung from the slums of the coastal town," is the most popular Puerto Rican folksong. It consists of a four-line refrain followed by a quatrain. The guitar, as in Spain, is the favorite accompanying instrument.

Trinidad

This southernmost West Indian Island, with Port-of-Spain the chief city, containing a heterogeneous polyglot population of many races and cultures, has produced a uniquely indigenous musical idiom, the calypso. The Spanish, French, English, Portuguese, Chinese, Creole, and, above all, the African Negro inhabitants have shaped the peculiar character of this song form.

Various theories have been suggested for the origin of calypso. To mention a few (after Crowley): *Kaiso* (an African word meaning "Bravo!"), *Carrousseaux* (a French word meaning "carouse," "debauch" from which the Creole words *cariso*, *calyso* and *cayiso* are derived), *Caliso* (a Venezuelan term for a topical local song), and *Carieto* (a Carib word for a joyous song). The calypsonians, dark-skinned Negroes, perform their songs—some prepared far in advance and others improvised at the moment—in tents from the end of the Christmas season until Carnival, two days before Ash

Wednesday. At Carnival time, the high point of the festivities, "all inhibitions go by the boards, imagination runs riot and the streets gyrate with a flowing stream of humanity." While a certain number of stock melodies are employed, the important thing is that the words must be fresh, related to topical events, derisive and satirical; interspersed with Creole slang words, with accents on important words falling on wrong syllables, and vowels and consonants frequently undergoing strange modifications. A favorite theme for all "calypsonians is woman, her attractiveness, her sexual voracity, her infidelity, and her sharp tongue." Calypso has been characterized as "strident, truculent, and breathless tunes . . . couched in naïf-grandiloquent jargon."

Formerly, the musical accompaniment consisted of *kalenda* (stickfighting) drum rhythms, *shak-shak* (maracas), bottle-and-spoon (or -stone), stringed instruments such as the *cuatro* or guitar, *tamboo-bamboo* (varying lengths of bamboo poles struck against the ground). In the tents the calypso singer is usually accompanied by stringed instruments, saxophones, clarinets and trumpets. However, the most popular band today consists of different tuned oil drums (thanks to Lend Lease!). Some extraordinary musical effects, in rhythm and melody, are produced by these ensembles. One Trinidadian aptly described the method of construction and tuning these steel bands:

> *Take oil barrel and cut it down,*
> *Take sledge hammer and beat it round.*
> *Heat it over fire,*
> *Tune as you desire.*

Calypsos usually consist of four verses of eight lines each, with the first two lines of the first verse repeated. A four-line chorus separates one verse from another. The melodies are set in 2/4 or 4/4 time, with frequent syncopations.

The Bahamas

A spiritual in which the elements of protest and the yearning for freedom are clearly evident. The leader-chorus pattern shows its African origin.

I Can't Stay in Egypt Lan'

2.
To-morrow mornin', baptisum day,
I cannot stay in de Egypt lan';
My gospel goin' from sho' to sho',
I can't stay in Egypt lan'.
Chorus:

3.
I looked on mi feet, mi feet looked new,
I cannot stay in de Egypt lan';
I swear by God I was runnin' too,
I can't stay in Egypt lan'.
Chorus:

Dominican Republic

A love song of intimate tenderness and sustained lyricism, displaying its Spanish origin through its melody and rhythm.

English version by
Charles Haywood

Adoración—Adoration

En si - len - cio __ te es - toy a - do - ran - do, ____
Si - lent - ly I __ a - dore you, be - lov - ed, ____

____ En si - len - cio __ me es - toy con - su - mien - do, ____
____ Si - lent - ly I'm __ with love's fire con - sumed, ____

____ En si - len - cio __ tam - bien voy su - frien - do. ____
____ Si - lent - ly I'm __ tor - ment - ed and an - guished. __

____ Du - ro gol - pe __ del ha - do fa - tal. __ En si -
____ Oh, how heav - y __ the blow fate did im - part. __ Si - lent-

55

tal. ___   Yo voy __ a mo - rir, _____   Yo voy __ a mo -
part. ___   I yearn __ for my death, _____   I yearn __ for my

rir, _____   Yo voy __ a mo - rir, Yo voy ___ a mo -
death, _____   I yearn __ for my death I yearn __ for my

rir,   Yo voy __ a mo - rir de un _ cró - ni - co
death,   I yearn __ for my death from the pain ___ in my

mal. _____   Yo voy ___ a mo - mal.
heart. _____   I yearn __ for my heart.

English version Copyright © 1966 by Charles Haywood

Haiti

The Haitians consider the Juba Dance (also known as *Martinique*) one of the oldest on the island, and one of the first African dances in the New World. According to Courlander, "the rhythm is played upon a single drum, called *tambour Martinique,* or *tambour Juba.* . . . Behind the drummer a *singalier,* or *catalier,* plays with sticks on the sounding board affixed to the body of the drum, or on the wood of the drum itself." The popularity of the Juba Dance extends throughout the Antilles, and is well known among the Creoles in Louisiana.

Danse Juba—Juba Dance

English version by
Charles Haywood

Moderato

Fé nans pi - lon pi - let, pi - let nans pi - lon!
Leaves in ___ the mor - tar, a man pounds in the

Ga' çon pi - let nans pi - lon, femme pas cou - man - dé! ___
mor - tar! A - gain pound - ing, no wo - man com - mands him! ___

Ma ba nou man - gé Pa - pa, loa Ci - ma - lo! ___
I give you food ___ Pa - pa, loa Ci - ma - lo! ___

Ma ba nou Vo - doun Pa - pa, loa Ci - ma - lo! N'a -
I give you Vo - doun Pa - pa, loa Ci - ma - lo! In -

pé so' - ti nans trou nous pou nous dan - sé ___ Zou -
to our cave we shall go, where we can dance the Ju -

ba! N'a - pé so' - ti nans trou nous pou nous dan - sé ___ Zou -
ba! In - to our cave we shall go, where we can dance the Ju -

ba! N'a - ba! A - go a - go! Hié, fé nans bois! ___
ba! In - ba! A - go a - go! Hié, leaves in the woods!

57

Cuba

A guajira is the name applied to a white female inhabiting the rural areas of Cuba. This particular one appears to be very pretty and sophisticated. The Spanish element, in rhythm and melody, is quite apparent.

English version by
Eleanor Hague

La Guajira—The Guajira

Moderato

Yo — soy gua - ji - ra Na- cí en Me - le - na, En —
I'm a nice gua - ji - ra, Born in Me - le - na, Near the

el in - ge - nio de Cu - ru - jey. Quin-ce a - ños ten- go, Me
su - gar- mill — of Cu - ru - jey. Of fif - teen sum-mers, I'm

lla - mo E - le - na; Soy ri - ca y bue-na co - mo el ma - méy. Me
called He - le - na, And I'm de - lect - a - ble like ma - méy. The

de-spier- tan las to - jo - sas, Sal - go al cam - po con el
birds ev' - ry morn- ing wake me, To the fields with the sun I

sol. Y voy a co - ger las ro - sas, Que a - le - gre
fly. I wan - der and gath - er ros - es, And for my

guar - do pa - ra mi a - mor. Si a mi - sa al pue - blo
love keep them hap - pi - ly. When I go in - to

58

voy, Mon - ta - di - ta en mia - la - zán, To - dos me di - cen que
town To — Mass, on my chest-nut mare, Then ev'- ry one says that

soy La más bo - ni - ta del ma - ni - gual.
I'm the belle, The fair - est of all the fair.

The significant role of African melody and rhythm in Cuban life and music is well illustrated in this *Lucumí* cult chant, based on the pentatonic scale.

Canto Lucumí de Iyá—Lucumí Cult Song

English version by
Charles Haywood

Iya', mo duk - pe fó ba ____ e.
Thank you, moth - er! I'm near ____ you!

O - ba nla to ba - ro, A - go - lo - na.
Ho - ly King! You can hear me, Be kind un - to me.

I - yá ____ mo duk - pe ya le ya lo ____ de.
Moth - er, ____ I thank you, I am close to you now.

HAND CLAPS

Jamaica

"They want to beat Isabella, so they put the skin-whip in water to soak before beating her. After the beating she is too lame to put on her clothes or walk or sleep at night." (Martha Beckwith)

Isabella

Is - a - bel - la, go skin in a soak - ee, Is - a -
bel - la, You kyan' walk a night, se - ka Is - a - bel - la,
You kyan' weah yo' frock, se - ka Is - a - bel - la, E - do, e -
do, Is - a - bel - la! You kyan' sleep o' night, se - ka Is - a -
bel - la, You kyan' weah yo' draw's, se - ka, Is - a - bel - la,
You kyan' put on yo' shirt, se - ka Is - a - bel - la.

Martinique

Here we have a fine example of the *cante fable*, a narrative tale interspersed with song, highlighting the most dramatic elements of the story. This folk tale, a variant of the "Brer Rabbit" cycle, recounts the manner in which a ewe saves her young from being devoured by "ferocious animals" through a clever stratagem. One finds many other interesting *cante fables* among the Negroes in the West Indies.

La Gue' Déclarée—War Is Declared

English version by
Charles Haywood

Allegro molto (♪=168)

Vie dans nos, vie dans, vie dans nos, vie mes dames.
Fol - low me, fol - low, fol - low me ev' - ry - one.

Vie dans nos, vie, la gué dé - cla - rée, mes dames.
Fol - low me now, the war is de - clared at last.

Vie dans nos, vie dans nos, vie dans nos, vie. La
Fol - low me, fol - low me, fol - low me now. The

gué dé - cla - rée, vie dans, vie dans nos, vie. Cab -
war is de - clared at last, fol - low me now. The

uite ca mon - té, vie dans, vie dans nos, vie.
lamb shout - ed loud - ly: O come, fol - low me.

English version Copyright © 1966 by Charles Haywood

Puerto Rico

A widely known children's song, supposedly of French origin, where it is sung as "Le petit navire." In Italy, it is known as "Il piccolo naviglio."

Era Una Vez—Once There Was

English version by
Charles Haywood

Allegretto

1. E - ra u - na vez un bar - co chi - qui - ti - to,
1. Once — there was a ti - ny lit - tle sail - boat,

E - ra u - na vez un bar - co chi - qui - ti - to,
Once — there was a ti - ny lit - tle sail - boat,

E - ra u - na vez un bar - co chi - qui - ti - to, —
Once — there was a ti - ny lit - tle sail - boat, —

— que no po - dí - a, que no po - dí - a, que no po -
— that was un - a - ble, that was un - a - ble, that was un -

dí - a ca - mi - nar. Pa - sa - ron u - na, dos, tres,
a - ble to set sail. And af - ter one and two and

62

cuat - ro, cin - co, seis, sie - te se - ma - nas, Pa - sa - ron
three and four and five, six, sev - en tri - als, And af - ter

u - na, dos, tres, cuat - ro, cin - co, seis, sie - te se -
one and two and three and four and five, six, sev - en

ma - nas, Pa - sa - ron u - na, dos, tres, cuat - ro, cin - co,
tri - als, And af - ter one and two and three and four and

seis, sie - te se - ma - nas ____ y los vi - ve - res, y los
five, six, sev - en tri - als, ____ still the lit - tle boat, still the

vi - ve - res em - pe - za - ron a es - ca - sear.
lit - tle boat, still the little boat could not sail.

2. *Los tripulantes de este barquito, (3)*
   se pusieron, se pusieron, se pusieron a pescar.
   Pescaron peces grandes, chicos, y medianos (3)
   y se pusieron, (3) a cenar.

2. The jolly sailors of this tiny little sailboat, (3)
   all decided, all decided, all decided to catch fish.
   They caught some big ones, fat ones, long ones, short ones, odd ones of
      all sizes, (3)
   and then prepared, and then prepared, and then prepared a tasty dish. (2)

Trinidad

The inconstancy of women, and that man is but an "innocent" victim of female allurements are common themes of calypso satirical songs.

Man Smart—Woman Smarter

1. Let us put man and wo - man to - geth - er, To find out which one is smart- er. ___ Some say man, But I say no, Wo - man got the man beat, I should know. _ Not me! But the peo - ple they say, The men are lead - ing the wo - men a - stray, But I say, That the wo - man of to - day, Smart - er than the man in ev' - ry way. ___

2. Ever since the world began,
   A woman was always foolin' Man,
   But if you listen to my story you will see,
   I will tell you how a woman made a fool of me.
   Chorus:

3. I had a girl named Caroline,
   She called me honey boy all the time.
   When every single thing was goin' fine,
   She was dealing me short with a friend of mine.

4. You attend a girl at a pretty dance,
   Thinking that you would stand a chance,
   But you take her home thinking she's alone,
   You open the door to find the next man home.

5. I had a girl quite fat and tall,
   She went to the masquerade-newspaper ball,
   But her dress caught afire and burnt her attire,
   Front page, sport page section and all.

6. Sampson was the strongest man long ago,
   None could have beat him as we all know,
   Till he sit with Deliah 'pon top of the bed,
   She found out all the strength was in the hair of his head.

Virgin Islands (Saint Croix)

The unsuspecting rats, seeing the cat, Broder Manyo, lying on the ground, apparently dead, hold a religious service for her, intoning this deeply expressive chant. Sly Broder Manyo, evidently respectful of the ceremonial last rites, waits until they are through, before pouncing upon them.

Broder Manyo

1. Bro-der Man-y-o is dead an' gone, Look a' his eye, way he tek see ah — we! Oh, ah, Bro-der Man-y-o is dead an' gone, Look a' his eye, way he tek see ah we!

2. Broder Manyo is dead an' gone,
   Look a' his w'isker, way he tek smell ah we!

3. Broder Manyo is dead an' gone,
   Look a' his mout', way he tek hol' ah we!

4. Broder Manyo is dead an' gone,
   Look a' his bellie, way he hol' ah we!

5. Broder Manyo is dead an' gone,
   Look a' his paw, way he paw ah we down wid.

66

Mexico

Mexican folk music, as in most of the Latin-American countries, is a fusion of indigenous Indian (or African) elements—depending on the continuing influence of native tribal culture—Iberian music, and musical elements contributed by other Europeans who have settled and integrated in the traditions of the New World. Speaking of the character of Mexican music, Carlos Chávez stated: "By Mexican music we mean Indian music of the ancient Mexicans; the music of Spanish or other origin imported into Mexico and, finally, a mixture of these elements. The Indian branch differs from the Spanish branch of Mexican music in that the Indian music since the conquest has remained static, while Spanish music continued its evolution."

The ancient *romances* (ballads) of Spain, some in variant forms, are still heard in Mexico today, as well as the more recent native topical ballads, the *corridos*. The latter are usually sung by two voices, in thirds or sixths, accompanied by the guitar. The alternation of 3/4 and 6/8 time is a delineating characteristic of Mexican and other Latin-American folk music. The predominance of the major mode in Mexican folksong is a distinctive feature.

French influence, during the brief Maximilian episode, brought into Mexico the *mariachi* songs, accompanied by the guitar, violin and trumpet or clarinet. The French introduced the European salon dance forms, such as the *waltz, polka* and *mazurka*, which became integrated into the native cultural idiom, adding ethnic melodic and rhythmic idiosyncrasies. Out of this fusion emerged a variety of dance-songs reflecting the spirit and character of Mexican folk life, such as the *canción, son, huapango, jarabe, zandunga,* and *jarana*. Influences of American jazz, with new emphasis on Afro rhythms, have had their impact on modern folk idiom in Mexico.

Costa Rica

Spanish influences have been the predominant factor in Costa Rican folk music. However, these elements, in the words of a native musician, "are filtered through the sands of our own soil." The general characteristics of this music are clearly stated in the January 1942 edition of the journal *Educación*: "Our country is not as rich in folklore as Mexico or Colombia, but it possesses its own musical form of expression. The guitar, the accordion, the mandolin, the marimba, are the favorite instruments of our people, and are found even in the remotest villages. One hears in the afternoon the strumming of the guitar and the plaintive voice of the villagers who seek to brighten their leisure with songs. Our marriage ceremonies and field festivals are conducted to the accompaniment of this music. The province of Guanacaste has given us that inimitable dance, *Punto Guanacasteco*, and there are other country airs."

The eminent Costa Rican musician Luis Dobles Segreda has given us a more detailed and nationally inspired description of these "other country airs": "Four types of popular music are represented in Costa Rica: *Callejeras, Patrioticas, Pasillos,* and *Danzas.* The music of *Callejeras* (literally, street songs) is voluble. Like a fickle woman, who flirts with anyone, the *Callejeras* assumes a hundred forms.

"Then come the patriotic songs, in a more subdued and more solemn manner, marking rhythms, exuding tobacco smoke and sweat, gunpowder and blood. . . . There is the *Pasillo Guanacasteco*, a dance quite different from the Colombian *Pasillo.* Musically, it is the most original of all, for in it the melody proceeds in compound binary time, while the accompaniment goes on in simple triple time. Finally comes the *Danza*; it is the old *Danza*, differing from the *Habañera* by its vivacious pace and salty flavor."

Guatemala

The Quiche Indians, making up the major part of the indigenous population, have enriched the musical folk life of this small country. Their songs and dances, as well as their ancient instruments, are still a vital part of the Guatemalan folk idiom. The other Central American states have, in varying degrees, been affected by similar musical and cultural factors. Thus, the ubiquitous *marimba*, the *xul* (vertical flute), and the *tun* (similar to the Mexican *teponaxtle*, a drum made out of a hollowed-out tree trunk), and other instruments are common to these countries. In the popular native song-dance, the *Son Guatelmateco*, the Spanish influence is apparent in the cross rhythms of triple meter and six-eights.

Honduras

Honduras, bordering on Nicaragua, El Salvador, and Guatamala, exhibits, to a considerable extent, the musical characteristics of its neighbors. Here, too, we find the *marimba*, the *maracas*, the *xul* (vertical flute), the *chirimía* (a wind instrument of the clarinet family), and the *teponaxtle* (horizontal drum). We can also hear the lively *pasillo*, the graceful *danza*, as well as other lyric songs of Spanish provenance. The aboriginal music of the pre-Columbian Maya-Quiche tribes, vocal and instrumental, still lingers.

A unique hybrid musical culture is represented by the Black Caribs, showing derivative elements of their West African origin—the rain forest homeland of their Carib and Arawak ancestors. They still perform their ancient ceremonies, chanting the old tunes, accompanied by various drums and gourd rattles, in rhythmic patterns, from the simplest to complex polyrhythms.

Nicaragua

Among the most popular dance-songs of Nicaragua may be mentioned the colorful *La Yegüecita*, performed on the 25th of July in honor of the patron saint of Managua; the elaborately costumed *Los Diabolitos*, accompanied by a tuba, *chirimía* (clarinet), *zul* (flute), *cacho* (trumpet), and the *juco* (a bull-roarer, "a barrel covered with a drumhead with a string passed through the membrane"); the humorous *El Zopilote* (the dancers dressed in the bird costume of the buzzard); the extravagantly costumed *Los Caballitos*, and the delightfully mimicking *Los Tincos* (in imitation of the blackbird or the parrot), one of the oldest dances of Managua. Spanish *jarabes* and *zapateos* are still favorites. The most popular instruments, besides those mentioned above, are the *marimba*, the *quijongo* ("a string supported by a movable bridge on both ends to an oblong sound box"), the *chilchil* (small bell), and *maracas*.

Panama

Small though the country is, it has shaped a rich folk tradition of many varied elements: the Indian, the Negro, and the whites (among the latter many Americans) residing in the Canal Zone. The Indians in the interior have kept to their primitive traditions, songs, dances, and instruments (mainly drums and flutes). The Negro element is apparent in many songs and dances, and in much popular music. The *cumbia* captures the underlying African characteristics in its rhythms and movements.

The acculturated musical forms are reflected in such native dance-songs as the *tamborito* (with solo and chorus), a lively number in duple meter in the major mode, punctuated by strong rhythmic drum accompaniment in triple meter. Close to the heart of the Panamanians is the *mejorana*, of varying speeds, tonalities, and rhythmic patterns, accompanied by two guitars, in seemingly improvisatory style. Its performance resembles the American square dance. Another favorite is the *punto*, also in lively rhythm, the melody in two-four time and the accompaniment in 6/8, in the major key. When performed in the minor key, the dance-song is known as a *coco*.

El Salvador

As in most Central American countries, the Indian musical culture presents, to a considerable degree, similar general characteristics in the melodic character, types of instruments, and the religious and social festivals. To these indigenous traditions the Spanish brought their folk idiom. These acculturative melodies, often producing strange, but always fascinating musical hybrids, are apparent in the numerous songs and dances heard today in El Salvador. Thus, at the same time that the Salvadorians, generally consisting of mestizos, continue to use the ancient *tun*, a drum similar to the Mexican *teponaxtle*, various ancient vertical flutes, and the marimba, they also enthusiastically participate in the popular *danzas*.

Mexico

This is a *corrido,* a topical ballad, from Oaxaca, describing the passionate adventures of a gay *caballero,* with intimations of tragic overtones.

Las Chaparreras—The Chaparreras

English version by
Charles Haywood

Allegro moderato

1. *Las mu - cha - chas de mi tier - ra, ___ é - sas sí sa - ben que - rer, de que muer - den el re - bo - zo ___ es pa - ra co - rres - pon - der. ____*

1. Sweet are the girls from my coun - try, ___ On - ly they know ___ how to love; See how they draw their shawls tight - ly, ___ And with fire their dark eyes rove. ___

Refrain:

Cha - pa - rre - ra, cha - pa - rre - ra, ___ cha - pa - rre - ri - ta de cue - ro; ___ vá - yan - se le - jos las güe - ras, ___ que yo a las mo - re - nas quie - ro. ___

Cha - pa - rre - ra, cha - pa - rre - ra, ___ Cha - pa - rre - ra of fin - est leath - er; ___ Blond girls are not to my lik - ing, ___ But the dark ones ___ I love bet - ter. ___

Las Chaparreras

The Chaparreras*

2. *Negrita de mis amores,*
   tus manitas voy a atar
   para que cuando te bese
   no me vayas a arañar.
   Tu marido está en la cama,
   vete tu a la cabecera,
   con el rosario en la mano
   ruega a Dios que ya se muera.
   Estribillo:

2. Fairest of all, I adore you,
   I will tie your lovely hands;
   When I will hold you and kiss you,
   You won't scratch, or twist, or prance.
   Calmly asleep lies your husband,
   Please go quickly to his bed;
   Piously clutching the rosary,
   Pray that he may soon be dead.
   Refrain:

* chaps, leggings

A popular love song from Jalisco. The rhythm of the opening measure should be maintained in the accompaniment, with occasional cross rhythms of two against three.

La Paloma Azul—The Sky-Blue Dove

English version by
Charles Haywood

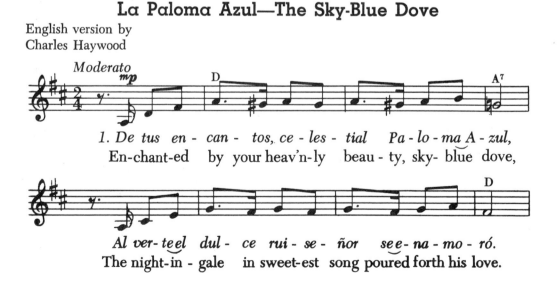

1. *De tus en - can - tos, ce - les - tial Pa - lo - ma A - zul,*
   En-chant-ed by your heav'n-ly beau - ty, sky- blue dove,

Al ver - te el dul - ce rui - se - ñor se e - na - mo - ró.
The night-in - gale in sweet-est song poured forth his love.

72

Dé-ja-lo tris-te ___ y a-pa-sio-na-do, ___
Oh, let his pas-sion ___ in sad-ness ling-er, ___

___ Mien-tras tú, a-man-te, llo-ras por el. ___
___ While you, be-lov-ed, weep for the sing-er.

Si al-gu-no pa-sa y te ju-ra a-mor, Que te que-
If an-y oth-er vows love to you, In fer-vent

rí - a te pro-me-tió; Pa-lo-ma
ac-cents yours to be true, Oh, tell him

blan-ca, di-le que no, Que me has ju-ra-do e-ter-no a-
quick-ly, this can-not be, Your heart, ___ fair dove, be-longs to

mor. ¡Ay, ___ Pa-lo-ma A-zul!
me. Ah! ___ my sky-blue dove.

2. Yo te suplico que vuelvas a querer
A otro tirano que se burle de tu amor.
Déjalo triste y apasionado,
Mientras tú, amante, lloras por el.
Si alguno pasa, etc., etc.

2. I long to hear you say, you love me, once again,
The other only mocks your love, your pain.
Oh, let his passion in sadness linger,
While you, beloved, weep for the singer. etc., etc.

Honduras

Although the Honduran navy cannot boast a mighty fleet, the sailor, at least in the eyes of a lovelorn maiden, is unequaled on land and sea—as a lover, of course!

Canción del Marinero Hondureño—
Song of the Honduran Sailor

English version by
Charles Haywood

Moderato

1. Ma-ri-ne-ro hon-du-re-ño que ya te vas __ a la mar, __ llé-va-me en tu ve-le-ro, llé-va-me en tu ve-le-ro, que quie-ro na-ve-gar.

1. Gal-lant sail-or from Hon-du-ras Who proud-ly sails __ the high seas, __ Take me when you go sail-ing, Take me when you go sail-ing, I too a-dore the breeze.

Refrain

Siem-pre char-lan-do, a-le-gre bai-lan-do, en ca-da puer-to __ va de-jan-do u-na la-di-na, u-na ru-bia, u-na mo-re-na, y u-na do-

He's al-ways pranc-ing, Most hap-py when danc-ing; At ev-'ry door-step __ All the maid-ens hear him sigh-ing A blond one or bru-nette; A doz-en more left

ce - na que-dan di - cien - - do. 2 Ma - ri - do. ___
wait - ing, To none love de - ny ing. 2 Gal - lant ing. ___

2. *Marinero hondureño*
   que ya te vas a la mar,
   tráeme en tu velero,
   conchitas de ultramar.

2. Gallant sailor from Honduras
   Who proudly sails the high seas,
   Bring me some colored sea shells,
   Tokens from the lands you see.

Costa Rica

A lover's plaint; when words fail him, he woos his beloved in a bird-like croon.

Yo Te Amo, Idolatro—Yes, I Love You

English version by
Charles Haywood

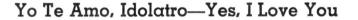

Yo te a - mo, ___ i - do - la - tro, ___ am - bi -
Yes, I love you, ___ i - dol - ize you, ___ and your

cio - no tu bel - dad, Yo ne sé por-qué la in -
beau - ty I a - dore. Tell me why you treat me

gra - ta ___ me cas - ti - ga sin pie - dad. ¡Ay! cu-ru-
harsh - ly, ___ why you scorn me ev - er more. Ah!

cú, cu - rú, cu - cú, cu - ru - cú, cu - rú, cu - cú.

Guatemala

The narrative aspect of this love song and its melodic character evoke a quality of the old Spanish ballads, the *romances*.

Nací en La Cumbre—A Mountain High-Top

English version by
Charles Haywood

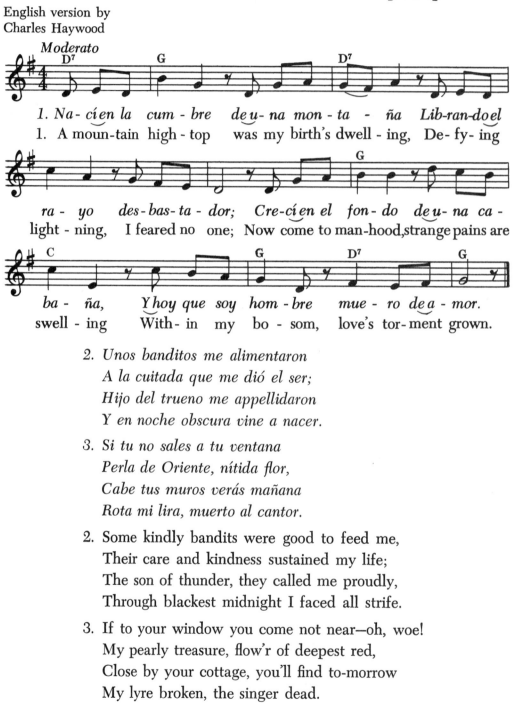

1. Na- cí en la cum - bre de u- na mon - ta - ña Lib-ran-do el
1. A moun-tain high - top was my birth's dwell - ing, De- fy- ing

ra - yo des-bas-ta - dor; Cre-cí en el fon- do de u- na ca -
light - ning, I feared no one; Now come to man-hood, strange pains are

ba - ña, Y hoy que soy hom - bre mue - ro de a - mor.
swell - ing With- in my bo - som, love's tor-ment grown.

2. *Unos banditos me alimentaron*
   A la cuitada que me dió el ser;
   Hijo del trueno me appellidaron
   Y en noche obscura vine a nacer.

3. *Si tu no sales a tu ventana*
   Perla de Oriente, nítida flor,
   Cabe tus muros verás mañana
   Rota mi lira, muerto al cantor.

2. Some kindly bandits were good to feed me,
   Their care and kindness sustained my life;
   The son of thunder, they called me proudly,
   Through blackest midnight I faced all strife.

3. If to your window you come not near—oh, woe!
   My pearly treasure, flow'r of deepest red,
   Close by your cottage, you'll find to-morrow
   My lyre broken, the singer dead.

Nicaragua

The insistent pleading of the youth and the cold rejection by the proud maiden are clearly conveyed by the melodic pattern and the alternating duple and triple rhythms.

No Puedo, Tengo Otro Dueño
No, Never Can I Go with You

English version by
Charles Haywood

Niña vamos al cam - po y cor - ta -
Let's hast - en to the field, my dear, To

re - mos u - na flor, a - rrea - re - mos el ga -
gath - er flow - ers there; We'll drive ___ the cat - tle

na - do, tu pas - to - ra y yo pas - tor. No
far and near, We're shep - herds, a hap - py pair. No,

pue - do, ten - go o - tro due - ño por e - so
nev - er can I go with you, my friend, For I

na - da te re - sol - ví, de - je - mos de tan - to em -
love some - one else, I do, For - get all de - sires, and

pe - ño de nin - gún mo - do se re - de - ti.
let's make an end, For I'll nev - er mar - ry you.

Panama

The *tamborito* is a very popular Panamanian folk air of old origin. It is in duple meter, and, most frequently, in the major mode. This tune is in minor, and belongs to the *tonada* type—that is, sung rather danced.

El Marido y La Piedra

English version by
Charles Haywood

The Husband and the Stone

1. Se - ño - res, ven-go a con - tar - les lo - que a
1. Friends, lis - ten to what I tell you, some - thing

mí me ha su - ce - di - do; Vi - nien - do de la mon -
strange in - deed has hap - pened; De - scend - ing from the high

ta - ña mi ma - ri - do se ha per - di - do.
mount - ain no - wheres could I find my hus - band.

De - ba - jo de la pie - dra lo bus -
I searched and searched be - hind each stone in

qué, — De - ba - jo de la pie - dra lo bus - qué.
vain. I searched and searched be - hind each stone in vain.

2. *Señores, vengo a contarles loque amí me ha sucedido;*
   Viniendo de la montaña mi marido se murió.
   Debajo de la piedra lo enterré.

2. Friends, listen to what I tell you something strange indeed has happened;
   Descending from the mountain my dear husband suddenly had died.
   Behind a stone I buried him, there to remain.

El Salvador

A jolly tune, popular with children and grown-ups.

Jeu! Jeu!

English version by
Charles Haywood

Allegro giocoso

Por a - quí pa - só u - na pa - va, _____
Watch the lit - tle tur - key run - ning, _____

Chi - qui- ti - tay vo - la - do - ra, _____
Ve - ry small and ve - ry cun - ning; _____

Qu'en las a - las lle - va flo - res, _____
On her wings the flow - ers bring - ing, _____

Y en el pi - cu mis a - mo - res. _____   ¡Jeu!   ¡Jeu!
With her beak my love she's sing- ing. _____

Argentina

Some commentators have remarked that a general spirit of lightness and gaiety permeates the Argentine folksongs. Like all generalizations, it is an oversimplification; at best, a half-truth that omits many vital and significant aspects of Argentine folk music. From the northernmost foothills of the Andes to the desolate and forbidding southern Tierra del Fuego, Argentine presents a varied panorama of musical folkways. Carlos Vega, Argentina's outstanding musical scholar, has traced in detail, in his numerous studies, the many influences that have shaped the spirit and pattern of the songs and dances of his country. While the Spanish cultural traits have perhaps been the strongest, the acculturative processes have also strongly affected the folk music of the French and Italian population, who have contributed much in the development of the Argentine nation. The rural areas, particularly in the northern provinces of Santiago del Estero and Tucumán, have maintained closer kinship with Spanish culture and folk traditions. Here the old *romances* (ballads) and their variants can still be heard.

The popular *tango*, the dance most always associated with Argentina, is quite different today from what it was known at the end of the nineteenth century. It exemplifies the influence of musical acculturation and synthesis of various ethnic elements: the Andalucian *tango*, the Cuban *habañera*, and the Argentine *milonga*; to which was added, in the twentieth century, the characteristic syncopated rhythmic pattern to give the *tango* the unique Argentine quality. Numerous other songs and dances show their kinship to Spanish musical idiom. According to Isabel Aretz, many dances of Llanos de la Rioja and Córdoba, especially the *cueca*, *chacarera*, and the *gato*,

80

still preserve the authentic Spanish rhythm and spirit. The *refalosa* bears close resemblance to the *seguidilla*.

In the northern regions of Argentina, which once was part of the Incan empire, the musical traditions of the ancient Indian culture continue. Carlos Vega traces the migration of numerous Argentine songs and dances via Peru. The frequency of melodies based largely on the intervals of major thirds, fourths, and fifths (some of these tunes are pentatonic, while others are closer to the heptatonic); the use of Peruvian instruments: the *antara* (panpipe) and the *quepa* (ocarina made of baked clay); the melancholy and plaintive *triste*, bearing close resemblance to the Indian *yaravi*; the *vidala*, a song in triple meter and moderate tempo, containing a blend of Quechua and Spanish elements, musically and linguistically—all these aspects show the influence of Inca culture on Argentine music and the importance of the continuing factors of acculturation.

Fact and fiction, blending into legend, have mirrored the life and exploits of the gaucho, the vagabond cowboy of the pampas. With his inseparable guitar, this "minstrel of the plains" possesses a wide and varied repertory of songs and dances: In a highly personal style the gaucho sings his *payadas* (songs) consisting of· old ballads, employing sixteenth-century literary forms and imagery; the *contrapunto*, a song contest between two gauchos, matching musical and dramatic wit and improvisatory skill; the lyrical and melancholy *vidalita* (in duple meter) and the four-line stanzaic *vidala*; the nostalgic *estilo* (with its slow first part in duple meter and the lively second part in triple meter); the spirited *chacarera* (with its alternating 3/4 and 6/8 rhythms, accompanied by guitar, violin and drum); the popular *pericón* (in triple meter, its dance pattern reminiscent of the North American *Virginia reel*); the bouncing *gato* (with its steady waltz-like triple meter, the waving handkerchiefs, and the vibrant *zapateo* [shoe dance]); the *gato con relaciones* (with verbal interpolations discoursing on a variety of topics). The seeming improvisatory freedom and the graceful, fluent bodily movements of the *gato* are contained within a formal and almost rigid musical structure. This is folk art at its finest and most expressive.

81

Bolivia

Together with Ecuador and Peru, the influence of the Incas still dominates the native musical idiom. Inaccessibility and economic primitivism have helped maintain a continuing, unbroken link with the past. The pentatonic character of its melodies, the plaintive *yaravi*, the festive *hualluncas*, the lyrical *huaiño*, and the Quechuan *chulló-chulló*, recapture the spirit of the pre-Columbian era.

Brazil

"Brazilian folk music continues to be determined by its Portuguese past, modified by the presence of the Negro element and, more subtly, by the remaining strain of the aboriginal Indians. The fusion of these diverse influences, or the predominance of one or the other of them, is evident in certain regions and in certain types of music common to a number of regions."

In the Amazon region the Indian population is the predominant group. Although they have shown a remarkable "psychological assimilation" with the Brazilian people, they still cling, by and large, to their tribal customs, beliefs, ceremonies, songs and dances. In the Northeastern Sertão we still find strong echoes of the *gaya ciencia* of the Provençal troubadours, the continuing active tradition of the ancient courtly *romances* (ballads) and the *desafía* (poetic debate), where improvisation plays a very important part. In the Northeastern Coastal region the light gaiety, infectious humor and biting satire of the people, influenced by Afro-Brazilian elements, are delightfully expressed in the *coco* and *embolada*, dance-songs involving quick repetition of short notes and rapid patter of text, requiring remarkable skill in articulation and performance. In the region of Algoas and Sergipe the tradition of "dramatic dances" reach their high degree of perfection both in context and interpretation. These elements find realization in the *autos*, sacred dramatic spectacles, in which Iberian, Negro, and Amerindian aspects are blended.

In the agricultural area from Bahia to São Paulo the Negro influence is the strongest. The African survivals manifest themselves in a folk music rich in rhythmic vitality, the solo and choral refrain, complexity and variety of percussion instruments, and in numerous ritual songs and dances, such as the *samba, jongo, macumba,* and *condobles.* The South Central region, comprising Minas Gerais, Goiás, Mato Grosso and Paraña, has close musical affinity with the Northeastern area: a free rhythmic style, melismatic ornamentation, and the singing of two voices in parallel thirds. The old Iberian forms and styles are remarkably preserved in the Southern Coastal region. Here one can still be stirred by the incisive rhythms of the *fandango,* or be deeply affected by the poignant lyricism of the *modinha.* And finally, the *gaucho,* or *troveiro,* holds sway in the Pampas, the region in Rio Grande do Sul. Accompanying himself on the guitar or the *gaita* (accordion), he recounts the dramatic events of the old country *romances* and the heroic exploits of Brazilian legendary and historical figures.

Colombia

Here, too, the traditional music shows the effects of three major cultural forces. The Spanish influence dominates in the melodic contour and rhythmic pulse of the country dances; the Negro culture manifests itself in the percussive, complex, interweaving rhythms, and the sustained pentatonic chants of the Indians are heard in their solemn ceremonies. The popular *bambuco,* with its graceful and alternating triple and 6/8 rhythms, is an outstanding example of Negro influence. In equal favor and popularity is the *pasillo,* of Spanish origin, in fast 3/4 syncopated rhythm. A native student of Colombian folk music, Emirto de Lima, described the essential characteristics of this dance in these words: "Its rhythm stresses the first beat in the classical manner, then abandons itself to the blandishments of a tender second beat, and joyfully explodes on the third and last beat. The *Pasillo* possesses the aristocracy and the distinction of the *Waltz,* the light cadence of the *Contradanza,* the winged subtlety of the *Gavotte,* and the serene grace of the *Minuet.*" Both the *bambuco* and the *pasillo* are usually accompanied by the favorite *tiple,* a small guitar-shaped instrument. The important role that Indian musical culture continues to play in Colombian life is to be observed in the use of native instruments, such as the pandean pipes,

83

and ancient drums: the *manguare*, the *cunnunu*, and the *bombo*, the conch trumpet, the *fotuto*, the notched gourd, the *guacharacas*, and the musical bow, the *timbirimba*.

Chile

Chilean folk music is predominantly Spanish, but other European settlers have contributed their share. In addition, there is also a notable indigenous music of the Araucanian Indians: in their ritual chants, such as the *canquen*, *ghul*, and *ñucprun* (threshing dance), and in the variety of instruments: *huada* (maracas), *trutruca* (bamboo horn), and others. The most popular song-dance is unquestionably the *cueca* or *zamacueca*, a couple-dance, accompanied by waving of handkerchiefs, clinking of silver spurs, guitars, harp and *tomboréo* (strumming on the back of the guitar). There is lively rhythmic vitality and bodily movement in the dance in 6/8 time, with vocal refrain superimposed in 3/4 time, and the handclapping is in 6/8. Other popular Chilean songs are the lyrical *tonada chilena* and the tender *esquinazo*.

Ecuador

As in Peru and Bolivia, and to a marked degree in Colombia, the cultural aspects of the Inca civilization are still vital elements in Ecuadorian folk music—in the native instruments and the pentatonic quality of the melodies. It is not surprising to find there the doleful *yaravi* and the festive *cachllapi*, accompanied on the *rondador* (panpipes of varying sizes), as well as religious and social songs and dances, such as the *abagos* and *yumbo*, accompanied by the strong accents of the *chil-chil* (rattles), and *churu* or *quipa* (horn made of a large conch), and the *pingullo* (vertical flute).

However slowly, the acculturative influence of Spanish life and folklore has had its inevitable effects on Ecuadorian folk music, readily discernible in the characteristic alternation of triple and duple meter. The national song, the *Sanjuanito* (after its patron saint, St. John), in duple meter and minor key, displays this lively rhythmic quality. As in the other northern countries of South America, the *pasillo* is very popular in Ecuador. It is in the minor key, differing from the one in Colombia which is in the major key.

Paraguay

The fact that the majority of the population of Paraguay are Indians, belonging to the Guaraní branch, explains the predominance of Indian lore and music in the cultural life of the country. The absence of African elements accounts for the lack of that particular rhythmic quality which the Negro has contributed. The Paraguayan melodies of Indian origin are "usually slow in tempo and melancholy in mood," simple, sustained pentatonic chants. Primitive instruments—wind and percussion—consisting of vertical flutes of varying sizes, drums and scrapers, add fitting accompaniment to the ritual songs and dances. European influences of the eighteenth and nineteenth centuries, in religious and salon music, have left their effect in such hybridizations as the *Polka Paraguaya*, flavored with an "Hispanic" touch. It consists of a slowly flowing three beat measure in two-four time. There is also an abundance of *waltzes*, *galops*, and *schottisches*.

Peru

As the stronghold of the Inca Empire, the Peruvian Indians, the main subdivisions being the Quechuas and the Aymarás, have, from the pre-Columbian days, participated in elaborate festivals and musical performances, involving large masses of people, singers and dancers, accompanied by a huge battery of percussion and wind instruments. This musical spirit and vitality still dominate present-day folk life in Peru. The basic quality of the ancient *Quechua* melody, the pentatonic scale, has remained unchanged through the centuries. "The songs of the Quechua are, as a rule, plaintive and melancholy. To his already naïvely sombre melodic scheme he adds a text that runs the gamut of all the tribulations of his simple life. Trees and stones, birds and llamas, the solitude of his pastoral life, his father and mother, the *coca*-leaves which he incessantly chews—all find a place somewhere in his poetry, which may take shape in the Quechua language, or in Spanish, or in a mixture of both." One can still hear the languidly expressive *yaravi*, the joyful *mulisa*, and the incisive rhythmic dance, the *huaiño*. The very names of the Indian dances evoke the mystery and glory of their past: the *aymatha* (a dance of the fields and fertility), the *guacon* (masked dance), the *kachua* (dance of young virgins), the *kirkita* (fast dance of the Aymarás), and the *silulo* (maypole dance). Many instruments in the highlands have remained unchanged for many centuries: the *kena* (vertical flute, most typical of Inca instruments), the *antara* (panpipes), various drums, and maracas.

Side by side, one hears in Andean music melodies based on the heptatonic scale (seven tone), a product of *criollo* influences, of the native Spanish, or the result of a fusion with Indian elements. An example of this type is the *triste*, a *criollo* version of the *yaravi*. The national song-dance of the Peruvian *criollos* is the *Marinera*, which is of the same character as the *Chilena*; both are derived from the *Zamacueca*. We also find in Peru the inevitable hybrid types, such as the *Inca fox trot*!

Uruguay

There is very little evidence today of the ancient musical tradition of the Indians who inhabited Uruguay, particularly the Churrúa and the Tupi-Guaraní. The early writings of Martin del Barco Centecera and Padre Antonio Sepp attest to the important role music played in their religious and social life. Today the folk music of Uruguay shares to a very marked degree the general characteristics of the folk culture of its large and powerful neighbor, Argentina. This is especially apparent in the importance of the Gaucho music—his lore, legend and song. The mainstream of the folk music of both countries came largely from Spain and, later on, enriched by other European immigrants. The transformation of the old country's folk material under the new indigenous conditions of Uruguay are well summed up by Raul A. Buccino and Luis Benvenuto: "Uruguay's dances and songs are taken from the wealth of Spain's music treasury. This music became acclimatized in the coastal provinces of the old state of Rio de la Plata, and gave birth to the popular music of Uruguay and Argentina. The *Triste, Cielito, Triunfo, Milonga, Jango, Vidala, Pericón*, and other airs and dances of Uruguay are intimately connected with the Argentina airs of the same name."

Venezuela

The continuing Spanish tradition in Venezuelan folk music can be traced to the dominant role the church has played in the lives of the people from the earliest Colonial days. It is not surprising to find many old traditional *romances* still sung, as well as the Spanish *villancicos*, or carols, called *aguinaldos*. The Old World melodies and rhythms are also discernible in the *canción* and *son*. Of the many songs and dances typical of Venezuela, the most popular is the *joropo*, in lively 6/8 rhythm. The *pasillo*, alternating between 3/4 and 6/8 time, similar to the one in Colombia, is also a favorite song-dance. A strikingly indigenous satirical ballad is the *guasa* in 6/8 or 2/4 meter, with a rhythmic accompaniment of a triplet followed by a duplet.

The isolation of the Indians in the Orinoco region has left their musical culture in a fairly pure condition. Their ritual songs, reflecting "the unmistakable racial spirit of the South American aborigines, a melancholy which finds its expression in mournful inflection and wistful monotonous rhythms," are sharply punctuated by the accents on their various jungle drums (*botutó*) and the shrill sounds of their flutes made from animal bones or bamboo reeds.

The Negro elements fused easily with the Spanish melody and rhythm, and this amalgamation gives the most characteristic aspects of Venezuelan music. As Juan Liscano aptly phrased it: "Our music is the daughter of Spain and Africa. Like our soil, it is rich and dark. It stems from the Spanish guitar and the Negro drum." Examples of these acculturative processes are found in the *zamuro* (dance of the vultures), in the *golpes* (songs accompanied by drums of various shapes and sizes producing complex polyrhythms), the lively *quichimba*, closely related to the *merengue*, and the tender and quiet *sangueo*, performed during the festival of Saint John.

Argentina

One of the very popular song-dances of Argentina is the *gato*, the favorite of the *gaucho*, the cowboy of the *pampa*. The gay rhythm, the spirited humor, and the verbal interpolations, the *relaciones*, reflect his hardy life and earthy exuberance.

Bailando el Gato—Dancing the Gato

Allegretto

1. Cuan - do los San Juan - in - os ba - jan — el a - gua, Cuan - a - gua, ba - jan en tro - pi - lli - ta co - mo las co - bras, co - mo las co - bras.

1. When San Juan folk from mount-ains come down — for wa - ter, When wa - ter, Spright- ly like goats they run down af - ter each oth - er, af - ter each oth - er.

CODA

Vi - van los San Juan - in - os, los Cor - do - bes - es y Men - do - ci - nos. Vi - van los San Juan - in - os, los Cor - do - bes - es y Men - do - ci - nos.

Long live the San Juan - in - os, the Cor - do - bes - es, and Men - do - ci - nos. Long live the San Juan - in - os, the Cor - do - bes - es, and Men - do - ci - nos.

2. *Cuando los Cordobeses bailan el gato,* (2)
   sacan la polvareda de adentro el rancho, de adentro el rancho.

3. *Cuando los Mendocinos bailan la cueca,* (2)
   yo he visto en las posturas canillas chuecas, canillas chuecas.

Relación:

Oido, vamos a ver la relación de costumbre.

Hay una criolla en rueda
que por ella me andó,
me andó muriendo de pena,
si he de ser correspondído
décime mi prenda, cuando?
Un·consejo le he dar,
desejé de andár paviándo
que esa prenda tiene dueño
no ve que está macaneándo, pó.

Coda:

Vivan los San Juaninos, los Cordobeses y Mendocinos.

2. When Cordoba folks are dancing their popular dance, "the gato,"(2)
   Watch their feet prancing, kicking up dust in the courtyard.

3. Mendoza folk are there too dancing their "cuecas," (2)
   Graceful their movements, swaying to musical accents.

Spoken (after 3rd verse):

Listen, now let's have the usual verses:
There's a pretty girl in the crowd
for her my heart cries out aloud;
I shall die broken-hearted
if my love is not returned.
Pray, tell me when, beloved?
Some good advice I offer you,
cease your pining, she is not true
To you, another claims this treasure;
he is her lover and her master.

Coda:

Long live the San Juaninos, the Cordobeses, and Mendocinos.(2)

Bolivia

This plaintive melody, a *yaravi*, expresses the deep humility and pious devotion of four weary pilgrims who have come from afar to pray at the famous shrine of *Nuestra Señora de Copacabana* on Lake Titicaca.

De Blanca Tierra—From Lands Far Away

English version by
Charles Haywood

De blan-ca tier-ra he-mos ve-ni-do, De nues-tra tier-
From lands far a-way we've wand-ered hi-ther, From snow-co-vered

ra he-mos ve-ni-do, Can-sa-dos, ren-
hills we've marched long dis-tance; So wea-ry, so

di-dos, por el Se-ñor! Y en-tre cua-tro he-mos ve-
tir-ed, all for our Lord! The four of us walked the roads to-

ni-do, Y en-tre cua-tro he-mos ve-ni-do, O-tro se ha
geth-er, The four of us walked the roads to-geth-er, But one, more

que-da-do en el ca-mi-no A ro- de-ar...
cu-rious, lin-gered by the road-side To wander a-bout...

Brazil

A *modinha,* an urban love song, of deep sentiment and passionate yearning.

Suspira, Coração Triste—My Heart Is Heavy with Sadness

English version by
Charles Haywood

Lento espressivo (♩=56)

1. Sus - pi - ra, co - ra - ção tris - te, Con - so - late_em sus - pi -
1. My heart is heav- y with sad- ness, In tears I find con - sol

rar. __ Sus - rar. __ Já que_a bel - la __ porquem
a - tion; My a - tion; Cru- el maid - en for __ whom I

mor - ro, Não tem dó __ do meu __ pe - nar. __ Já que_a
lan - guish Has no pi - ty, no __ com - pas - sion. Cru - el

bel - la __ porquem mor-ro, Não tem dó __ do meu__pe-nar. __
maid- en for__whom I lan-guish Has no pi - ty, no__com-pas-sion.

2. Bate coração, bate,
   Arrebenta—me este peito!
   Como cabem tantas maguas
   N'um espaço tão estreito?

3. Lá sa vae meu coração,
   Partido em quatro pedaços;
   Meio vivo, meio morto
   Quer acabar, nos teus braços.

2. Beat fast heart of mine,
   Oh, break within my bosom.
   How can grief, and so much torment
   In my heart be held imprisoned?

3. No longer my heart sustains me,
   In fragments it bursts asunder.
   Breathing life, or despairing, dying,
   Let it end in your arms, together.

91

The humor of this song lies in the onomatopoeic sounds of the word *pêga* (woodpecker), and the variations upon it, and *péla* (plumage)—especially when *the speed is increased*. For the sake of euphony and maintaining the rhythmic verve, the original Portuguese words were retained in the translation. This dance-song is known as a *côco* (the *embolada* is also quite similar in character), an admixture of African and Brazilian elements.

Ô, Tres Pêga—Oh, Three Pêga

English version by
Charles Haywood

paia _ Lá na ru - a d'A- ta - la - ia nin -guem po- di - a pas-
no-thing, In the streets of A - ta - la- ia no one now can pass at

sá! Ô, tres pê - ga, re - pe - pê - ga, pe - le _
all. Oh, three pê - ga, re - pe - pê - ga, pe - le —

lê - ga! Pe-guei na pê - ga, dei a mu - lher pra pe-
lê - ga, I took the pê - ga to a wo- man for a pê -

lá! Ô, tres pê - ga, re - pe - pê - ga, pe - le-
la. Oh, three pê - ga, re - pe - pê - ga, pe - le-

lê - ga! _ Pe-guei na pê - ga, dei a mu-lher pra pe - lá!
lê - ga, _ I took the pê - ga to a wo-man for a pê - la.

Colombia

This dance-song is known as a *bambuco*, one of the most characteristic of Colombian airs. In rhythm (an alternation of 6/8 and 3/4 meter) and melody it shows the influence of various cultures. In the words of a Colombian poet, the *bambuco* reflects "the combined strains of Indian melancholy, African ardor, and Andalusian valor."

Por Un Beso de Tu Boca—For a Tender Kiss

English version by
Charles Haywood

Allegro moderato

Por un be - so de tu bo - ca, Yo no
For a ten - der kiss, be - lov - ed, All pos -

sé lo que da - rí - a, Tal vez en mi fie - bre
ses - sions I would give up; In my burn - ing pas - sion,

lo - ca Al be - sar - te mo - ri - rí - a.
no doubt, Kis - sing you would make my heart stop.

No sé que me pa - sa - rí - a Por un be - so de tu
Oh, what long-ing stirs with-in me For a ten - der kiss, be -

bo - ca. No sé que me pa - sa - rí - a Por un
lov - ed. Oh, what long - ing stirs with - in me For a

94

be - so de tu bo - ca. En tu bo - qui - ta de
ten - der kiss, be - lov - ed. In your ru - by lips en -

gra - na Ha - lla - rán los co - li - brí - es
tic - ing, Filled with hon - ey o - ver - flow - ing,

El néc - tar to - do que ma - na De un ma -
All the hum - ming birds in - vit - ing Your sweet

no - jo de a - le - li - es, Por-que hay miel cuan-do te
love - li - ness a - dor - ing. For your smile is full of

rí - es En tu bo - qui - ta de gra - na. Por-que hay
hon - ey And __ your ru - by lips en - tic - ing, For your

miel cuan-do te rí - es En tu bo - qui - ta de gra - na.
smile is full of hon - ey And your ru - by lips en - tic - ing.

English version Copyright © 1966 by Charles Haywood

95

Chile

English version by
Charles Haywood

El Tortillero—The Tortillas Vendor

Allegretto

1. No-che os-cu - ra, na - da ve - o Pe - ro lle - vo
1. Dark the night is, to - tal black-ness, With a lan - tern

mi fa - rol,___ Por tus puer-tas, voy pa - san-do, Y can-
in my hand, Near your dwell-ing, my heart swell-ing With a

tan - do con a - mor. ___ Mas ___ voy can-tan-do ___
song of love re - sounds. _ Loud ___ is my sing-ing,_

___ Con ___ har - ta pe - na,___ Quien com-pra mis_
___ All ___ hear it ring-ing: ___ Come, buy my fresh_

___ tos - ta - i - tas,___ Tor - ti - llas bue - nas.
___ tos - ta - i - tas,___ Deli - cious tor - ti - llas.

2. *Bella ingrata, no respondes*
   A mi grito placentero
   Cuando pasa por tu casa,
   Pregonando el tortillero.
   Refrain:

3. *Ya me voy a retirar*
   Con mi canasto y farol,
   Sin tener tu compasion
   De este pobre tortillero.
   Refrain:

2. Heartless beauty does not answer
   To my lusty, joyful cry,
   When I walk near your house, my dear,
   Begging all my food to buy.
   Refrain:

3. I've gone far now down the long road
   Carrying basket and lantern too;
   But no pity have you shown
   On this poor tortillero.
   Refrain:

Ecuador

The pentatonic melodic contour and rhythmic inflection of this old Indian melody, a *yaravi*, recaptures the musical world of the ancient Quechuas, who constituted the major group of the Inca empire. Here, with few exceptions, it is sung in their native tongue.

En Sumag Palacio—In My Spacious Palace

English version by
Charles Haywood

2. *Sumag pan de huevo,*
   —Kušniko—
   Mikuxungi mi;
   Ñoeka sara kamiča,
   —Kušniko—
   Yuyaringi mi.

2. The tastiest foods you'll have,
   —Let us eat—
   As much as you want;
   Our humble meals of corn,
   —Let us eat—
   You will remember.

Paraguay

The highly exquisite lace made by the women of Paraguay is called *Ñandutí*, derived from its delicate structure imitating the spider's web (ñandu-tí). The lace is always worked in circle patterns, and each motif has a secret meaning and a special name of identification. The women sing the song while at work.

La Tejedora de Ñandutí—The Weaver of Ñandutí

English version by
Charles Haywood

Moderato

1. A - quí bien le - jos, A - quí bien le - jos de nues - tra
1. Far from my coun-try, Far from my coun - try and all my

pa - tria, Tie - rra del ma - té, Tie - rra del
peo - ple, Land of the ma - té, Land of the

ma - té y a - za - har, Yo quie - ro en
ma - té and or - ange groves; In songs of

ver - sos, Yo quie - ro en ver - sos can - tar te u - fa - na, ___
glad - ness, In songs of glad - ness I'll sing so proud - ly, ___

a tempo

___ Mu - jer her - mo - sa, mu - jer her -
___ Of the love - li - est wo - man, the love - liest

mo - sa del Pa - ra - guay. ___
wo - man of Pa - ra - guay. ___

2. *Cuando en las tardes siento nostalgias*
   De nuestros campos y el naranjal,
   En ti yo leo todo un poema
   De las florestas del Paraguay.

2. I'm filled with longing for my dear country,
   Its hills and valleys and orange trees;
   You are my poem and sweetest music,
   Oh wondrous land of Paraguay.

Peru

A beautiful blend of Indian (Quechua) and Spanish elements; a haunting pentatonic melody of tender expressiveness and rhythmic subtlety. "Wetata," in Quechuan, means tender flower.

Rio de Avenida—Overflowing Torrent

English version by
Charles Haywood

Ri - o de a - ve - ni - da, __ dé - ja - me pa - sar,
Riv - er, over - flow - ing tor - rent, __ oh, do let me pass,

A mi pa - lo - mi - ta __ la quie - ren ma - tar
My sweet dove a - waits __ me, __ they'll kill her, a - las!

Con pis - to - la de o - ro, __ ba - la de cris - tal.
A gold - en __ pis - tol, load - ed __ bul - lets of crys - tal.

We - ta - ta, We - ta - ta, ma - ra - vi - lla we - ta, We - ta - ta!
We - ta - ta, We - ta - ta, mar - vel - ous we - ta, We - ta - ta!

Uruguay

The *estilo*, also widespread in neighboring Argentina, is a song consisting of two parts: the first, slow and "melancholy" in 2/4 time, and the second, fast and spirited, in 6/8 (or 3/4) time. This song is in ballad style, in *decima* (ten-line, octosyllabic verse) structure. José Artigas is the national hero of Uruguay, whose valorous exploits for his country's independence have become legendary.

Estilo

English version by
Charles Haywood

1. La au - ro - ra em - pie - za a bri - llar ___
1. The sky is a - glow in the morn - ing,

y a - lum - brar el sol de ma - yo,
Greet - ing the dawn with its sun - shine,

a es - te pa - trio - ta u - ru - gua - yo
Stir - ring the hearts of Uru - gua - yans

que a - quí pre - ten - de can - tar; ___
In songs of de - vo - tion re - sound - ing.

Hoy em - pie - za a mur - mu - rar ___
Hark to the voi - ces chant - ing

el u - ru - guay cau - da - lo - so, _____
U - ru - guay's great - ness and splen - dor; _____

y en - tre el con - cier - to ar - mo - nio - so _____
Hymns filled with beau - te - ous won - der _____

de flo - res, a - ves y es - pi - gas, _____
Of flow-ers, and rich fer - tile val - leys, _____

re - sue - na el nom - bre de Ar - ti - gas,
Proclaim - ing the name of Ar - ti - gas,

co - mo un e - co mis - te - rio - so.
The coun - try's most glo - rious de - fend - er.

2. Artigas fué el gran guerrero
   que luchando en cien batallas,
   a estas playas uruguayas
   libertó del extranjero;
   él fué deseado lucero,
   que en la patria apareció;
   al criollo puro alumbró
   en las noches de sus penas,
   para romper las cadenas,
   con que un rey lo esclavizó.

2. Artigas fought with great valor,
   Hundreds of battles he conquered;
   Treacherous enemies he vanquished,
   Freedom he brought to our shore.
   Bright as a morning star,
   Shining upon our dear country;
   No more's the Creole unhappy,
   Darkness and suffering no longer,
   Royal chains broke asunder,
   Free from oppression and slavery.

Surinam

The music of the Surinam Negroes displays their African origin in the tonal mode, range and structure, harmonic combination, rhythm and instruments. This song is repeated with other names substituted for Gado, such as Papa, Mama, etc.

Lĕba Gado—Lĕba God

English version by
Charles Haywood

4 times with minor variations

Venezuela

This dance-song is in the characteristic Venezuelan *llanero* ("melody of the plains") style: lyrical, smoothly flowing Spanish rhythm, within the tonal range of an octave.

Bogando á La Luz del Sol—Rowing Toward the Sunlight

English version by
Charles Haywood

Moderato con molto sentimento

So - plan la bri - sas de la___ ma - ña - na, Ri - zan-do el
Gent - ly ca - res - ses the breeze in the morn-ing With rip - pling

la - go mur - mu - ra - dor, Y por o -
mur - mur the silv' - ry lake; The east - ern

rien - te su faz a . - so - ma Cual ra - ro in -
sky - line with lights a - glow-ing In fie - ry

cen - dio la luz del sol. Y por o -
bril - liance the sun ap - pears. The east - ern

rien - te___ su faz a - so - ma___ Cual ra - ro in -
sky - line___ with lights a - glow-ing___ In fie - ry

cen - dio___ la luz del sol.___
bril - liance___ the sun ap - pears.___

Europe

United Kingdom

ENGLAND: The English folksong, characterized by unadorned simplicity and straightforward rendition, reflects the varied activities on the farm, village and town; seafaring life and religious activities; children's games and songs and the pursuit of soldiering and travel, as well as love songs. Traditional ballads (first carefully studied and analyzed by the indefatigable Francis James Child in his monumental work *The English and Scottish Popular Ballads*, whose classification is known to students as the "Child Ballads"), are among the richest treasures of the English folksong. They recount heroic deeds, bold adventure, gruesome tragedies, humorous incident, and fanciful invention. Many of their variants are found in the United States and in numerous countries on the Continent. These melodies are often in modal tonalities, with a predominant number in the Ionian mode, our modern major scale. One also encounters melodies in the Aeolian mode (a to a on the white keys of the piano), Dorian mode (d to d on the white keys), and Mixolydian mode (g to g on the white keys). Cecil Sharp, leading scholar of English folksong, characterized the essential aspects of its melodies as being "remarkable for their large compass, the unexpectedness and width of their intervals, and the boldness and vigour of their melodic curves."

SCOTLAND: While the folk music of the Scottish Lowlands is closely identified with that of England, the musical idiom of the Highlanders and the inhabitants of the Isles of the Hebrides shows affinity to the Gaelic spirit and temperament. The wealth of their folksong is reflected in the numeous traditional, historical, and national ballads, proclaiming with patriotic fervor the heroic deeds of their

Scottish leaders; work songs, love songs, humorous songs, and the vibrant accompaniment of the fiddle and bagpipe, punctuated by strong accent and the so-called "Scottish Snap." These old melodies, wedded to the folk poetry of Robert Burns and other gifted poets, have been made accessible to the world at large.

The antiquity of Scottish music is evidenced in the modality and pentatonic character of the tunes, predating Celtic cultural influences. The austerity, loneliness and "mystery" of Hebridian social existence and pursuits are subtly reflected in their haunting melodies. Their folksongs range "from Eastern-like hypnotic croons to big sweeping airs with a range of nearly two octaves, rapturous sea-chanties, processional refrain songs, labour lilts, and mystic chants filled with the glow of love and exultation of light."

WALES: Wales' rich musical heritage, dating from the pre-Christian era, had been transmitted by their ancient bards and harpers. The importance of music in the lives of the Welsh, and the high degree of their musical accomplishments, have been attested by many historians. The oft-quoted comments of Giraldus Cambrensis of the twelfth century highlights this musical vitality: "In their musical concerts they do not sing in unison like the inhabitants of other countries, but in many different parts; so that in company of singers, which one frequently meets in Wales, you will hear as many different parts and voices as there are performers who all at length unite with organic melody, in one consonance, and the soft sweetness of B flat." A great deal of this Cymric or Welsh musical tradition has been lost and disseminated after centuries of political, religious and social change. The peasantry is still the main source of this folk heritage, having retained, to a large degree, its ancient language, customs and folk music. The distinctive quality of Welsh folk melody is, according to Alfred Daniel, the descendant of a *recitative* or recitation scale, full of quarter tones and augmented or "grave" intervals, resembling the Dorian mode. The rhythm of Welsh folk melody is strongly affected by the speech accents, where words of more than one syllable have their stress on the penultimate syllable.

Ireland

The songs of Ireland fall under two major classifications, those of the Irish (Gaelic) speaking people, and the English-speaking people. The Gaelic songs, expressed in vivid poetic imagery, deal with every aspect of the people's activities: their daily labors—plowing, milking, spinning; religious songs, laments, love songs, drinking songs, lullabies, humorous songs, narrative airs, and many others. A distinctive feature of Gaelic folk poetry is the prevalence of assonantal rhyme: the repetition of identical vowel sounds in every stressed syllable of the poetic pattern. The occurrence of these assonances on the accented beats of the musical phrase produces an effect of graceful motion and lyrical intensity. As with all people—bound to the land, eking out subsistence from an unyielding soil, enduring foreign oppression—the Irish folk music expresses profound grief and deep yearning. Yet, at the same time, there is also a compensatory release in boundless laughter, rollicking humor, and hopeful enthusiasm. The spirited rhythms of the songs, and dances: the reels, the jigs, and the hornpipes, accompanied by the pipers, fiddlers, and fifers—all bear witness to the true Gaelic spirit.

The Anglo-Irish folksongs often lack the poetic and musical merit of their Gaelic forebears. "The poetic fancy, choice diction and variety of themes, which are marked features of the songs of the Irish, have here no counterpart, and the words too often are an ill match for the airs in terms of beauty . . . they represent the attempts of the people to express themselves in a language with which they had an imperfect and recently acquired acquaintance." In spite of these critical observations, one can still find an abundant number of tunes that capture the spirit of the folk both in text and melody. The Irish variants of the old English and Scottish ballads afford the student of comparative folksong interesting aspects and valuable data on the problems of ballad migration and diffusion.

The Netherlands and Belgium

THE NETHERLANDS: The widespread diffusion of folksongs among the various ethnic groups in the Netherlands and neighboring

Germany and France, may be attested by the fact that the leading Dutch composers of the fifteenth and sixteenth centuries made freqent use of them in their extended polyphonic compositions, secular and sacred. Furthermore, due to close economic and political contacts between Elizabethan England and Holland, one finds in the latter country many folksongs of English origin. Among the many valuable source books of early Dutch folksongs is the *Nederlandtsche Gedenckclanck* of Adrianus Valerius (1626). There is also an unmistakable close affinity of the Dutch folk music with that of the German *Volkslied*. In both instances the tunes usually begin on the upbeat, with the musical rhythm determined by the word-accent, and a great number of the melodies possessing a strong harmonic determining element. These common aspects led one of the earliest students of German folksong to state: "The German and the old Netherland folksongs are indistinguishable, for from the last half of the 15th to the end of the 16th century they had a fund of folk poetry in common. And among the songs contained in the Netherland collections many were written in High and Low German." (Frederick Böhme)

BELGIUM: The folk music of Belgium reflects the bilingual ethnic groupings, the Flemish and Walloon. The former have close affinity with the Dutch, while the latter are culturally linked to the French. Indeed, this folk music displays many of the general characteristics of their southern neighbors: flowing grace, lilting dancelike movement, a predilection for satirical texts, as well as abundant examples of old traditional ballads with their frequent use of modal melodies.

Germany

German folk music has been greatly affected, in its tonal structure and manner of interpretation, by the cultivated fine art music. Perhaps more than any other European country, it shows the influence of Western musical composition. Thus, part-singing appears early, as well as "artistic expression." A general prevalent characteristic of German folksong is the use of the upbeat, and a rising motion of the melodic line. The melodies generally show symmetrical construction, moving toward the dominant, with a recapitulation, or with slight variation, ending on the tonic. The tunes are usually in the major mode, with straightforward syllabic division, and with rare melismatic embellishment. Regional ethnic characteristics are still found in Bavaria, Westphalia, Swabia, and Silesia.

As in other countries, the folk music of Germany shows strains of other peoples and cultures. Indeed, the traditional links of the past, from the primitive Indo-Germanic race down to the Mediterranean civilizations, are still evident in certain tunes and texts. The old ballads, among which many English and Scottish variants are to be found, recount stirring historical events, as well as local happenings, shedding much light on traditions, customs and beliefs. Old village instruments—the dulcimer, the hurdy-gurdy, bagpipes and shawms (primitive oboe)—usually accompanied the ballad singer. All major events in Germany's history—social, political, economic, religious and military—find ample expression in their great repertory of folksongs. To mention but a few: the apprentice and journeymen songs, soldiers' and students' songs, songs of the various occupations, songs of the seasons, lyrical and love songs, songs of the homeland (*Heimat*) and Alpine (*Schnadahüpfl*) songs. The *Ländler* and *Polkas* are favorite folk dances.

The forces that have brought a change, and, to some observers, a decline, in the continuing vitality of German folk music, are the same that have influenced the songs of other highly developed industrialized countries. According to Walter Wiora, the German folk music has been replaced "by other forms of popular music: church and social songs, political propaganda songs, hits for the masses[!], ballroom dances and popular entertainment music." Wiora, distinguished scholar that he is, laments the shift from rural to urban centers, and fails to recognize the emergence of a new, and equally vital, folk music reflecting contemporary social change.

Austria

While the chief characteristics of the various types of Austrian folksongs—the sacred songs, the ballads, and the songs of daily life—are quite similar to those of southern Germany, the most indigenous ones are the *Alpenlieder* (Alpine songs). The most popular of these are the *Yodler* of Tirol. Close to the heart of all Austrians are the *Schnadahüpfl*, a dance-song consisting of one stanza of four lines, sung to the tunes of the *Ländler*, the progenitors of the waltz. While the texture and content of a great many of the Austrian folkways reflect the wealth and variety of the lives and activities of the people, certain characteristic qualities are observable. These are, briefly, a prevailing emphasis on the major mode, a diatonic sequence of melodic configuration, a regular pattern of tonal structure, a close correlation of syllabic stress with accented beats of the bar, and a strong predilection for part-singing.

In Austria the fine art of the "cultivated" musicians was always in close contact with the folk, and many of their compositions show the strong influence of folk music. This close affinity was aptly stated by one observer: "The success of the Vienna waltz was also in great part due to the fact that both Lanner and the 'Strauss dynasty of musicians' had sprung from the people, and knew how to create in a popular way."

Within the folk music of this relatively small Austria of today, there not only echo the ethnic memories of its geographic and political past, but also the rich variety of the folk culture in each of its present nine provinces. There is an abundant heritage and creative continuity of songs, dances and instrumental patterns. These reflect all aspects of life—in Burgenland, in the southeast, with its Croat and Hungarian traditions; in Tirol, reflecting the vital effects of Swiss and Italian influences. The same amalgation of cultural factors is to be found in Niederoesterreich, Kärnten, and in the other provinces.

France

The crosscurrents of various peoples and cultures—after many years of wars, conquests and intermingling—have left their imprint on the folk music of France. Indeed, the various provinces still show effects of these contacts in language, customs, folksongs and folk dances, and type of instruments. Thus we find Celtic (Welsh, Scottish, and Irish) elements in the folk music in Brittany; in southwest France the Basque influence, in melodic contour and rhythmic pulse, is quite evident; the essential characteristics of Flemish folk music are still heard in the north; the Germanic Rhineland of the east left its mark. The diffusion among the French of many old ballads, lyric songs, and dances of outside origin attest further to the rich heritage of the country's folk tradition.

All the various activities of the French people: on the farm and in trade, on land and sea; their religious life and their hours of contemplation and gaiety, family life, with its pleasures, sadness and merrymaking—all these are vividly reflected in their folk music. We can hear the lusty sea songs of the region of Cotentin in Basse-Normandie; the plaintive and insisting *briolée*, or plowing song, of Berry; the lyrical melodies of Provence, some still reminiscent of the courtly troubadour spirit of the twelfth century, as well as the sustained or melismatic church chant; the plaintive laments and wailing songs of Corsica. The delicate dancelike lilt and the delightfully insinuating texts of the *pastourelles* (many of these found their way into the popular theater and "vaudevilles") are favorites in many regions of France, as well as the tender *berceuses* (lullabies), and the abundance of contemplative and joyful *Noëls* (Christmas songs).

Switzerland

This small country, resplendent in natural beauty of mountains and lakes, presents as rich a variety in folklore and folksong. Within its borders one finds four distinct geographic-ethnic regions: the German-speaking area of the north, east and center of the country; the French-speaking section of the Alpine chain; the Italian area south of the Alpine chain, and Romanic Switzerland on the Grisons in the southeastern part. Each of these regions has produced a folk music reflecting the linguistic, ethnic, and cultural traits of the people.

The life of the mountaineers and shepherds is reflected in many songs and dances. Songs of the shepherds express every facet of their life: their toil, their ardent patriotism, their love, despair and pleasures. They have a rich repertoire of ballads, *Kuhreihen* (*ranz de*

111

vaches), dance songs, yodeling songs, patriotic and homesickness songs, love songs (especially in German-Switzerland), the so-called *Kilt* (songs of nocturnal visits by lovers to their girls, with their parents' consent!), songs of mockery and ridicule, songs of seasons, and religious songs, capturing in pointed simplicity and lyrical tenderness the various holidays in their church calendar. Their religious zeal is reflected in the many choral part-songs, a distinctive feature of their spiritual togetherness; cradle songs, spinning songs, serenades and morning songs, and soldiers' songs. Most of their songs are in the major mode. One readily associates the Alpine folk with the "yodel," and its accompanying instrument the "alphorn." It is not easy to define the "yodel," and its particular manner of execution. It may be said to be an "exuberant vocalise; a sense of joy and pride, in harmony with nature; perhaps, a primitive outburst of exultation."

Italy

The various provinces of Italy, formerly separate and independent states, have developed distinct cultural, social and ethnic characteristics, as well as different dialects. These idiosyncrasies are reflected in the songs of the people and their various activities. The Italians have been rightly called "the singiest folk"; their very speech, as one aptly put it, is "operatic." Their folksongs display the perfect fusion between word and melody, between the musical rhythm and bodily movement.

Each province has shaped, through the centuries, individual qualities peculiar to itself. Thus, the Piedmontese, an agricultural people, show predilection for the historical dramatic narrative, while the Tuscan stresses the strongly personalized, introspective lyrical song, illustrated in the *rispetti*. Venetian love songs have a simple and homely quality, "often in a mood of half-playful cynicism." They do not indulge in parody or burlesque, or the "luxuriant imagination" frequently found in Sicilian folk lyrics. Nor do the Venetian songs possess the intense refinement of the Tuscan serenader. The traditional ritual and songs connected with the christening of the newborn child, the tender lyricism of the cradle songs (*Ninna-nanna*), the

112

gondolier's nostalgic love song and the rhythmic chant of the Lido fisherman are some of the songs expressing the manifold activities of the Venetians.

Sicily, the crossroad of many cultures and historic events, has been, according to some scholars, "the original fountainhead of Italian popular poetry and the source of the greater part of songs which circulate through Italy." One still hears the Sicilian peasant sing the old historical ballads and various religious songs of great antiquity. He expresses his love sentiments in the *ciuri* (called in Tuscany *stornelli*), couplets or triplets beginning with the name of a flower, with which the other line or lines have to rhyme, and *canzuni*, consisting of eight lines. As in all parts of Italy, one finds in Sicily an abundance of nursery songs and rhymes. Contact with Greece and the Arabic influence of Northern Africa have left their imprint— in melodic contour, microtonal intervals, elaborate melisma and rhythmic pattern—on Sicilian folksongs.

However, one must not overlook a very striking similarity of folksong tradition and performance practice found in many different regions of Italy. Thus, polyphonic forms, in various degrees of complexity, are heard in the *canti a vatoccu* (bell-like imitation) in Marche, in the *lamintari* (lamentations) in Sicily, in the *canti battipali* (pile drivers) of Venice, in the *serenate* and *stornelli* in the south, in the *sostenores* (shepherds' songs) in Sardinia, and the *trallalero* (mariner's song) of Liguria. Similar practices have also been heard in Lazio, Umbria and Sicily. The importance of cultivated musical forms, such as the opera and the popular *canti*, particularly in urban centers, has strongly influenced the melodic and rhythmic aspects of many Italian folksongs.

Spain

The vitality and variety of Spanish folk music is the product of the intermingling of many different cultures, aided by the natural physical topography of the Iberian peninsula. Each region has contributed its own specific ethnic flavor and spirit—in melody, rhythm and text—to the quality of the Spanish folksong and dance. Thus, the folk music of Andalusia, considered by foreigners the most "typical" of Spanish music, reflects strong Oriental influences: the Byzantine chant, Moslem melody, Gypsy music, and Hebraic cantillation. These factors are superbly reflected in the passionate and intense *cante hondo*, or deep song—in the sliding vocal line, iterative embellishments, the insistent repetition of a simple tune, the clapping, and the "Olé's!"; the subtle alternation of rhythmic accents in the *falsetas*, the instrumental interludes performed on the guitar. The wide variety of *flamenco* music—*malagueñas, alegrias, granadinas, sevillanas* and others—mirrors all the subtle nuance, the joyous abandon and utter despair of Spanish folk life.

The folk music of Murcia shows the effect of contact on the western side with the complex *flamenco* style of southern Andalusia, and the more simple, triple-meter, major-tonality melodies of their Valencian-Catalan neighbors to the east. This general influence of regional culture contact is apparent in all other areas of Spain. Thus, while a great body of Extremaduran folk music shows the effect of long domination by the Moslems, its own northern and eastern neighboring regions, León, and Old and New Castile, have left their imprint in the numerous *tonadas* (ballad tunes), *aradas* (plowing songs), Christmas carols, and children's games. This vitality of regional change is also apparent in the subtle variations in the *seguidilla* of New Castile, achieving uniqueness in La Mancha, subtly changing in Murcia and Andalusia to *seguidillas sevillanas* and *seguidillas boleras*, each adding a nuance of its own. The distinctive flavor of Catalan music is the product of ancient French troubadour melodies, an admixture of complex Mediterranean elements, and Basque and Castillian influence. The *sardana* eloquently captures the spirit and temperament of the Catalan. Galicia's proximity to Portugal shows the inevitable effects on its speech and song—in the *alalá* (melody based on the ballad stanza) and the *muiñeira*, in 6/8 meter, accompanied by the *gaita gallega* (bagpipe).

Portugal

Although some of the Portuguese folksongs, especially those of the

114

eastern provinces, show considerable affinity with the folk music of Spain, the remarkable fact is the extraordinary individuality and variety that distinguish them from those of its larger neighbor. It is no more possible to generalize on the characteristics of the folk music of a relatively smaller country than on one occupying a greater area.

Portuguese folksong research has long been obscured by romantic oversimplification and unverified sentimental attachment to Spanish idiom. Sober investigation has discovered that the folksongs and dances of Portugal possess distinctive features and qualities having no relation or affinities to Spanish music. "It is sufficient to cite the *corais* from Alentejo, the *cramóis* of Minho, certain religious songs from Beira and a large number of songs whose 'exotic' flavor is absolutely distinctive and constitutes one of the greatest surprises of the latest investigations."

The songs of the peasantry, the *cantigas*, and *cançòes*, show the influence of many diverse sources: the Arabic, "chanting in a minor key, with a pointless, halting measure and vague rhythm"; and the medieval church modes and highly ornamented Gregorian chant. The growth of urban life and the effect of popular music (gramophone, radio, and American jazz) have not only affected the authentic ethnic regional melodies, but have also commercialized the *fado* (popular dance-song, consisting of strongly rhythmic, symmetrically alternating patterns between tonic and dominant), and the lyrical, sentimental *modinha*.

Norway

Norway's awareness of its folk heritage was strongly influenced by the country's national awakening and political separation from Denmark in 1814. Fired by national pride, Norway's scholars rediscovered their country's long-neglected cultural treasures. The peasantry yielded a rich harvest of native folk music: songs, dances, and indigenous instruments.

The valorous deeds and bold adventures of their national heroes are immortalized in their ancient ballads, the *kjempeviser*. Many of those bear strong resemblance to the old traditional English and

115

Scottish ballads.

All the various activities of the Norwegian folk find expression in characteristic tunes and rhythms. Delightfully captivating are the melodies connected with the summer cheese farms (*saltermelodier*), and the cattle calls (*lokk*) sung by the milkmaids. Equally representative are the songs and dances connected with spinning, weaving, courting, lullabies, humor, and religion.

Sweden

The folk music (*folkvisa*) of the Swedish peasants is rich in traditional ballads, many of them showing strong affiliation with those of England and Scotland, herdsman's calls, and occupational songs connected with the farm and cattle. The haunting quality of the shepherd's cow calls, played on the long pipe-shaped wooden horns, has given that special melancholy characteristic to its music. A lighter, happier ring to Swedish folk music is conveyed by the milkmaid's *spilopipa*, a recorder-like instrument made of pinewood.

The violin, which influenced its dance tunes and rhythms, may be rightfully claimed to be its national instrument. The fiddler is the center of peasant festivals, weddings, dances, and holy days. The tradition of the strolling fiddlers is still strong in spite of the increasing impact of the radio and television.

Various other factors have shaped the character of the Swedish folksongs. Among them may be mentioned the solemn majesty of the German chorales brought to the country by the Reformation, the French court dances of the seventeenth century, and the folk music of Sweden's Scandinavian neighbors.

Denmark

The geographic position of Denmark, and its small size, made it easy prey for conquest by various European countries in their numerous struggles for political, national and economic power. They all culturally affected the native Danes in varying degrees. Their folklore and folksong reflect these ethnic and cultural influences. Thus, we find many Swedish, French, English, and German melodic strains and textual similarities in Danish ballads, work songs, soldiers' songs, religious tunes and children's songs and games. Love lyrics particularly show strong affiliation with German song-poetry.

Iceland

The cultural influences—in language, traditions and music—of Iceland's mother country, Norway, remained comparatively the same from the first settlements in the ninth century to more recent times. The old declamatory style, strongly affected by the medieval chant, is still heard in the epic ballads narrating the heroic exploits of its folk heroes. These ballads are characterized by direct simplicity and austerity of melodic line, mostly cast in the Lydian mode (f to f on the white keys of the piano). The contemporary Icelandic folksong, still an offshoot of old Norwegian folk patterns, reflects all facets of life and mood.

Finland

The ancient Finnish ballads recounting the fearless deeds of its mighty heroes, chanted to the recurrent trochaic pulse of its expressive melody, the *runo*, reflect "the land of a thousand lakes, the vast stretches of moors, silent forests and long, dark winters." Indeed, there is no better instance of the remarkable synthesis of text and melody reflecting the physiographic characteristics and cultural traits of a people. The changing moods of the folk, as with the landscape, are discernible in the varying quality of the *runo* melody; epic in the *Kalevala*, and lyric-romantic in the *Kanteletor*.

Foreign influences have inevitably affected the ancient melodies and introduced new tunes and rhythmic patterns into the Finnish folk tradition. Of these, the Russians, Swedes, and Germans, both in their folk music and cultivated art forms, left their strongest imprint.

The *kantele*, a psaltery, is their favorite instrument both for vocal accompaniment and for dancing. The violin, clarinet, the accordion, and various horns and pipes play an important part, singly or in ensemble.

The Soviet Union

A great deal of the Russian folksong is rooted in the ancient Slavic pagan rites. In spite of church restrictions and social change, they have persisted in the folk traditions for many centuries. These origins can be traced in the funeral laments, wedding songs and in the calendar songs. The dramatic element—from the simple, lyrical to the complex and passionate—can be found in each of these categories. The epic narrative ballads (*byliny*), a product of the Kiev period, have left a rich legacy of custom, tradition, historical and social events, and heroic characters of Russia's past. After the Tatar invasions of the eleventh and twelfth centuries, the cultural center shifted to Novgorod. The Northern *byliny*—of short vocal range, rarely exceeding an octave, with frequent intervals of a fourth and sixth—were sung in a sustained declamatory manner. Other distinctive features of the melodies of these ballads are their modal character, the frequent occurrence of the triton (augmented fourth or diminished fifth—b to f), and also certain tritonic features such as fragments of a tone-semitone scale and passages of diminished triads (e-g^b). These epic ballads reflected every phase of life.

During the Muscovite period, from the fifteenth to the seventeenth centuries, the "historical song," akin to the *byliny*, played a dominant role. The songs dealt with the events and destiny of Russia's historical personages. The *khorovod* (round dance), formerly associated with the calendar spring cycle, now assumed independent vocal existence, with melodies of wide range and greater ornamentation. The most characteristic of Russian folksong, the "lyrical protracted song," with its "expressive melody and its great rhythmic freedom," achieved a significant place in the folk tradition. Similarly, songs of political nature, protest and satire emerge.

The great social and economic changes of the eighteenth century yielded a rich harvest of folk music: town songs, military songs, songs of peasant rebellions, humorous songs, and lyrical songs. This national awakening and cultural enthusiasm stimulated the first attempts at collecting and studying the folksong expression of the Russian people. The gathering of this material was zealously continued in the nineteenth century, with more scientific methods and critical techniques in analysis and arrangement of this material.

Russian folksongs are usually diatonic; they are devoid of any chromatic embellishments, so characteristic of Near Eastern music. However, one often encounters chromatic passing notes, but not in succession. Furthermore, there is no insistence that the song end on the tonic. Indeed, a Russian folksong can end on any degree of the scale. Most of the songs use the natural major (c-c') and minor scales (a-a'), with some modifications. It is these modifications—the use of the flattened supertonic in the minor scale (the second note, b♭) and the sharpened submediant (the sixth note, f♯), in the natural major scale the sharpened subdominant (the fourth note, f♯), and the flattened submediant (the sixth note, a♭)—that distinguish the Russian folksongs from all others. These alterations, in various sequences and combinations, evoke that special tonal idiosyncrasy and "flavor" of Russian folk music. The old liturgical scale (*znamenny chant*), containing a major third in the lower octave and a minor third in the upper, influenced many folksongs. Vocal polyphony is also an inherent characteristic of the Russian folksong. The leader-chorus manner of performance is very common in Russian folk singing. An interesting feature of the choral style is the improvisational manner and seeming independent motion of the various voices (*heterophony*), yet retaining its main outline, producing at various points two-, three-, and four-part harmony, gravitating toward a unison at the cadence.

The Baltic States (U.S.S.R.)

ESTONIA, LATVIA, LITHUANIA: These three Baltic states have many common cultural traits, and these are abundantly manifested in their folkways and folk music. With some inherent linguistic variations and rhythmic changes, there are great similarities in the types and structure of folksongs, dances and instruments used. Epic ballads describing the heroic deeds of their historic forebears, and those dealing with adventures of a more personal and lyric quality, if not less dramatic, are the common stock of all three countries. Some bear resemblance to the Finnish *runes*. Moreover, a number of these ballads are based on the same motifs as those of the Scandinavian, Celtic and English-speaking countries.

The most popular folksong, and also frequently used for dancing, is the *daina*. It consists of four short, unrhymed lines, in trochaic or dactylic meter, of eight syllables, and often making use of alliteration and assonance. Parallelism is a distinguishing characteristic of the *daina*, in which the first two lines contrast with the last two; they can be on personal matters, between a youth and a maiden, or a confrontation on ethical or moral problems—nature and human life, the world of the flesh and the spirit. They are usually sung in unison. Since the meter is dependent upon verbal accents, there is great variability and rhythmic changes in the melodies, from 5/4 to 3/4, are quite common. The tonalities of the older *dainas* are frequently based on the old modes. The *daina* mirrors, more than any other song, the various nuances of social and spiritual life of the humble folk.

It is important to note that songs glorifying war and cruelty are rare. Nor do they treat the love theme with intense passion and fervor, nor yield to the violent changes from utter resignation to jubilant exultation, that one finds in the folksongs of their Slavic neighbors. Rather, there is an aloofness, or coldness in its treatment. According to Balys, "The word *milestiba*, love, is a very great rarity." However, some of the most pregnant utterance is in the orphan songs. The wedding songs are both melancholy and cheerful, with the former mood predominating, as in the Lithuanian wedding dirges, *verkavimai*. Work songs reflect both the hardships of toil and the joyful satisfaction in accomplishment. Songs and dances of the harvest are abundant; it is an occasion for communal effort and spirited merrymaking, such as the Latvian *talka* and the Lithuanian *dzukai*. These get-togethers also provided opportunity for singing the *sutarinés*, Lithuanian choral rounds, now only kept "alive in the northeastern part of the country and sung by women." Some religious songs, particularly those of Christmas and Calendar festivals, still retain many pre-Christian customs, beliefs, and ritual, showing their origin in fertility rites and pagan symbolism. These people, living at the sea and dependent upon it for their livelihood, have a large repertory of fishermen's songs, reflecting every aspect of their toilsome labors.

Armenia (U.S.S.R.)

The folk music of Armenia, among the most ancient musical cultures, is a blend of European and Arabic elements. The rich admixture continues from the songs of the early rhapsodic *ashugs*, the bards and minstrels, reaching its zenith in the time of Haroun al Raschid, to their modern counterparts, extolling the achievements of the local heroes on the collective farms in Soviet Armenia. The heroic epics of the *ashugs*, accompanied on the *saz* (a guitar-shaped instrument of Persian origin), were most eloquently expressed in one of the various appropriate musical forms known as the *mukhgam*. The element of improvisation was an important feature. The rhapsodic quality of ancient Armenian music was performed and transmitted to the folk by the *vipisani* and the *gusani*, who, in former days, entertained the nobility. Today their musical offspring glorify life under Communism.

As with the folksong of all people, the Armenian expresses every aspect of life—his happiness and despair, his daily hard toil and the exuberant joys—in singing, dancing and instrumental music. Since the Armenian, until recently, was closely associated with ancient methods of farming and the life of a shepherd, his songs depicted every aspect of these activities. The most expressive of these songs are the *orovels*, associated with plowing, accompanied with onomatopoeic sounds "imitating such noises as the squeaking of plow-wheels, the clanking of chains, or the snorting of draft-cattle."

Poland

The influence of the church and ritual on Polish folk music has been a vital factor from the tenth century, when Poland embraced Catholicism. Equally important were the contacts with Western music and culture. This is particularly true in the southern part of Poland, where the musical idiosyncrasies of Germany, Hungary, Byelorussia and Ukraine are to be found. Even Scandinavia left impressions on Polish music.

121

Certain marked characteristics appear in many old Polish folksongs: the range rarely exceeds a seventh—"the smaller the range the older the tunes"—the repetition and alteration of short motives, and the frequent initial skip of a seventh. The songs are usually monophonic, and are of irregular structure, consisting of 6, 7, 9, 10 or 11 bars. Some of them are full of ornamentation, and, in the case of the old melodies, are based on the pentatonic mode—"the crux of the Polish melos." Moreover, Western influences, from the folk and cultivated sources, have produced many melodic, rhythmic, and structural changes. The tunes are predominantly in triple meter, although southern and eastern regions "succumb" to duple meter. The tempi frequently consist of fast sections counterbalanced by *tempo rubato* (a slowing up). An authentic Polish folk singer can easily be recognized by his distinct manner of singing. As one student of Polish folklore aptly described it: "high intonation and clamorousness are much favored, as well as a laryngeal emission (somewhat constricted tone quality) of the voice."

Czechoslovakia

As the name implies, the people of this country are divided into two ethnically distinct culture areas. "The drawing line along the river Morava," according to Karel Vetterl, "cuts the country almost in half. West of the river, the Czechs, Moravians, and the Bohemians display strong Occidental European characteristics, such as regular melodic construction, definite tonality, well-defined rhythmic periods and symmetrical form. On the other hand the folksongs east of the Morava [Slovakia] show a free construction, melodically and harmonically as well as rhythmically. A very close connection between words and tune, and melismas, free modulation, short melodic phrases and motives derived from prosody are conspicuous. Folksong thus approaches Oriental musical culture by way of the curve of the Carpathian Mountains to the Balkans and the domain of the old Byzantine music. . . . Ethnographical sources show that the Czech and Slovak folk music must originally have been identical and linked by common roots to the music of other Slavonic tribes and nationalities. This common Slavonic origin is proved chiefly by the *koledy*, ancient Christmas carols, as well as the New Year's and Easter songs of felicitation, accompanied by archaic rites to secure longevity and good fortune, ceremonies which point back to a pre-Christian origin."

Czech melodies usually are diatonic, in triple meter, in the major mode. The accompanying instrument associated with Czech folksongs is the shepherd's pipe, the *dudy*, or bagpipe. Its affiliation with Western musical style is evident in the extensive use of the *clarinet* in the instrumental accompanying bands. A general spirit of gaiety seems to permeate many of their songs. In contrast, the Slovak folk melodies are most frequently in duple meter, in the minor mode, and express deep sentiments of sadness and resignation, influenced no doubt by their Byzantine and Oriental tradition.

Hungary

The major characteristics of Magyar folk music, according to Bartók and Kodály, may be briefly summarized: Most of the tunes are connected with special occasions and special functions, many are derived from ancient ritual customs and ceremonies—such as those related to the harvest, marriage and death. These contain melodies of the old style: sharply defined rhythmic structure; a four-line stanza, varying from eight to twelve syllables per line; predominantly in the *pentatonic* (five-tone) scale; some (the slow melodies) performed in a free (*rubato*) and highly ornamented declamatory (*parlando*) manner, or in a more decisive (*giusto*) rhythmically accented *tempo* (speed)—found in quick melodies and dance tunes.

Another class of songs belongs to the new style. These tunes have a great deal in common with those mentioned in the preceding classification. However, the melodic structure, in relation to the four-line stanza, tends to be more exact and clear, with the characteristic melodic-rhythmic patter of ♪ ♩. ♩, that has become almost synonymous with all Hungarian folk music. In this group the melodies make greater use of the ecclesiastical or medieval modes. A third general category employs melodies of mixed characteristics: influences of foreign styles in melody, rhythm, structure, and tonal sequence.

Yugoslavia

The folk music of Yugoslavia is a hybrid of many cultural forces, European and Oriental, with the Slavic element a predominant factor. The two great crosscurrents of the Serbs, Croats and Slovenes, on the one hand, and that of western Europe and the Orient, on the other, have produced a cultural pattern reflecting the major characteristics of the Yugoslavian folksong.

The music of the southern Slavs resembles in many aspects the Russian folksong, in subject matter, melodic contour, and sense of harmony. There is also close kinship with the Russian heroic and historical ballads, sung to the accompaniment of the native instrument, the *gusla* (related to the violin). These traditional melodies are still performed, with deep intensity and dramatic fervor, by the blind beggars, the *gusylari*. In Slovenia, western Yugoslavia, the German influence predominates, in the use of the major and minor modes, the lyrical quality, and symmetrical structure. Although some strains of European contact have affected the songs of the Croatians in Medjimurye, bordering Hungary, they, nevertheless, represent perhaps the purest strain of indigenous Yugoslavian folk music, with their "broad and melancholy" melodies, small intervals, and with a range rarely exceeding a sixth.

A unique flavor, evoking the dim past and an older culture, is found in the folksongs of Istria and Dalmatia. These are frequently performed by two voices, moving in parallel thirds and sixths, ending in unison or in the octave. Arabic influences, through the Turks, dominate much of the music of Bosnia and Herzegovina, particularly that of Serbia and Macedonia. The Oriental augmented second occurs in many of their tunes, as well as the characteristic ornamentation and sudden intervallic leaps. The *svedalinke*, Bosnian love songs, with their broad expressive melodies, are eloquent examples of this cultural contact, and a product of acculturative factors. Moreover, in Serbia and Macedonia one also finds elements of Greek, Rumanian, Albanian, and Tatar melodic configuration.

Bulgaria

Many cultures left their traces and influences on the life and folklore of the Bulgarian people, the dominant one being that of the Slavs. Through historic and social changes the tradition of singing and dancing to the accompaniment of the *gusla* (one-stringed bowed instrument) continued. The predominant character of the dance-songs, with their residual symbolism of pagan ritual, is still retained today in their epic ballads, the *tlaki* (evening songs), the *horo* (chain dance), *sedenka* (night watch), *prepevki* (question-and-answer type of song), and others.

The most common structure of the Bulgarian folk tune, essentially for solo voice, is frequently a two-line diatonic melody, with the most characteristic intervals of a fourth and fifth, in the minor mode, symmetrically constructed, with a wealth of rhythmic variety, in measures displaying such varied metric groupings as five, seven, nine and eleven beats. Their dances have the same rhythmic subtlety and momentum. Indeed, "the organizing force of the rhythm is the leading element which faultlessly directs the dancers."

Rumania

The Rumanian folk music reflects, in varying degrees, the rhythmic, melodic, structural and interpretive characteristics and patterns of the different ethnic groups. Their Latin affiliation is clearly discernible not only in their language but also in the persistence of many qualities of French and Italian music. Slavic elements have had their influence on Rumanian folksongs and dances. The Hungarians have also contributed their share, but not as much as it was once believed. All these factors have been so remarkably assimilated that they give unique individuality to Rumania's musical folk expression.

Rumanian folk music, as that of other countries, has been best preserved in the isolated, mountainous areas, where residual pagan traditions, though somewhat admixed with Christian ritual, still persist. The amazing prowess of its heroes, the *Haidouques*, can still be heard, chanted to melodies derived from the old church modes. Songs of poignant melancholy and despair, the *doinas*, with their many trills and embellishments, or the wailing songs, the *voceri*, are balanced by songs and dances of abandoned gaiety, laughter, and humor, in the *horas, cantece*, and *colinde*.

Albania

Albanian folk display a great deal of the musical characteristics of the other people of the Illyrian territory. However, the style of diaphonous singing (a piquant clashing of seconds), still found in some of the neighboring countries, is remarkably preserved in Albania. This distinctive manner of performance has been lucidly described by A. L. Lloyd, based on the original investigations of Ramadan Sokoli. We take the liberty of quoting some of Mr. Lloyd's pertinent observations.

"Generally, within each district, three styles are found: the old-style (*pleqërishte*), the young folk's style (*djemurishte*) and the women's style (*grarishte*). The old-style songs are sung rather in the manner of plain chant, with a forced throaty tone and an epic-elegiac utterance. The *djemurishte* style is more vivacious, higher-pitched, rather open in tone. The two styles differ in polyphonic structure. In old-style songs, the lead singer may open with an ornamented flourish around the pedal note before displaying the melodic theme. A second solo voice replies, and following that the rest of the group roll out the ison. In most *djemurishte* songs, however, the theme is stated at the outset by the soloist, and the drone group in more or less from the start. Throughout the Albanian polyphonic area, women's songs are sung in different fashion from those of the men, even if the texts are identical. Thus in Pogradec and Korcë, the women sing in two parts, the men in three. In Labëri, the women sing in three parts, the men in four. If by chance men and women find themselves singing together, each sex keeps to its proper form. For example, in the neighborhood of Fier, the men sing in diaphony and the women answer in unison—but always in another pitch, sometimes a fifth higher. Among many attractive forms of group-singing described by Sokoli, the three-part style in which the second voice repeatedly breaks into yodel-like flourishes is worth particular mention."

126

Greece

Modern Greek folk music exhibits a multiplicity of influences of varying intensity and persistency: the glorious era of ancient Hellas, the Orient and Byzantium, the Near East, the Ottoman rule, the nationalist awakening of the nineteenth century, the Balkans and the Mediterranean. All these peoples and cultures strongly influenced the folk expression of the Greeks. Strains of ancient Hellenic melodies, reminiscent of the Homeric epic or the glories of Pericles, are still heard, however faintly, in the mountain recesses or among the isolated islanders. Every phase of the people's lives is reflected in their folksongs.

Of the historical songs those connected with the heroic struggle against Ottoman rule and with the War of Independence of 1821 are the most celebrated. These deal with the legendary feats of the Greek leaders, the *Klephts*, who fled to the mountains, and express their determination to free the land from Turkish oppression. The songs describe their valorous deeds, their ardent devotion, and love for freedom and their country. "Many of these Klephtic songs have a heroic tone, others have a delicate feeling of tenderness and love, and often a nostalgic yearning for peaceful life." There is a free, spontaneous and improvisatory quality in their long melismatic melodies.

The folk music of the Greeks exhibits not only their ancient traditional heritage in their persistent employment of ancient Greek modes and tonal systems, but also a considerable use of Oriental chromaticism as well as Western European diatonic influences. The general range of a great number of Greek melodies rarely goes beyond the octave or the ninth; structurally clearly defined, with a preponderant use of seven-part time (7/8, or 7/4) to a measure, "the Greek national time *par excellence*."

United Kingdom

This favorite ballad (Child, 286) appears in many melodic and textual versions, with the enemy being Turkish, French and Spanish. In one version the hero is Sir Walter Raleigh.

The Golden Vanity
(England)

1. A ship I have got in the North Coun - try And she goes __ by the name __ of the Gold - en Van - i - ty, O I fear she will be tak - en by the Span - ish Ga - la - lie, __ As she sails ____ by the Low - lands low, As she sails __ by the Low - lands low, by the Low - lands low, As she sails __ by the Low - lands low.

2. To the Captain then up spake the little Cabin-boy,
    He said, What is my fee, if the galley I destroy,
    The Spanish Galalie, if no more it shall annoy,
        As we sail by the Lowlands low?

3. Of silver and gold I will give you a store,
    And my pretty little daughter that dwelleth on the shore,
    Of treasure and of fee as well, I'll give to thee galore,
        As we sail by the Lowlands low.

4. Then the boy bared his breast, and straightway leaped in,
    And he held in his hand an augur sharp and thin,
    And he swam until he came to the Spanish Galleon,
        As she lay by the Lowlands low.

5. He bored with the augur, he bored once and twice,
    And some were playing cards, and some were playing dice,
    When the water flowed in, it dazzled their eyes,
        As she sank by the Lowlands low.

6. So the Cabin-boy did swim to the larboard side,
    Saying, Captain! take me in, I am drifting with the tide!
    I will shoot you! I will kill you! the cruel Captain cried,
        You may sink by the Lowlands low.

7. Then the Cabin-boy did swim all the starboard side,
    Saying, Messmates, take me in, I am drifting with the tide!
    Then they laid him on the deck, and he closed his eyes and died,
        As they sailed by the Lowlands low.

8. They sewed his body up, all in an old cow's hide,
    And they cast the gallant Cabin-boy over the ship' side,
    And left him without more ado adrifting with the tide,
        And to sink by the Lowlands low.

The old English custom of wassail (meaning *be hale*) singing, of ancient Saxon origin, was performed on January 5th, the eve of Epiphany. Drinking, merrymaking and exchange of gifts were part of the celebration.

Wassail
(England)

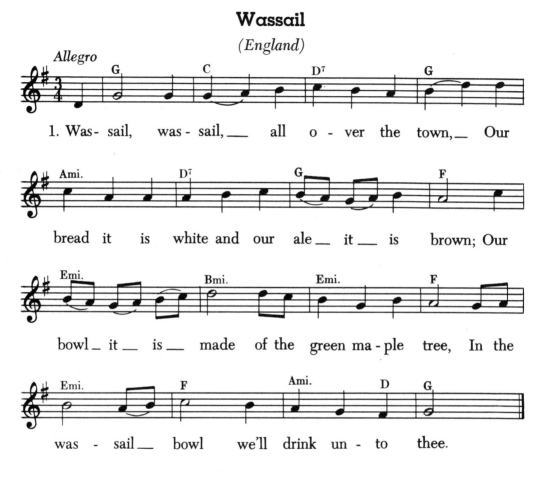

1. Was-sail, was-sail,__ all o-ver the town,__ Our bread it is white and our ale__ it__ is brown; Our bowl__ it__ is__ made of the green ma-ple tree, In the was-sail__ bowl we'll drink un-to thee.

2. Here's a health to the ox and to his long tail,
   Pray God send our master a good cask of ale;
   A good cask of ale as e'er I did see,
   In the wassail bowl we'll drink unto thee.

3. Come butler come fill us a bowl of the best,
   Then we pray that your soul in heaven may rest;
   But if you do bring us a bowl of the small,
   Then down shall go butler, bowl and all.

4. Then here's to the maid in lily white smock,
   Who tripped to the door and slipped back the lock,
   Ans slipped back the lock, and pulled back the pin,
   For to let these jolly wassailers walk in.

Widely known nursery song. Some commentators have attempted to interpret it as political satire on the Restoration Court of Charles II.

The Carrion Crow

(England)

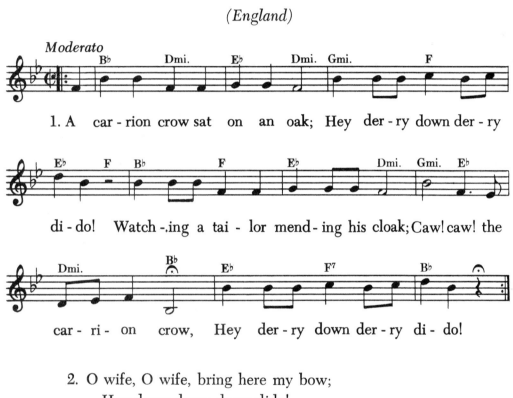

1. A car-rion crow sat on an oak; Hey der-ry down der-ry di-do! Watch-.ing a tai-lor mend-ing his cloak; Caw! caw! the car-ri-on crow, Hey der-ry down der-ry di-do!

2. O wife, O wife, bring here my bow;
   Hey derry down derry dido!
   That I may shoot this carrion crow;
   Caw! caw! the carrion crow,
   Hey derry down derry dido!

3. The tailor he fired but missed his mark,
   For he shot the old sow right bang through the heart.

4. O wife, O wife, bring brandy in a spoon,
   For our old sow is down in a swoon.

5. The old sow died, and the bell did toll,
   And the little pigs prayed for the old sow's soul.

131

This Scottish (Lowlands) border ballad is believed to have been inspired by the execution of Cockburn of Henderland, a border freebooter, who was hanged over the gate of his own tower by James V in 1529. The melody is based on the pentatonic scale g-a-b-d-e. To convey a truer harmonic color, the occasional omission of the third of the chord is suggested.

The Border Lament

(Scotland)

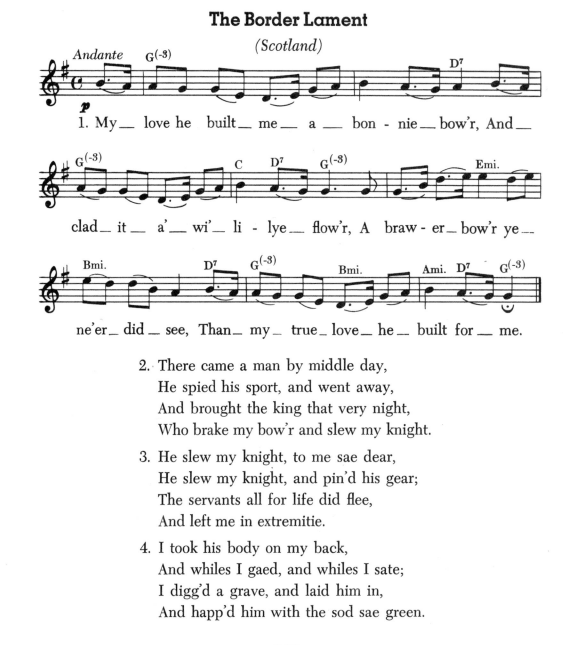

1. My __ love he built __ me __ a __ bon - nie __ bow'r, And __ clad __ it __ a' __ wi' __ li - lye __ flow'r, A braw - er __ bow'r ye __ ne'er __ did __ see, Than __ my __ true __ love __ he __ built for __ me.

2. There came a man by middle day,
   He spied his sport, and went away,
   And brought the king that very night,
   Who brake my bow'r and slew my knight.

3. He slew my knight, to me sae dear,
   He slew my knight, and pin'd his gear;
   The servants all for life did flee,
   And left me in extremitie.

4. I took his body on my back,
   And whiles I gaed, and whiles I sate;
   I digg'd a grave, and laid him in,
   And happ'd him with the sod sae green.

132

5. But think na ye my heart was sair,
   When I laid the mool on his yellow hair,
   O think na ye my heart was wae,
   When I turn'd about, away to gae?

6. Nae living man I'll love again,
   Since that my lovely knight is slain,
   Wi' ae lock o' his yellow hair,
   I'll chain my heart for evermair.

A lullaby of intimate tenderness and poignancy, so characteristic of the stark and somber life of the Hebridean islanders. The modal structure of the tune makes the mere chord suggestion for the accompaniment but a faint reflection of the inner quality of the song. With such elusive tunes, unaccompanied performances are, perhaps, the most successful.

English version by Margaret F. Shaw
Adapted by Charles Haywood

Gille Beag Ó—Little Lad, Oh
(Scotland—Hebrides)

Gill - e beag ó, gill - e lag ó, Gill - e beag ó nan caor-ach.
Lit - tle lad o, feeb- le lad o, Lit - tle lad o, with your sheep.

Tha mi sgìth 'gad alt - ra - mas, A' srac - adh mo chuid aod - aich.
I'm tired of nurs - ing you, And tear - ing all my cloth - ing.

Nam bu mhac duín ua - sail thu, Gu faigh - inn luach mo chaor-ach.
If you were of no - ble birth, I would get more for my sheep.

133

There are many folksongs expressing the passionate yearnings of a lovelorn youth and the feigned indifference of a "coldhearted" maiden, but there is hardly one to match the innocent simplicity and the lyrical poignancy of this song. The shifting harmonies in the dialogue from e minor to b minor underscore its intimate charm and beauty.

Lliw Gwyn Rhosyn Yr Haf—White Rose of My Heart

English version by
H. Idris Bell

(Wales)

1. Dyd da fo i ti, ser - en ol - eu, Lliw gwyn
1. A fair good mor - row, love - ly maid-en, White wild

rhos - yn yr haf! Ty - di yw'r gyw - rain ferch __ a gar - af,
rose of my heart! For you my soul is sor - row la - den,

Lliw gwyn rhos - yn yr haf! Wel, cau dy geg yr __
White wild rose of my heart! Nay, cease, dull oaf, your __

hen of - er - ddyn, Y cas - a fu 'rioed ar
i - dle chat - ter, The sil - li - est bab - ble

wyn - eb y tir! Mi grog - af fy hun cyn
ev - er I heard! You and your oaths are

dof __ i'th gan - lyn Mewn gair, dyn - ai ti'r gwir.
no __ great mat - ter, That's truth in a sin - gle word!

134

2. *Y mae gusan di, f'anwylyd,*
   Lliw gwyn rhosyn yr haf!
   'Run fath a diliau mêl bob munud,
   Lliw gwyn rhosyn yr haf!
   Ac felly mae dy gusan dithau,
   Y casa fu'rioed ar wyneb y tir!
   Yn ail i gamamil i minnau—
   Yn hen geg, dyna i ti'r gwir!

3. *Os wyt ti'n mynd i'm troi i heibio,*
   Lliw gwyn rhosyn yr haf!
   Wel, dyro gusan cyn ffarwelio,
   Lliw gwyn rhosyn yr haf!
   Wel, 'waeth im ddweyd y gwir na pheidio,
   Y mwynaf erioed ar wyneb y tir!
   Cest ddwy o'r blaen, cei bymtheg eto,
   Mewn gair, dyna i ti'r gwir!

2. *He:* Your kiss is sweeter far than honey,
   White wild rose of my heart!
   Such nectar ne'er was bought for money,
   White wild rose of my heart!
   She: And yours, for all your fond devotion,
   The silliest babble ever I heard!
   As loathsome as a doctor's potion—
   That's the truth in a single word.

3. *He:* Ah me! salt tears, you'll still be flowing,
   White wild rose of my heart!
   But kiss me once and I'll be going,
   White wild rose of my heart!
   She: Oh, no, my love, I cannot grieve you,
   A tenderer speech you never have heard!
   I gave you two, fifteen I'll give you—
   That's the truth in a single word.

135

Ireland

This well-known ballad expresses the anguish and longing for the beloved who has departed to battle on foreign soil. It originated in the time of the "Wild Geese" or Irish Brigade, in the years 1691 to 1745, when many young Irishmen went to enlist in the French army.

Shule Aroon—Come, Oh Love

2. I'll sell my rock, I'll sell my reel,
   I'll sell my only spinning wheel,
   To buy for my love a sword of steel.
   Is go dee tu mavourneen slaun.
   Shule, shule, shule aroon, etc.

3. I'll dye my petticoats, I'll dye them red,
   And round the world I'll beg my bread,
   Until my parents shall wish me dead.
   Is go dee tu mavourneen slaun.
   Shule, shule, shule aroon, etc.

The insistent, but fruitless, pleadings of a lover to be admitted to his sweetheart's chamber (always on a cold wintry night) is a frequent theme in folksong. Compare Brahms' "Vergebliches Ständchen," as an example in art song literature.

Barney and Katey

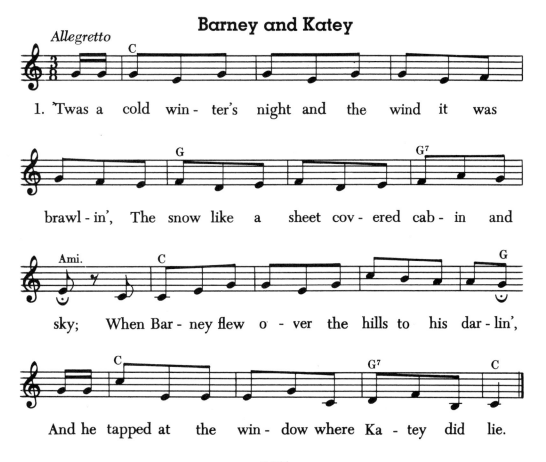

Barney and Katey

2. "Arrray, jewel", says he, "are ye sleepin' or wakin'?
   'Tis a bitter cold night and me coat it is thin;
   The storm is a-brewin' and the frost is a-bakin',
   O, sweet Katey, darlin', won't ye please let me in?"

3. "O, Barney", says Katey, she spake through the winda,
   "Why do ye come talkin' me out of me bed?
   To be sure it is a shame and a sin to ye,
   'Tis whiskey, not love that's got into yer head.

4. "O think of the time of me name ye'd be tender,
   Consider it's night and there's nobody in.
   What has a poor girl but her name to defend her?
   Ray no, Barney Avouren, I won't let ye in."

5. "O cushla", says he, "in me eyes there's a fountain
   To weep for the wrong I would lay at yer door.
   Yer heart is as pure as the shnaw on the mountain,
   And Barney would die to preserve it as pure.

6. "I'll go to me home though the winter winds face me,
   I'll whistle them off for I'm happy within;
   And the words of my Katey shall comfort and bless me,
   'Ray no, Barney Aver, I won't let you in'."

The Netherlands

A satirical song, poking fun at the lazy, capricious girls of Kieldrecht.

English version by
Charles Haywood

Te Kieldrecht—In Kieldrecht

1. Te Kiel - drecht, te Kiel - drecht, Daer zyn de meis - kens
1. In Kiel - drecht, in Kiel - drecht, The girls are ve - ry

koe - ne, Zy vry - en tot den mid - der - nacht En
free and gay, They flirt un - til the mid - night hour, And

sla - pen tot den noe - ne. Ik maei, is dat niet
sleep 'til noon next day. I say, is that ve - ry

fraei? En sla - pen tot den noe - ne.
nice? And sleep 'til noon next day.

2.

Als ze op staen, als se op staen,
Dan kyken ze in de wolken,
Zy zeggen: "wol hoe laet is't al?
Myn koe staet ongemolken."
 Ik maei, is dat niet fraei?
Myn koe staet ongemolken.

2.

When they wake up, when they wake up,
Upon the clouds their eyes are set,
And then they ask: "What time is it?
My cow has not been milked as yet."
 I say, is that very nice?
My cow has not been milked as yet.

3.

En als zy komen in de wei,
Zy zeggen: "koeiken blare!
Ik ben hier met myn lieveken,
En zal u dat niet varen?"
 Ik maei, is dat niet fraei?
En zal u dat niet varen?

3.

And when they come into the field.
They greet their cows most warmly:
"You need not fear us, dearest friends,
We'll treat you ever kindly."
 I say, is that very nice?
We'll treat you ever kindly.

Belgium

This song describes the popular custom during the Christmas season, when youngsters, appropriately costumed, go from house to house carrying a wooden pot, covered with pig's bladder (*rommelpot*). A stick is inserted into the pot, and, when moved up and down, makes a loud sound (*rommelt*); this acts as an accompaniment to their singing. They are rewarded with food mentioned in the song.

English version by
Charles Haywood

De Rommelpot—The Rommelpot

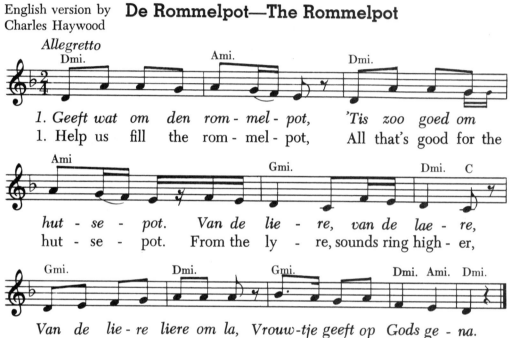

Allegretto

1. Geeft wat om den rom - mel - pot, 'Tis zoo goed om
1. Help us fill the rom - mel - pot, All that's good for the

hut - se - pot. Van de lie - re, van de lae - re,
hut - se - pot. From the ly - re, sounds ring high - er,

Van de lie - re liere om la, Vrouw-tje geeft op Gods ge - na.
From the ly - re, lyre om la, All God's bless-ings on you now.

2. *Geef wat spek en geef wat worst,*
   Geef wat bier al voor den dorst.
   Van de liere, van de laere, etc.

2. Give us sausage, give us lard,
   Give us beer 'gainst thirst to guard.
   From the lyre, sounds ring higher, etc.

3. *Geef ons eene rib of twee,*
   Geef ons dat voor moeder mee.

3. Give us ribs as many you can spare,
   Give us that for our mother dear.

4. *'T Verken heeft een langen staart,*
   En is ook het eten waard.

4. Pigs have tails quite long and fine.
   Splendid food for all to dine.

5. *Karbonaden op den disch,*
   Dan is 't huis ook kerremis.

5. For our table chops are good,
   Home is festive with such food.

6. *Vrouwtje geef zooveel gy kunt,*
   Hemelsvreugd wordt u gegund.

6. Kind, fair lady give all you can,
   Health and joy to you, Amen.

140

A passionate serenade: the insistent lover urging his beloved to come to him in the darkness and stillness of night.

English version by Charles Haywood **Léonore**

Allegretto con tenerezza

Tan - dis __ que tout __ som - meil - le, ___ À l'om - bre
While all is in slum - ber en - fold - ed, ___ In peace and

de __ la nuit, __ L'a - mour __ qui tou - jours veil - le, __
quiet __ of night, __ The voice __ of love clear - ly sound - ing __

__ L'a - mour, __ qui nous __ con - duit. __ Me dit tout bas: Viens,
__ In - vites __ us both __ to flight. __ Soft - ly he calls: Oh,

suis __ mes pas __ Où la __ beau - té __ t'ap - pel - le.
come fol - low me __ Where beau - ty and love __ a - waits. _____

Voi - ci l'in - stant de ren - dez - vous, Pro - fi - tons
This is the mo - ment for pleas - ure, Waste not the

ce mo - ment, si doux; Moi, __ pour é - car - ter __ les
chance, dear treas - ure. The __ jeal - ous in - trud - ers I'll give full

ja - loux, Je me fe - rai sen - ti - nel - le.
meas - ure, As I stand guard bat - tling the fates. __

Germany

One of the great masterpieces of sacred folksong. The downward motion of the melodic phrases conveys a feeling of inner resignation. The symbolic significance of the stern Reaper (death) and the fragile flower (man) is widespread in folk tradition.

Es Ist Ein Schnitter—Behold the Reaper

English version by
Charles Haywood

1. Es ist ein Schnit - ter, der heisst Tod, Hat G'walt _ vom
1. Be - hold the reap - er call - ed Death, God - grant - ed

höch - sten Gott. ____ Heut wetzt er das Mes - ser, Es
pow - er he hath. ____ He sharp - ens his long knife The

schneid't schon viel bes - ser, Bald wird er drein schnei-den Wir
bet - ter to cut life; Soon our own is tak - en, Yet our

müs - sen's nur lei - den: Hüt' dich, schön's Blü - me-lein!
faith nev - er shak - en. Guard thee well, fair - est flow'r!

2. *Was heut noch grün und frisch da steht,*
   Wird morgen weggemäht:
   Die edel Narzissel,
   Die englische Schlüssel,
   Die schön Hyacinth,
   Die türkische Bind:
   Hüt' dich, schöns Blümelein!

142

3. *Viel hunderttausend ungezählt,*
   Da unter die Sichel hinfällt:
   Rot Rosen, weiss Lilien,
   Beid' wird er austiligen,
   Ihr Kaiserkronen,
   Man wird euch nicht schonen:
   Hüt' dich, schöns Blümelein!

4. *Trutz Tod! Komm her, ich fürcht dich nit!*
   Trutz, komm und tu ein Schnitt!
   Wenn er mir verletzet,
   So werd ich versetzet,
   Ich will es erwarten,
   In himmlischen Garten.
   Freu dich, schöns Blümelein!

2. All that grows and blooms today
   Will wither, die, and fade away:
   The noble narcissus,
   The English primrose,
   The lovely hyacinth,
   The sturdy terebinth.
   Guard thee well, fairest flow'r!

3. Unnumbered thousands Death obeyed,
   Cut down by the scythe's sharp blade:
   Red roses, white lillies,
   Uprooted are both these,
   Proud crown imperials
   From death no denials.
   Guard thee well, fairest flow'r!

4. Grim Death, come here, I fear thee not!
   I humbly accept my lot.
   Were I accused harshly,
   My fate I accept gladly;
   Awaiting my sentence
   In God's holy presence.
   Rejoice thee now, fairest flow'r!

This song captures the exuberant humor of a young lad who will not be tempted into marriage. In the seventeenth century, this song was also known as "The Shoemaker's Song."

Ich Ging Emol Spaziere—One Day I Went A-Walking

English version by
Charles Haywood

1. Ich ging e-mol spa-zie-re, na-nu, na-nu, na-
1. One day I went a-walk-ing,

nu! Ich ging e-mol spa-zie-re, na-nu, na-nu, na-
One day I went a-walk-ing,

nu! Ich ging e-mol spa-zie-re, bums, val-le-
One day I went a-walk-ing,

ra! Und tät ein Mä-del füh-re,
With a girl who did much talk-ing,

ha-ha-ha-ha-ha,____ ha-ha-ha-ha-ha!

2. *Sie sagt, sie hätt viel Gulde,(2)*
   'S warn aber lauter Schulde.

2. She said she had much money,(2)
   But these were big debts only.

3. *Sie sagt, ich sollt sie nehme,(2)*
   Sie mach mir's sehr bequeme.

3. She said she'd like to marry me,
   And make me very happy. (2)

4. *Der Sommer ist gekomme,(2)*
   Ich hab' sie nicht genomme.

4. When summer sky was shining,
   I felt her lovelorn pining. (2)

A favorite children's song; dressed in hunter's garb, astride a sturdy (wooden) horse, aiming his deadly weapon (a stick), and galloping through the meadows (the living room or the sidewalk), the child experiences the rich and exciting life of the bold hunter.

Ein Jäger aus Kurpfalz—A Hunter from Kurpfalz

English version by
Charles Haywood

1. Ein Jä - ger aus Kur - pfalz, Der rei - tet durch den
1. A hunt - er from Kur - pfalz, Who gal - lops through the

grü - nen Wald; Er schiesst das Wild da - her, Gleich
for - est green, He shoots with per - fect aim All

wie es ihm ge - fällt. Ju ja, ju
wild - life he has seen. Ju ja, ju

ja, gar lus - tig ist die Jä - ge - rei, All
ja, for hunt - ing is a mer - ry game, O'er

hier auf grü - ner Heid', all hier auf grü - ner Heid'.
mead - ow all a - round. O'er mead - ow all a - round.

2. *Auf, sattelt mir mein Pferd,*
   Und legt darauf den Mantelsack,
   So reit ich ihn und her
   Als Jäger aus Kurpfalz.
   Ju ja, ju ja, usw.

2. Go saddle me my horse,
   And tighten the leather bag,
   I boldly ride about,
   The hunter from Kurpfalz.
   Ju ja, ju ja, etc.

Luxembourg

A love song of exquisite lyricism and sustained tenderness. The structure and the melodic line show the influence of the Romantic German *Kunstlied* (art song).

D'Piirle vum Da—Dewdrops on Leaves

English version by
Charles Haywood

D'Piir - le vum Da, ___ Dat sin déng Di - a - man - ten;
Dew- drops on leaves, _ These are thy pre - cious dia - monds,

D'Blum- men um Feld, _ Déi sin dain Hoch-zäits- klèd; _ An
Flow - ers in field, _ These are thy wed- ding gown; _ Sweet

d'Nuech - te - gai - ler cher, ___ Dat sin déng Mu - si - kan - ten;
song of night - in- gales, ___ Thy band of gay mu - si - cians;

An däin treit Hierz ___ As méng Gléck-sei - lech - keet. ___
Thy faith-ful heart, ___ No great - er joy yet known. ___

An däin treit Hierz ___ As méng Gléck-sei - lech - keet. ___
Thy faith-ful heart, ___ No great - er joy yet known. ___

Austria

A song of lusty humor and cynical commentary on the hard life of an apprentice. This was a favorite song of the blacksmiths around Steyer, whose swinging hammers, accompanying the tune, were heard resounding from the early hours till sundown.

English version by
Charles Haywood

Der Blaue Montag—Blue Monday

1. Der Mon - tag, der Mon - tag, der muss ge - fei - ert
1. On Mon - day, on Mon - day, a day of cel - e -

wer - den, Und was vom Sonn- tag ü - ber- bleibt, das
bra - tion, And what from Sun- day is left o'er, we

muss ver - sof - fen wer - den! So ist's recht, so muss's sein,
drink in good old fash - ion. That is right, you'll a - gree,

lus - tig wolln wir le - ben, Wenn das Geld ver -
life en - joy · as we know, When the mon - ey

sof - fen ist, nach Hau - se wolln wir gehn!
is all spent, straight-way to house we go!

2. Am Dienstag, am Dienstag, da schlafen wir bis neune,
   Dann kommt das Meistertöchterlein und legt sich zu uns eini.
   So ists recht, usw.

2. On Tuesday, on Tuesday, we then can sleep 'til nine,
   Then comes the master's daughter fair, snugs into bed of mine.
   That is right, you'll agree, etc.

147

3. *Am Mittwoch, am Mittwoch, da sind die Bänk zerbrochen,*
   Und wann der Meister neue schafft, so nennt man's Mitt' der Wochen.

3. On Wednesday, on Wednesday, the money is all gone,
   And when the master finds new work, Midweek again 's begun.

4. *Am Donnerstag, am Donnerstag, da fängt sich an die Wochen,*
   Und wann das Fleisch gefressen ist, so frisst man auch die Knochen.

4. On Thursday, on Thursday, the week begins in earnest,
   And when the meat is eaten up, the bones can taste the finest.

5. *Am Freitag, am Freitag, da bäckt die Meistrin Fische,*
   Und wenn wir auch nichts g'årbeit håm, so setzen wir uns zu Tische.

5. On Friday, on Friday, the mistress bakes the fish then,
   And even tho' we did not work, we join at dinner with them.

6. *Am Samstag, am Samstag, da geht die Woch' zu ende,*
   Und wenn das Glöcklein ein Uhr schlägt, so waschen wir uns die Hände.

6. On Saturday, on Saturday, the week at last is ended,
   And when the bell strikes one o'clock, our hands are washed and cleanèd.

7. *Am Sonntag, am Sonntag, da tun die Meister prahlen,*
   Und wenn die Zeit zum Rechnen kommt, dann können sie nicht zahlen.

7. On Sunday, on Sunday, the master's boasts are mounting,
   But when it comes to add our pay, he is not good at counting.

English version Copyright © 1966 by Charles Haywood

A song of derision, in which the proud Tyrolean ridicules the clumsiness and incompetence of the inhabitants of the town of Pinzgau.

Die Binschgauer Wallfahrt—The Binschgauer Pilgrimage

English version by
Charles Haywood

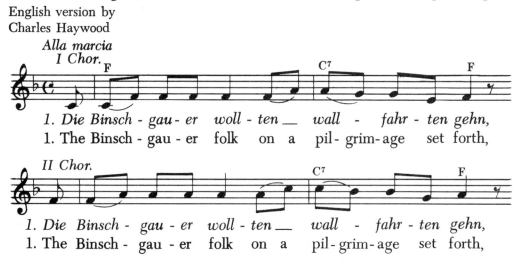

Alla marcia
I Chor.

1. *Die Binsch - gau - er woll - ten __ wall - fahr - ten gehn,*
1. The Binsch - gau - er folk on a pil - grim-age set forth,

II Chor.

1. *Die Binsch - gau - er woll - ten __ wall - fahr - ten gehn,*
1. The Binsch - gau - er folk on a pil - grim-age set forth,

I C
Sie ta - ten ger - ne sin - gen und kunn - ten's nit gar schön.
They liked to sing to - geth - er, but their sounds were not much worth.

II C
Sie ta - ten ger - ne sin - gen und kunn - ten's nit gar schön.
They liked to sing to - geth - er, but their sounds were not much worth.

Zscha - hi! zscha - he! zscha - ho! _____ die Bins - ger sind schon
Zscha - hi! zscha - he! zscha - ho! _____ the Bins - ger on the

do! _____ Jetzt schau fein, dass ein Je - der Je - der
go! _____ Now look how love - ly each one each one

Je - der Je - der Je - der Je - der sei
each one each one each one each one with his

Rän - zel - le - ho! _____ sei Rän - ze - le - ho!
lit - tle knap - sack, ho! _____ with his lit - tle knap - sack, ho!

2. *Die Binschgauer gängen um den Dom her um, (2)*
   Die Fahnestang is broche, jetzt gängens mit dem Trumm. (2)
   Zschahi! zschahe! zschaho! usw.

2. The Binschgauer folk are marching round the Dom, (2)
   The flagpole now is broken, they're banging on the drum. (2)
   Zschahi! zschahe! zschaho! etc.

France

This old ballad reflects the ancient feud and long-drawn-out wars between France and England. However, the recalcitrant French princess changes her mind after the nuptial night, and decides to remain with her "accursed" Englishman. Love conquers all! This ballad appears in many melodic and textual versions in various parts of France.

La Princesse Mariée à un Anglais—The Princess Wed to an Englishman

English version by
Charles Haywood

1. C'é - tait la fille au Roi Fran-çais, __ La __ veut don-
1. Fair - est __ daugh - ter of the King of France __ Was __ bid to

ner à un An - glais. __ Mon __ père, oh! ne m'y ma - ri -
wed an Eng - lish - man. __ Fa - ther, oh, do not make me

ez Mal à mon gré. __ J'ai - me - rais
wed The one I dread. __ Rath - er a French

mieux sol - dat Fran - çais Que roi An - glais. __
sol - dier my love I'd give, Than Eng - land's King. __

150

Mais si l'ont prise et l'ont mené,	Forcefully taken, led away
De dans Paris elle a passé.	Through the streets of Paris in dismay.
Toutes les dames de Paris.	Women of Paris seeing her pass
En ont pleuré	Wept in distress;
D'y voir mener la fill' du Roi	Their beloved Princess gone from them
Par un Anglais.	With an Englishman.
Quand ce vint au bord de la mer,	When the seashore they had neared,
L'Anglais lui veut les yeux bander.	Seeking her to blindfold he appeared.
Bande les tiens et laisse moi,	Blindfold thine own, no, mine ne'er can,
Maudit Anglais!	Accursed Englishman!
Puisque la mer me faut passer	When we cross the rolling sea
Je la verrai.	My sight be free.
Et quand la mer était passé,	When they had reached the other shore,
Tambours, violons, de tous cotés.	Drums and fiddles sounded far and near.
Retirez-vous, ô tambourniers	Stop the beating drums, of that no more,
Et violoniers!	Nor sounds of fiddlers here!
Ce ne sont pas les beaux tambours	This is not the music of my land,
Du Roi Français.	Nor the royal band.
Quand ce fut l' heure de souper,	When they prepared to dine and feast,
L'Anglais lui coupe pour manger.	He carved meat for her to eat.
Coupe pour toi, et laisse moi,	Carve for thee, but not for me,
Maudit Anglais!	Accursed Englishman!
J'ai bien des gens de mon pays	My own kinsmen serve me best
Pour me servir.	Than you ever can.
Quand ce fut l'heure de coucher,	When the hour had come to retire,
L'Anglais voulut la déchausser.	He sought to help remove her attire.
Déchausse-toi et laisse-moi,	Take off thine, but ne'er touch mine,
Maudit Anglais!	Accursed Englishman!
J'ai bien des gens de mon pays	My own kinsmen serve me best
Pour me servir.	Than you ever can.
Et quand ce fut la matiné,	Next morning early at break of day,
La belle s'est mise à pleurer.	She was a-weeping in dismay.
Mes chers amis, embrassons nous	Press me fondly, dearest friends, adieu,
Et quittons nous.	I say to you.
Puisqu'à l'Anglais on m'a donné,	Since I wed the Englishman,
Il faut l'aimer!	I'll love him best I can.

A dance-song of infectious humor and lively rhythm. The young maiden's coquettish and flirtatious character is "innocently" conveyed through the suggestive sounds. With the song ending unresolved, on the dominant, one may even question her true affection for the shepherd boy.

L'Autre Jour en Voulant Danser—While I Was Dancing the Other Day

English version by
Charles Haywood

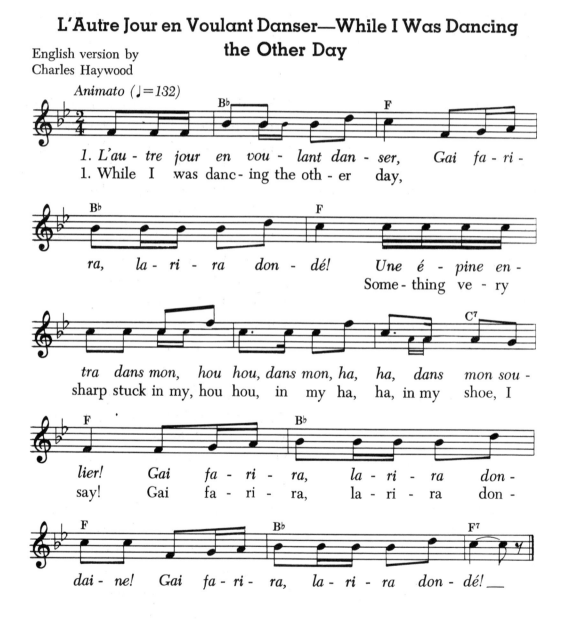

Animato (♩=132)

1. L'au - tre jour en vou - lant dan - ser, Gai fa - ri -
1. While I was danc - ing the oth - er day,

ra, la - ri - ra don - dé! Une é - pine en -
Some - thing ve - ry

tra dans mon, hou hou, dans mon, ha, ha, dans mon sou -
sharp stuck in my, hou hou, in my ha, ha, in my shoe, I

lier! Gai fa - ri - ra, la - ri - ra don -
say! Gai fa - ri - ra, la - ri - ra don -

dai - ne! Gai fa - ri - ra, la - ri - ra don - dé! __

2. *Un officier voulut m' l'ôter,*
   Et pour sa peine il voulut, hou hou, voulut
      ha, ha, prendre un baiser!

3. *Je n'embrass' pas les officiers,*
   Mais, j'embrasserais bien mon, hou, hou, bien mon
      ha, ha, bien mon berger!

4. *J'embrasserais bien mon berger,*
   Et surtout quand il me fait, hou, hou, me fait,
      ha, ha, me fait danser!

2. Let me remove it, an officer did say,
   For my daring effort, I want, hou hou, may I have
      ha, ha, a kiss, if I may!

3. I will not kiss you, oh, no, ne'er,
   I like to embrace my hou, hou, and my
      ha, ha, my shepherd fair!

4. I will embrace my shepherd boy,
   Anytime he tries to make, hou hou, make me
      ha, ha, dance with joy!

Switzerland

A yodel-song expressing the joy and contentment of the Alpine dairy-men in their work and their friends.

Mir Senne Heil's Lustig—We Are Happy and Merry

English version by
Charles Haywood

Allegretto

1. Mir— Sen - ne — heil's— lu - stig, mir— Sen - ne heil's
1. We are hap - py — and — mer - ry At our Dai - ry - men's

guet, Hei— Chäs und— hei — An - ke, das— git üs guets
trade, With our cheese and— fine — but - ter The— best ev - er

Bluet.
made. Hu - di - ri - a - ho - lei - e, hu - di - ri - a - ho-

lei - e, hu - di - ri - a - ho - lei - e, hu-di-ri - a - ho - li - oh!

2. *Und chum i zur Hütte,*
   rüeft d's Bethli mir zue:
   "Chum hurti, mi Hausli,
   wenn i heirati du!"
      Hu-di-ri-a, etc.

2. When I reach the small cottage,
   Bethli calls me inside,
   "You can share my whole household
   When you'll be my bride."
      Hu-di-ri-a, etc.

3. *Und e nigel-nagel-neues Hausli,*
   und e nigel-nagel-neues Dach,
   und e nigel-nagel-neues Fenster
   mit Hudle vermacht!
      Hu-di-ri-a, etc.

3. And a new shining cottage,
   And a new shining roof,
   And a new shining window
   With rags to weatherproof.
      Hu-di-ri-a, etc.

A love song of appealing tenderness; the smooth-flowing rhythm accentuates the gondolier's warm affection for Ninetta.

È Mi Son Chi in Barchetta—In My Little Boat

English version by
Charles Haywood

Moderato

1. E mi son chi in bar - chet - ta
1. I am a - lone in my lit - tle boat,

e ti su in ti __ mo - nel - la, Ques-ta l'è l'o - ra
You are not bu - sy, I know, Oh, what a per - fect

bel - la per far l'a - mo - re con te. Che bel-la
hour __ this is My love and pas - sion to show. The night is

not - te che fa in gon-do - let - ta, si va col - la Ni -
love - ly, My gon-do - la is read - y To sail with my Ni -

net - ta a res - pi - rar. Che bel - la rar.
net - ta Far o'er the sea. The night is sea.

2. *Vieni, Ninetta bella,*   2. Come my beloved Ninetta,
   vieni mio solo bene,   Fairest of all I adore,
   Che remeremo insieme   Come row beside me, the better
   e parlerem d'amore.   To speak of love evermore.
   Che bella notte, etc.   The night is lovely, etc.

Italy

This ballad, among the oldest in Italian folk tradition, first recorded in the early seventeenth century, and found in other parts of the country, is a variant of "Lord Randal." (*See*: p.39 and also p.169)

L'Avvelenato—The Poisoned Lover

English version by
Charles Haywood

Andante

1. Do - ve si stà jer - si - ra, Fi - gliuol mio ca - ro, fio - ri - to e gen - til? Do - ve si stà jer - si - ra? Son stà dal - la mia da - ma, Si - gno - ra ma - ma, mio co - re stà mal! Son stà dal - la ___ mia da - ma! Ohi - mè! ch'io mo - ro ohi - mè!

1. Oh, where were you last eve - ning, my son, My dear - est and fair - est young man? Oh, where were you last eve - ning? I went to see my sweet-heart, Dear moth-er, I am so sick at my heart; I went to see ___ my sweet - heart, Woe's me! I'm sick at heart!

2. —Cossa v'halla da de cena,
   —On 'inguilletta arrosto,

3. —L'avì mangiada tutta,
   —Non n'ho mangia che mezza,

4. —Coss'avì fa dell' altra mezza?
   —L'ho data alla cagnola.

5. —Coss'avì fa della cagnola?
   —L'è morta drê la strada.

6. —Mandé a ciama 'l notaro, (parlato)
   —Perche vorri ciama 'l notaro?
   —Per fare testamento.

7. —Cossa lassè alla vostra Mama?
   —Ghe lasso 'l mio palazzo.

8. —Cossa lassè alli vostri fratelli?
   —La carozza coi cavalli.

9. —Cossa lassè alla vostra dama?
   —La forca da impicarla.

2. —Oh, what had you for supper, my son,
   —I ate a roasted eel,

3. —Did you eat all of that, my son?
   —I ate but half the portion.

4. —What did you with the rest, my son?
   —I gave it to my dog.

5. —What happened to your dog, my son?
   —He died upon the street.

6. —Please send for the lawyer. (spoken)
   —Why must I call the lawyer, my son?
   —To make my final will

7. —What will you leave your mother, my son?
   —I leave to her my palace.

8. —What will you leave your brothers, my son?
   —The carriage and the horses.

9. —What will you leave your sweetheart, my son?
   —The gallows for to hang her.

A fisherman's song well known in Mediterranean ports, probably of
Sicilian origin. A young maiden pleads with the fisherman to help
her "fish out" the ring that fell in the water. He refuses all promised
rewards—he only wants a kiss. . . . The Corsican fishermen chant this
tune while they haul in their nets.

Pescator dell'Onda—The Gallant Fisherman

English version by
Charles Haywood

Moderato scherzando

1. O pes - ca - tor dell' on - da, O Fé - dé - ri! O
1. O fish - er - man so gal - lant, O Fé - dé - ri! O

ri! Vie - ni pes - car in quà, Col - la tu - a bel - la
ri! Come do your fish - ing here. In your boat that's built so

bar - ca, La tua bel - la se ne va. Fé - dé -
stur - dy I will glad - ly sail with you. Fé - dé -

Chorus

ri, lin, la! Vie - ni pes - car in
ri, lin, la! Come do your fish - ing

quà Col - la tu - a bel - la bar - ca, La tua
here. In your boat that's built so stur - dy I will

bel - la se ne va. Fé - dé - ri, lin, la!
glad - ly sail with you. Fé - dé - ri, lin, la!

158

2. *Vieni à pescar mio annello,*
   O Fédéri!
   Che mi è caduto in mar,
   Colla tua bella barca,
   La tua bella se ne va. } (2)
   Fédéri, lin, la!

3. *L'annello è già pescato*
   O Fédéri!
   Cosa mi vo donar?

4. *Ti daró cento scudi,*
   O Fédéri!
   Sta borsa ricama.

5. *Non vole cento scudi*
   O Fédéri!
   Ne borsa a ricama.

6. *Vole un bacin d'amore,*
   Il tuo Fédéri!
   Che quello pagherá.
   Colla tua bella barca,
   La più bella se ne va.
   Fédéri, lin, la!

2. Come help me fish my gold ring,
   O Fédéri!
   It fell into the sea.
   In your boat that's built so sturdy
   I will gladly sail with you. } (2)
   Fédéri, lin, la!

3. The ring I've fished out for you,
   O Fédéri!
   Now what will you give me?

4. I'll give you hundred pennies,
   O Fédéri!
   You will be very rich.

5. I don't want hundred pennies,
   O Fédéri!
   Nor being very rich.

6. I want a kiss, my darling,
   Your Fédéri!
   That's the only way to pay.
   In your boat that's built so sturdy
   I will gladly sail with you.
   Fédéri, lin, la!

Spain

An exuberant declaration of love for the pretty baker maiden. (The preciseness of "La panaderita" is well-nigh untranslatable into English.) To describe her exquisite charm, the ardent lover can find no better comparison than a "tasty breadcrumb"!

La Panaderita—The Baker Maiden

English version by
Charles Haywood

1. A la en-tra-da del pue-blo y a la sa-li-da,___
1. When I en-ter the vil-lage, or on my way out,___

hay u-na pa-na-de-ra, pa-na-de-ri-ta, pa-
There's a young bak-er maid-en, a sweet bak-er maid, none

na-de-ri-ta. ¡ Qué pa-na-de-ra lin-da y chi-qui-
pret-tier a-bout. She is so love-ly, de-light-ful to

ta, Qué pa-na-de-ra, pa-na-de-ri-ta!
see, Oh, what a dar-ling, sweet ba-ker is she!

2. *Al besarla le ha dicho hoy, su abuelita:*
   eres sabrosa, niña, como la miga, como la miga.
   ¡ Qué panadera linda, etc.

2. I am longing to kiss her, her granny knows that,
   She is tasty like breadcrumbs, refreshing, and good without doubt.
   She is so lovely, etc.

This languid, plaintive melody, with shifting from minor to major and the cadential melismas, shows the strong Arabic influence on the Andalusian folk idiom.

English version by
Charles Haywood

Nina, Nana—Lullaby

1. A la na - ni - ta, na - ni - ta,
1. Lis - ten, my child, to the lull - a - by,

a la na - ni - ta de a-quel _____ que lle -
Sweet lull-a - by of a man _____ Who led his

vó el ca - ba - llo al a - gua, y lo
horse _____ to the wa - ter, And yet

tra - jo sin be - ber. _____
could not make him drink. _____

2. Duérmete, niño chiquito,   2. Sleep, dearest child, close your weary eyes,
   duérmete y no llores más,   Sleep, do not cry, my beloved;
   que reirán los angelitos   Let your guardian angel smile
   para no verte llorar.   When he sees you do not cry.

The popularity of this Christmas song dates from the Middle Ages, and it is widely known, in variant forms, in other European countries. It was usually sung by children's choirs after Midnight Mass.

English version by
Charles Haywood

Baile de Nadal—Christmas Dance-Song

2. *A vinticinc de Desembre,*
   fum, fum, fum, } (2)
   Es el dia de Nadal
   molt principal.
   Quan eixirèm de Matines
   farèm bones restolines.
   fum, fum, fum!

2. On the twenty-fifth December,
   fum, fum, fum, } (2)
   Is the happiest holiday,
   'Tis Christmas day!
   From the church they hurry quickly,
   To bake cakes that taste most sweetly.
   fum, fum, fum!

Slowly and painfully the skeletal horse pulls the reins attached to the circular stone grinding the corn. Round and round he goes. Despairingly, the equally tired Mallorcan peasant coaxes the weary animal.

Cançó de's Batre—Threshing Song

English version by
Charles Haywood

(Mallorca)

si no fos p'es ca - rre - tó
No hi hau - ri - a cap so - me - ra,
Your days are o - ver, good horse,
Now you are bon - y and old,

p'es ca - rre - tó   Que vá da - rre - ra, da -
cap so - me - ra,   Que ba - tés un ca - va -
o - ver, good horse,   Once you were stur - dy and
bon - y and old,   Hide look - ing rag - ged and

rre - ra,   ¡Ah!
yó.
live - ly;
mould - y.

¡A - rri!

Portugal

A *modinha*—a deeply expressive, romantic and sentimental love song.

English version by **Canção a Lua—Song to the Moon**
Charles Haywood

Moderato, molto espressivo

1. Vai al - ta g noi - te vem ver a lu - a, co -
1. Be - hold the moon shin - ing thro' the dark night, In

mo flu - ctu - a no ver - de mar. Sa - be que é
grace - ful calm sails the emer - ald sea. The glori - ous

be - la que é pra - te - a - da e en - ver - go -
splen - dor, her silv' - ry beau - ty In mod - est

nha - da vem ver - seao mar. __ Sa - be que é be - la
won - der ob - serves the sight. __ The glori - ous splen - dor,

que é pra - te - a - da e en-ver-go-nha-da vem ver-seao mar.
her silv' - ry beau - ty In mod-est won-der ob-serves the sight.

2. *Penso que a noite es conderia*
   ninguem veria seu meigolhar.
   Atraico ouse a inocente
   inconsciente com seu brilhar. } (2)

2. I thought the blackness of night would hide her,
   That no one might see her lovely face.
   Her guileless innocence, alas, betrayed her
   By the shimmering brilliance in her heavenly race. } (2)

The *fado,* a hybrid, urban folksong—combining African, Brazilian, and Portuguese melodic and rhythmic elements—expresses the despair and yearning (*saudade*) and the native sentimental fatalism of the people. It is characterized by a predominant use of duple meter, syncopated rhythm, and binary (two-part) structure. The guitar is always associated with the *fado.*

English version by
Charles Haywood

Emilia

Andante doloroso

Já tu - do dor - me vai a noi - te em mei - o,___
In mid - night still - ness and peace - ful slum - ber___

Já tur - va a lu - a vem sur - gin - do a - lem;___
The moon glides smooth - ly through cloud - y sky;___

Tu - do é si - len - cio só se vê na ___ cam - pa, __
From top the grave - stone the ___ si - lence is bro - ken___

Pi - ar o mo - cho ao cru - el des - dem. __
By fear - ful sound of the owl's pierc - ing cry. __

Tu - do é si - len - cio só se vê na
From top the grave - stone the si - lence is

cam - pa, ___ Pi - ar o mo - cho ao cru - el des - dem.
bro - ken ___ By fear - ful sound of the owl's pierc - ing cry.

Emilia

2. *Despois um vulto de roupagem preta*
   No cemiterio com vagar entrou,
   Junto ao sepulcro curvandose a meio, }
   Com tristes fados nesta voz fallou. } (2)

Emilia

2. A spectral figure attired in black robe,
   With solemn footsteps he nears the stone;
   Then bending low in tortured movement beside the grave,}
   Pours out sad fados in mournful tones. } (2)

Denmark

A lover's plaint—pleading with his beloved to restore calm to his agitated mind and heal the wound of his broken heart.

Gaaer Jeg Udi Skoven—In Forest and Meadow

English version by
Charles Haywood

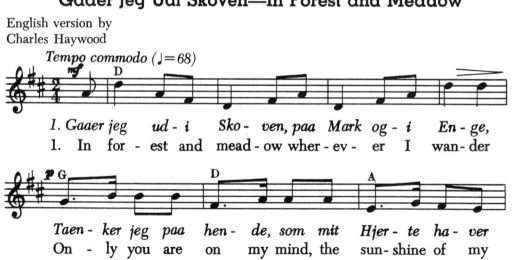

Tempo commodo (♩=68)

1. *Gaaer jeg   ud - i   Sko - ven, paa Mark og - i   En - ge,*
1. In   for - est and   mead - ow wher - ev - er   I   wan - der

Taen - ker jeg paa   hen - de, som mit   Hjer - te ha - ver
On - ly you   are   on   my mind, the   sun - shine of   my

166

kjaer; De dei - ligs - te Frug - ter paa Trae - er - ne
life; The trees bend - ing low, filled with fruit heav - y

haen - ge; Men jeg gans - ke ro - lig la'er dem
lad - en, Fill with joy the heart of all, but

haen - ge - der. Fug - gle - ne for -
mine is full of strife. Birds are sing - ing

nøi - e sig, syn - ge saa fry - de - lig;
joy - ful - ly, sport - ing gai - ly all a - round,

Kun jeg a - le - ne maa be - kym_____ re mig!
what pains you so, my heart, and why in sor - row bound?

2. Ja, kunde med Tilden det sig saa for andre,
   At jeg kunde tale med min kjaereste igjen!
   Da vilde jeg unden Bekymringer vandre,
   Søge og omfavne dig, min trofaste Ven!
   Gid du var mig saa naer, som du nu langt borte er;
   Det er mit Ønske og almin Begjaer.

2. Oh, when will the time come when all this is altered,
   Once again to hold you close, and rest my heart on thine!
   When will my despair and my yearning be ended,
   All my longing be at rest, the sun at last to shine!
   Were you but near to me as I not far from you,
   We would be joined in love, my dreams would all come true.

English version Copyright © 1966 by Charles Haywood

167

Norway

A children's singing game.

Karusellen—Carrousel

English version by
Charles Haywood

Allegretto

Jom - fru, jom - fru, jom - fru, jom - fru skjær.
La - dy, la - dy, la - dy, la - dy fair. The

Her er ka - ru - sel - len som skal gå til kvel - den.
car - ou - sel is read - y. To - night it leaves, hold stead - y.

Ti for de voks - ne og fem for de små. Skynd deg
Ten for the grown - ups, And five for the small. Hur - ry

på, skynd deg på, for i kveld skal den gå.
up, hur - ry up, For to - night you come all.

Ha, ha, ha, det går jo bra for
Ha, ha, ha, it rides a - way, For

An - der - sen og Pe - ter - sen og Lund - strøm å ja!
An - der - sen and Pe - ter - sen and Lund - strom, Hur-rah!

Sweden

This ballad belongs to "The Croodlin Doo," a nursery branch of the "Lord Randal" group. (*See* p.39) The more widely known form of this ballad is the one in which the child is poisoned by the step-mother, often associated with evil and witchcraft. However, in this instance, it is the nurse who shares the guilt with the stepmother. (*See also* p.156)

English version by
Charles Haywood

Den Lillas Testamente
The Child's Testament

1. Hvar har du va't så län - ge, Lil - la dot - ter
1. O where have you been so long, Dear - est daugh- ter

kind? Jag har va't hos Am - ma, Styf - mo - der
mine? I stayed with my old nurse, Step- moth- er

min, Aj, aj, ondt haf - ver jag, aj!
mine, Ah, ah, how great my pain, ah!

2. Hvad fick du der att äta,
   Lilla dotter kind?
   Stekter ål och peppar,
   Styfmoder min,
   Aj, aj, ondt hafver jag, aj!

3. Hvad gjorde du af benen?
   Kasta dem för hundarne.

4. Hvad kommo de hundarne?
   Remma i femton stycken.

5. Hvad ger du då din fader?
   Godt korn i lador.

2. What did you get for dinner,
   Dearest daughter mine?
   Eels broiled with pepper,
   Stepmother mine,
   Ah, ah, how great my pain, ah!

3. What did you with the bones?
   To my dog I gave them.

4. What happened to the fine dog?
   He went wild with madness.*

5. What do you wish your father?
   Finest corn a-plenty.

6. *Hvad ger du då din moder?*
Himmelen den gode.

6. What do you wish your mother?
Heavn'ly joy and blessing.

7. *Hvad ger du då din broder?*
Vida skepp i floder.

7. What do you wish your brother?
Biggest ships a-floating.

8. *Hvad ger du då din syster?*
Gullskrin och kistor.

8. What do you wish your sister?
Coffers full of gold.

9. *Hvad ger du då din styfmoder?*
Helvetes bojor!

9. What do you wish your stepmother?
To suffer hell's damnation.

10. *Hvad ger du då din amma?*
Helvetes samma!

10. What do you wish your old nurse?
To burn in hell forever.

* *Original text: "He jumped in fifteen pieces."*

The spirit of Christmas jollity is delightfully conveyed in this song. There may be other holidays and festivals, but none has the universal appeal of the Christmastide.

English version by
Noel Wiren
Con moto

Nu Är Det Jul Igen
Christmas Is Here Again

1. Nu är det jul i - gen, och nu är det jul i - gen, och
1. Christ-mas is here a - gain, And Christ-mas is here a - gain, And

ju - len va - ra skall till på - ska. på - ska.
Christ-mas goes right on till East-er. East-er.

Så är det påsk i - gen, och så är det påsk i - gen. Och
Then East-er's here a - gain, And East-er is here a - gain, And

pås - ken va - ra skall til ju - la.
East - er goes right on till Christ - mas.

170

Iceland

A joyful and exalted reflection on the beauties of nature unfolded in the summer season. The Norwegian melodic influence is apparent.

Nú Er Vetur Úr Boe—Now the Winter Is Past

Allegretto

1. Nú er vet - ur úr boe, rann í sef - groen - an
1. Now the win - ter is past With its keen i - cy

soe, og par sef - ur í djúp - i - nu voer - a, en
blast In the depth of the sea it re - pos - es. But

sum - ar - io blitt kem - ur fag - urt og fritt meo - ur
sum - mer's de - light Reigns with life - giv - ing light, And the

fjör - gjaf - ar ljós - in - u skoer - a.
lin - ger - ing sweet - ness of ros - es.

2.

Brunar kjöll yfir sund,
flýgur fákur un sund,
kem ur fugl heim ur suorinu heita.
Nú er vetur úr boe,
rann í sefgroenan soe,
nú er sumrinu fögnuð að veita.

2.

Now the keel ploughs the main,
And the steed feels the rein,
And the bird from the southland is winging.
Now the winter is past
With its keen icy blast,
And the welcome of summer is ringing.

3.

Pegar lauf skryðir björk,
pegar ljósgul um mörk
rennur liflandi kornstanga moða,
pá mun farið af stað,
pá mun peyst heim á hlað
til hans porgeirs i lundinum göða.

3.

When the forest is green,
And the billows are seen
In the fields, where the breezes are playing;
Then 'tis ho and away,
At the dawn of the day,
To our friends in the country a-maying.

Finland

English version by Charles Haywood

Suomen Salossa—The Finnish Forest

Con spirito (♩=92)

Hon - ka - en kess - kel - lä mök - ki - ni sei - soo,
Deep in the for - est in cool shad - y grove, ___

Suo - me - ni so - re - as - sa sa - los - sa,
There stands my house in fair Su - o - mi - land;

Hon - ka - en vä - lil - tä siin - ta - vä sel - kä
Clear are the wa - ters that flow gent - ly by, ___

Vilk - ku - vi ko - it - te - hen va - los - sa.
Mead - ow in frag - rance with ___ flowers a - round.   *Hoi*

poco sost.   *pp echo*

laa - ri laa - ri laa,   Hoi laa - ri laa - ri laa,   Hoi

echo   *pp*

laa - ri laa - ri laa,   Hoi laa - ri laa - ri laa,

Kai - ku mun su - loi - nen Suo - me - ni maa!
Joy - ful the song of our fair na - tive land!

172

The Soviet Union

A song of childlike simplicity and sweet remembrance; a yearning for the love that is no more; the ending on the dominant harmony (and the second note of the scale) emphasizes the mood of unfulfillment.

Kui Mina Alles Noor Veel Olin—When I Was But a Small Young Laddie

English version by
Charles Haywood

Allegretto   *(Estonia)*

Kui mi - na al - les noor veel_ o - lin, noor veel o - lin,
When I was but a small young_ lad - die, small young lad - die

Lap - se - põl - ves män - gi - sin,___ män - gi - sin,
Games I would play, and al - ways read - y; al - ways read - y.

Ei mi - na tead - nud muud, kui_ se - da, muud kui se - da,
Ev' - ry - thing I saw with_ pleas - ure, saw with pleas - ure,

Mis mi - na nä - gin sil - ma - ga,___ sil - ma - ga.
Filled my_ mind with un - told treas - ure, un - told treas - ure.

Mei - e e - lu on siin_ il - mas, on siin il - mas
I was hap - py, free and_ jol - ly, free and jol - ly,

Na - gu_ lin - nul ok - sa pääl,___ ok - sa pääl!
Like the_ birds on ev' - ry tree, ___ ev' - ry tree!

A song of lively satire. A young Latvian maiden, who is indifferent to the attractions near home, soon discovers, to her sad disappointment, that the allurements in Prussia only mean backbreaking hard work and no pleasure.

Diw' Laiwinas—Two Little Boats

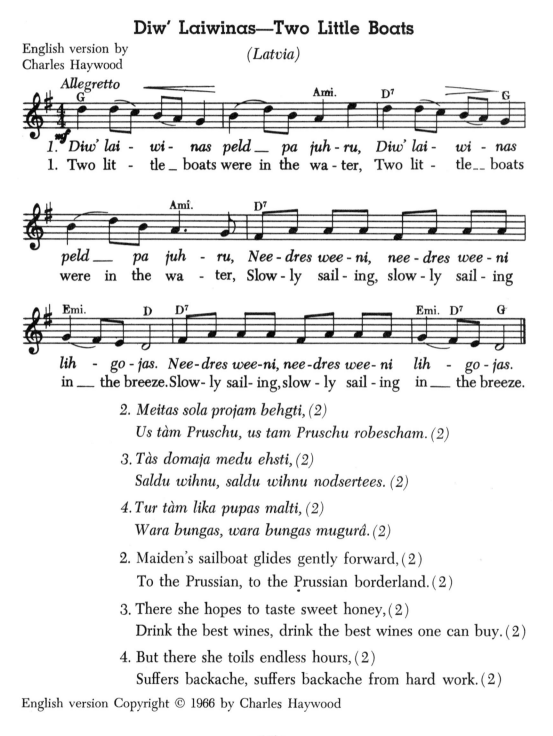

English version by
Charles Haywood

(Latvia)

1. Diw' lai - wi- nas peld __ pa juh-ru, Diw' lai- wi - nas
1. Two lit - tle _ boats were in the wa - ter, Two lit - tle __ boats

peld __ pa juh - ru, Nee - dres wee - ni, nee - dres wee - ni
were in the wa - ter, Slow - ly sail - ing, slow - ly sail - ing

lih - go - jas. Nee-dres wee-ni, nee-dres wee- ni lih - go-jas.
in __ the breeze. Slow- ly sail- ing, slow - ly sail -ing in __ the breeze.

2. *Meitas sola projam behgti, (2)*
   Us tàm Pruschu, us tam Pruschu robescham. (2)

3. *Tàs domaja medu ehsti, (2)*
   Saldu wihnu, saldu wihnu nodsertees. (2)

4. *Tur tàm lika pupas malti, (2)*
   Wara bungas, wara bungas mugurâ. (2)

2. Maiden's sailboat glides gently forward, (2)
   To the Prussian, to the Prussian borderland. (2)

3. There she hopes to taste sweet honey, (2)
   Drink the best wines, drink the best wines one can buy. (2)

4. But there she toils endless hours, (2)
   Suffers backache, suffers backache from hard work. (2)

This love song exemplifies the finest qualities of the *daina*: a deeply expressive melodic line (in the Aeolian mode), the alternation between 4/4 and 5/4 time, and the two-part structure. The symbolic flowers attest to his undying love.

Kol Jauns Nevedęs Buvau—

English version by **Quite Young and Carefree Was I**
Charles Haywood

(Lithuania)

2. *Rašiau as paš tevęlį* ⎱ (2)
   Margą gromatęlę: ⎰
   Ar galiu šimet vest margelę?
   Fale rale riloš raloš,
   Ar laukt da metelius?

2. A letter to her father ⎱ (2)
   I wrote with trembling hand: ⎰
   May I this year wed your daughter?
   Fale rale rilosh ralosh,
   Or yet wait another year?

3. *Mano tęvelio sode,* ⎱ (2)
   Stovi du medeliu. ⎰
   Ant vieno auga tik korintai.
   Fale rale riloš raloš,
   Ant kito gvazdikai.

3. In my dear father's garden ⎱ (2)
   Two bushes proudly bloom, ⎰
   On one there blooms currants,
   Fale rale rilosh ralosh,
   Carnations on the other one.

A dance-song. Tchaikovski uses this theme in the "1812 Overture."

Ai, Dunaii Moy—Ah, My Belov'd Dunaii

English version by
Charles Haywood

(RSFSR)

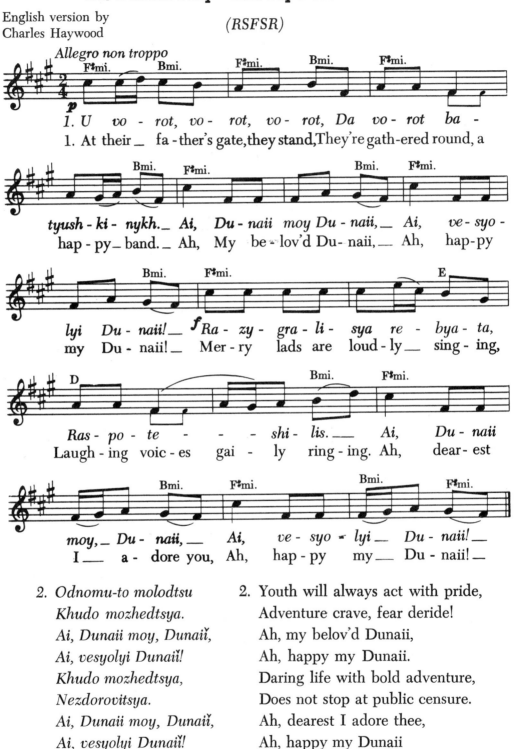

Allegro non troppo

1. U vo - rot, vo - rot, vo - rot, Da vo - rot ba -
1. At their _ fa -ther's gate, they stand, They're gath-ered round, a

tyush - ki - nykh. _ Ai, Du - naii moy Du - naii, _ Ai, ve - syo -
hap - py _ band. _ Ah, My be - lov'd Du - naii, _ Ah, hap - py

lyi Du - naii! _ Ra - zy - gra - li - sya re - bya - ta,
my Du - naii! _ Mer - ry lads are loud - ly _ sing - ing,

Ras - po - te - shi - lis. _ Ai, Du - naii
Laugh - ing voic - es gai - ly ring - ing. Ah, dear - est

moy, _ Du - naii, _ Ai, ve - syo - lyi _ Du - naii! _
I _ a - dore you, Ah, hap - py my _ Du - naii! _

2. *Odnomu-to molodtsu*
   Khudo mozhedtsya.
   Ai, Dunaii moy, Dunaiĭ,
   Ai, vesyolyi Dunaiĭ!
   Khudo mozhedtsya,
   Nezdorovitsya.
   Ai, Dunaii moy, Dunaiĭ,
   Ai, vesyolyi Dunaiĭ!

2. Youth will always act with pride,
   Adventure crave, fear deride!
   Ah, my belov'd Dunaii,
   Ah, happy my Dunaii.
   Daring life with bold adventure,
   Does not stop at public censure.
   Ah, dearest I adore thee,
   Ah, happy my Dunaii

A wedding song, expressing the loneliness and despair of the young maiden about to leave her home and friends to meet the man of her father's choice.

Chi Ya V'luzi Ne Kalina Bula?—Was I Not a Flower in the Meadow?

English version by
Charles Haywood

(Ukraine)

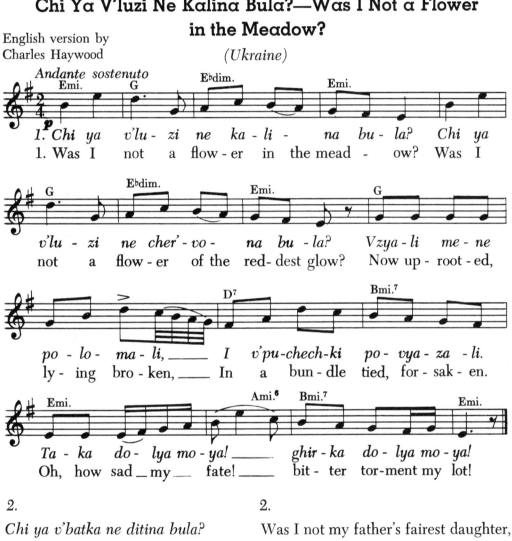

Andante sostenuto

1. Chi ya v'lu - zi ne ka - li - na bu - la? Chi ya
1. Was I not a flow - er in the mead - ow? Was I

v'lu - zi ne cher' - vo - na bu - la? Vzya - li me - ne
not a flow - er of the red - dest glow? Now up - root - ed,

po - lo - ma - li, _____ I v'pu - chech - ki po - vya - za - li.
ly - ing bro - ken, _____ In a bun - dle tied, for - sak - en.

Ta - ka do - lya mo - ya! _____ ghir - ka do - lya mo - ya!
Oh, how sad _ my _ fate! _____ bit - ter tor - ment my lot!

2.

Chi ya v'batka ne ditina bula?
Chi ya v'batka ne kokhana bula?
Vzyalizh mene povinchali,
I svit meni zavyazali.
Taka dolya moya! ghirka dolya moya!

2.

Was I not my father's fairest daughter,
Treated kindly, angered never?
Forced to wed a man I love not,
Now my world is dark, life's shut.
Oh, how sad my fate! bitter my lot!

A Tatar love song of utmost tenderness and inner fervor. The undulating melody, based on the oriental or harmonic minor, appropriately intensifies the mood; should be sung softly and expressively, in *mezza voce* (half voice).

Bakhchalarda—In My Garden

(Crimea)

English version by
Charles Haywood

1. *Bakh- cha - lar - da gul __ lya - le men __ e - la - dim __*
1. In my gar - den ros - es bloom, Tho' __ the __ au - tumn __

yash __ a - re; Sen - den ba - na fie - da - nok
rains __ are __ near; Pain - ful long - ing fills __ my __ heart,

kar - shim da - dur - ma __ ba - re.
Wand'- ring __ sad - ly __ in __ de - spair. A, _____ a, ___

a, _____ a, ___ a, _____ a, ___ a, ___ a, _____ a.

2. *Bakhchalarda gul nahne,*
   kul oldum yane, yane;
   Alkiz seni derdin den,
   oldum deli divane.

   A, a, a, ...

2. In my garden roses grow,
   All paths lead to final death;
   No one is more fair than thou,
   Praised and blessed by the Prophet.

   A, a, a, ...

A folk dance, beginning slowly, softly and languidly, gradually increasing in tempo and dynamics, building up to a "wild" presto and crescendo. Repeat many times until the desired effect is produced.

Vorira
(Kazakhstan)

Vo-ri-ra ri-ra vo-ri-ra-ra, Vo-ri-ra ra-ra,

Vo-ri-ra ri-ra vo-ri-ra ra, Vo-ri-ra ra-ra!

This folksong came out of the Civil War period in the 1920's in Russia. It is a tragic commentary upon the ravages and destruction of one's fair homeland.

English version by
Charles Haywood

Dagestan
(Azerbaidzhan)

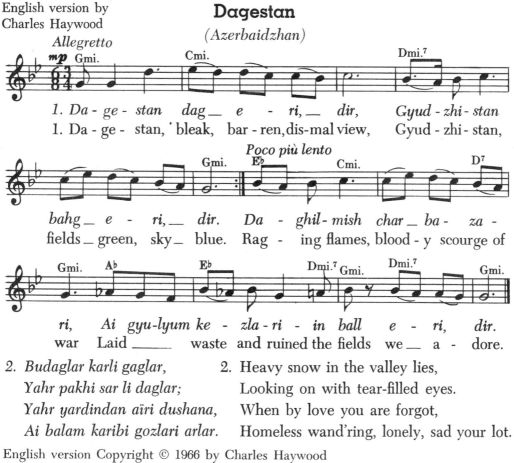

1. Da - ge - stan dag _ e - ri, _ dir, Gyud - zhi - stan
1. Da - ge - stan, bleak, bar - ren, dis-mal view, Gyud - zhi - stan,

bahg _ e - ri, _ dir. Da - ghil - mish char _ ba - za -
fields _ green, sky _ blue. Rag - ing flames, blood - y scourge of

ri, Ai gyu-lyum ke - zla - ri - in ball e - ri, dir.
war Laid _____ waste and ruined the fields we _ a - dore.

2. Budaglar karli gaglar,   2. Heavy snow in the valley lies,
   Yahr pakhi sar li daglar;   Looking on with tear-filled eyes.
   Yahr yardindan aïri dushana,   When by love you are forgot,
   Ai balam karibi gozlari arlar. Homeless wand'ring, lonely, sad your lot.

A street singer or wandering bard, accompanying himself on the *tari* (a long lute), is ready to entertain and bring joy to all for a small token.

Kabak da Boynuma—Striking a Tune

English version by
Charles Haywood

Allegretto grazioso

1. Ka - bak da boy - nu - ma ta - ka - rim, _____
1. Strik- ing a tune on my faith- ful ta - ri,

Gahm - mü mikh - ne - ti a - ta - rim.
Glad - dens my heart,_ bring- ing com - fort to me.

Iz - ni - niz _____ o - lur i sě, _____
Grant me a to - ken, be - lov - ed, of va - lue,

Sǐ - ze ka - bak cha - la - rim bu - ghi - dzhe.
I will play and sing _ the whole night_ through.

Refrain

Ka - tin - ga din - ga din - ga din - ga - la, _____

Äy bah - di sa - ba _ din ka - bak.

180

2.

2.

Kabaghima kirish tokarim,
Khovardaii gözünden chakarim.
Egher manghir veriseniz,
Sĭze kabak chalarim bughidzhe.
    Katinga dinga dinga, etc.

All hearts I sway with my tuneful tari,
Pleasure for all who listen to me.
Will the fair one pay me, I beg you!
I will play and sing the whole night through.
    Katinga dinga dinga, etc.

3.

3.

Karshidan ghelirmisin?
Sen beni severmisin?
Göksündeki gül ichün,
Dzhanimi da veririm senin ichün.
    Katinga dinga dinga, etc.

Why are you dressed in your finest gown?
Queenly attired, are you going to town?
Fairest maiden, give me a flower,
Songs I will sing to gladden the hour.
    Katinga dinga dinga, etc.

English version Copyright © 1966 by Charles Haywood

Yehrgeenkun Ahmbel Eh—Gray Clouds Engulf the Sky

English version by
Charles Haywood

(Armenia)

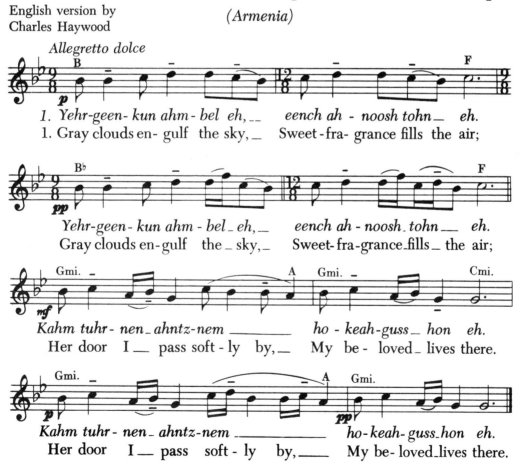

1. Yehr-geen-kun ahm-bel eh,__ eench ah-noosh tohn__ eh.
1. Gray clouds en-gulf the sky,__ Sweet-fra-grance fills the air;

Yehr-geen-kun ahm-bel_eh,__ eench ah-noosh_tohn__ eh.
Gray clouds en-gulf the_sky,__ Sweet-fra-grance_fills_ the air;

Kahm tuhr-nen_ahntz-nem_____ ho-keah-guss_hon eh.
Her door I__ pass soft-ly by,__ My be-loved_lives there.

Kahm tuhr-nen_ahntz-nem_____ ho-keah-guss_hon eh.
Her door I__ pass soft-ly by,___ My be-loved_lives there.

181

Yehrgeenkum Ahmbel Eh

2. Yehrgeenkum ahmbel eh,
   kedeeneh tatz eh.   }(2)
   Yares kunel eh,
   yehresh patz eh.   }(2)

3. Yehrgeenkum ambel eh,
   eench ahnosh yehrag.   }(2)
   Sirdees metch luhtzav
   mee pooreh guhrag.   }(2)

4. Yehrgeenkum ahmbel eh,
   kedeen shagherov.   }(2)
   Yes kez seerel yem
   ahnoosh khagherov.   }(2)

Gray Clouds Engulf The Sky

2. Gray clouds engulf the sky,
   Deep shadows the earth obscure, }(2)
   My love in sleep doth lie,
   Her face heavenly pure.   }(2)

3. Gray clouds engulf the sky,
   Soft drops fall gently down,   }(2)
   Tormented, anguished am I,
   Fearful my beloved may frown.   }(2)

4. Gray clouds engulf the sky,
   Earth scented odors rise,   }(2)
   Exulting my song soaring high,
   For you my heart cries.   }(2)

Poland

This is a *mazurka*—a dance in triple meter, consisting of two or four parts of eight measures, each part repeated, with a strong accent on the third beat of the bar. The dance is performed by four or eight couples; the tempo is usually much slower than the waltz.

Podkóweczki Dajcie Ognia—Click Your Heels

English version by
Adam Harasowski

1.Dziś, dziś, dziś, dziś, dziś, dziś, dziś dziś!

Pod - kó- wecz - ki __ daj - cie og - nia, __ Bo dziew-czy - na __
Click your heels till __ sparks are fly - ing, __ Let your dance be __

te - go god - na, A czy god - na, __ czy nie-god - na! __
bright and snap - py, Your girl's nice, there's __ no de - ny - ing, __

Pod - kó - wecz - ki __ daj - cie og - nia!
She is worth it, __ make her hap - py.

Nu - że ży - wo, nu - że da - lej, Bo pod-ków - ki
Keep on go - ing, fast and dash - ing, Click your heels, boys,

sa że sta - li, Byś - my og - nia __ wyk - rżé - sa - li, __
show your spi - rit, Oth - er pairs be - hind you rush - ing, __

Hej - że ży - wo, __ nu - że da - lej!
Rous - ing is the __ tune, let's hear it.

2.

Hej, zawracaj od komina,
A uważáj której nie ma,
Jest tu Kasia, jest Marysia,
Tylko Zosi nie ma dzisiaj.

Grajże, grajku, będziecz w niebie,
A basista koło ciebe ciebie,
Cymbalista jeszcze dalej,
Bo w cymbały dobrze wail.

2.

From the chimney starts our journey,
Our fair partners we'll be kissing,
Kate and Mary, to the tourney,
Where is Sophie? she is missing.

Come, play on, you stalwart drummer,
Fiddle, bass, a merry measure,
Every swallow makes a summer,
Heaven's yours who give such pleasure.

183

Czechoslovakia

A spiritual song of innocent charm and lyrical enthusiasm. It is not often that a village deacon evokes such warm affection by his simple, good deeds.

Milínkej Pan Děkan—Our Village Deacon

English version by
Charles Haywood

(Czech)

Moderato

1. Mi - lín - skej pan dě - kan do - bře ká - že;
1. Our vil - lage dea - con is one of the best,

do - bře ká - že; roz - dá - vá ob - ráz - ky
one of the best, He gives us ho - ly cards,

u ol - tá - ře. u ol - tá - ře.
pret - ty and blest, pret - ty and blest.

Allegro

Hej du - dy du - dy duj - da, duj - da, duj - da,

hej du - dy du - dy duj - jda, duj - da, dy - dum.

2. *Ta na to kázání taky půjdu,*
   o jeden obrázek prosit budu.
      Hej dudy dudy dujda, etc.

3. *Čoz jest ten pan děkan milostivý,*
   on mně dal obrázek on byl živý.
      Hej dudy dudy dujda, etc.

4. *Dám ho do modliteb nevejde se,*
   dám-li ho truhly u-dusí se.
      Hej dudy dudy dujda, etc.

5. *Dám ho do postýlky pod peřinu,*
   budu se s ním tesit celou zimu.
      Hej dudy dudy dujda, etc.

2. I will go gladly his sermon to hear,
   And ask for holy cards bringing good cheer.
      Hej dudy dudy dujda, etc.

3. No kinder deacon can ever be found,
   He gave us a holy card, the liveliest around.
      Hej dudy dudy dujda, etc.

4. If put in the prayer book, it will jump out,
   Placed in a box, it will choke without doubt.
      Hej dudy dudy dujda, etc.

5. I'll tuck it in gently right under my quilt,
   Enjoying it wintertime up to the hilt.
      Hej dudy dudy dujda, etc.

185

Mary, a young, innocent maiden, having fallen in love with a hunter
(and one needs be careful of hunters . . .), allays her mother's fears
by asserting that this hunter truly and honestly loves her.

English version by   **Starej Breclavy—Near Breclav**
Olga Paul
                     (Slovak)

1. U sta - rej Bre - cla - vy na hrá - zi,
1. Near Bre - clav, near by the riv - er - side,

My - sli - ve - ček sa tam pro - chá - zí;
There was a hunt - er who walked with pride;

Stre - lil na li - šku, Tre - fil Ma - ry - šku;
Hunt - ing for pleas - ure, He found a treas - ure;

Ma - ry - ška uz le - ží na bri - šku.
Ma - ry so trim, fell in love with him.

2. *Prišla kni mamenka, plakala,*   2. Mother came running in velvet skirt,
   Že jelí hlavěnka bolavá;   "Daughter, I fear that your head is hurt!"
   Ne plač, mamenko,   "Mother, don't hurry,
   Moje srdenko;   Don't always worry!
   Už je má hlavěnka zhojená.   He was polite, and my head's all right!"
   Ne plač, mamenko,   "Mother, don't hurry,
   Moje srdenko;   Don't always worry!
   Už je má hlavěnka zhojená.   He was polite, and my head's all right!"

186

Hungary

To the strong rhythm of the *czardas*, the bold hussar, in bright uniform and clicking spurs, proclaims his undying love.

Ázert Hogy én Huszár Vagyok—Look at Me, A Gallant Hussar

English version by
Charles Haywood

Danza energico

Az - ért hogy én hu - szár va - gyok, Kin - csem ró - zsám
Look at me, a gal - lant hus - sar, Treas - ure, rose - bud,

ga - lam - bom, Ok - tó - ber - ben ab - fü - ru - lok,
lit - tle dove; Gai - ly danc - ing in Ok - to - ber,

Kin - csem ró - zsám ga - lam - bom; Sár - ga - réz sar -
Treas - ure, rose - bud, lit - tle dove. See the spar - kling

kan - tyus cziz - mám Hu - szá - ros - san
spurs I'm wear - ing, Mark - ing hus - sar's

ösz - sze - pen - ge - tem; De - sok - szor meg -
no - ble bear - ing. Man - y times I

ö - lel - te - lek, So - ha el nem fe - led - lek.
held you close - ly, Un - for - get - ful ne'er I'll be.

Abandoned and brokenhearted the unhappy maiden bemoans her sad fate. A most expressive example of the contrasting slow (*parlando*) first and third part of the song, and the fast (*giusto*) tempo of the middle section.

Ablakomba—Through My Window

English version by
Charles Haywood

Ab - la - kom - ba, ab - la - kom - ba, be - sü - tött a
Thro' my win - dow, thro' my win - dow, bright - ly shines the

hold - vi - lág, A ki ket - töt, hár - mat sze - ret
silv' - ry moon, Lov - ing man - y, heart in - con - stant,

so - sincs ar - ra jó vi - lág. Lám én csak e -
sad - ness it will bring you soon. Yes, I love you,

gyest sze - re - tek, Még - is de so - kát szen -
on - ly you dear, Great my an - guish when you're

ve - dek, Ez az ál - nok bé - res
not near; You've de - ceived me, left me

le - gény csal - ta meg a szi - ve - met.
pin - ing, Bro - ken heart - ed, lone - ly, crying.

188

Yugoslavia

An anxious and love-stricken soldier is returning from war, eager to see his beloved, yet fearful if she still loves him.

English version by
Charles Haywood

Tri Dni—Three Days

(Croatia)

Allegro moderato

1. Tri dni mi je · kak sam do - šel sta - bo - ra;
Three days aft - er war was o - ver home - ward bound;

pa - la mi je ko - nju zno - ge pot - ko - va.
One shoe from my stur - dy horse had fal - len down.

Tri dni mi je kak sam do - šel sta - bo - ra;
Three days aft - er war was o - ver home - ward bound;

pa - la mi je ko - nju zno - ge pot - ko - va.
One shoe from my stur - dy horse had fal - len down.

2. *Kovac majster, potkovaj mi konjica,* } (2)
   Kaj bum jahal, tam 'de moja grlica. }

4. *Ne ce meni svetli mesec svetiti,* } (2)
   Ne ce mene moja draga ljubiti! }

2. O dear smithy, put another horseshoe on, } (2)
   To my sweetheart I must hurry before dawn. }

4. Sudden clouds have darkened moonlight, woe is me, } (2)
   For I know not if she loves me faithfully. }

The desperate pleadings of a frustrated wife for her husband to leave the bar and bottle and return home. The oriental minor scale, with the augmented second (b flat to c sharp), adds to the poignancy of the song.

Kad se Jangin—Hear Me, Dearest

English version by
Charles Haywood

(Serbia)

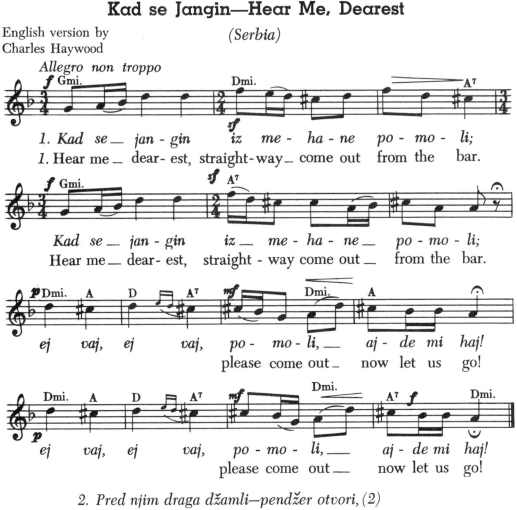

2. *Pred njim draga džamli—pendžer otvori, (2)*
   ej vaj, ej vaj, otvori, ajde mi haj! (2)

3. *I kroz pendžer b'jele ruke promoli, (2)*
   ej vaj, ej vaj, promoli, ajde mi haj! (2)

2. Through the window flung open, crying out; (2)
   ej vaj, ej vaj, flung wide open, now let us go! (2)

3. Through the window hands imploring to her man; (2)
   ej vaj, ej vaj, hands imploring, now let us go! (2)

Bulgaria

A dance-song variant of the "Barbary Allen" ballad, in the Aeolian mode.

English version by
Charles Haywood

Elenke

Allegro vivo

1. E - len - ke, E - len - ke, mom - ko ti eh bo - len!
1. E - len - ke, E - len - ke, come to your sick lov - er!

Gor - ko - mu, dosh - lo - mu, ne - ka bo - len le - zhi!
Is he sick, let him be, this does not con - cern me!

Kho - ro nye o - sta - vyam mom - ko da si gle - dam,
I'll not leave this mer - ry danc - ing for a mo - ment,

Se - ga eh kho - ro - to ta - mam nai - do - bro - to!
Here I'll stay, go a - way, danc - ing makes me hap - py!

2. *Elenke, Elenke, momko ti umira! (2)*
   Gorkomu, doshlomu, neka da umira! (2)
   Khoro ne ostavyam momko da si gledam, (2)
   Sega eh khoroto tamam naidibroto! (2)

2. Elenke, Elenke, I fear your lover's dying!(2)
   If he dies, let him die, this does not concern me!(2)
   I'll not leave this merry dancing for a moment,(2)
   Here I'll stay, go away, dancing makes me happy!(2)

Rumania

A poignant lament at the death of a young son. The melody is in the Phrygian mode; the shifting of the interval of the major to augmented second (a^b b^b–a^b b) adds considerably to the expressiveness of the tune.

Bucurâ t'e Ţintirim—Oh, Rejoice, Thou Frightful Grave

English version by
Charles Haywood

2. *Nu răsăď'im să 'nflorea,*
   Nu răsăď'im să 'nflorea,
   D'e 'n pământ să putredea.
   D'e 'n pământ să putredea.

2. Not to bloom, alas, 'tis planted,
   Not to bloom, alas, 'tis planted,
   She lies helpless, faded, and dead.
   She lies helpless, faded, and dead.

Albania

Lament for a young bride, who must leave home and her friends, and face the hardships of married life. The reference to the silken apron, about to be "torn and destroyed," is the loss of her maidenhood.

English version by
Charles Haywood

Pliot Mola Lülé
The Apple Tree

Andante espressivo

1. Pliot mo - la lü - lé të bër- dë, të bër- dé ____
   ____ pliot ____ mo la, Frü - vié - ra, é - ranë bër-
   dé moi bër - dé ____ é pliot mo - la, Del
   im - blid moï mous - se é ré moï é ré é ____
   ____ é pliot mo - la, Éim - bléd moï po skam në sé. ____

1. The ap - ple tree, with white blos-soms, white blos - soms ____
   ____ stands ____ proud - ly, The wind sweeps and scat - ters
   them all a - bout, ____ stands lone - ly; Thus
   go young bride, so sweet and in - no - cent, so fair, ____
   And gath - er the blos-soms, all you can bear. ____

2. É në podiá, moï podiá vëu kadüfé,
   Ëschtë é olë é grissété ëschtë sërma é,
   Prishëtë, é lé të prishét lë të,
   Sehrétonét édé në ziar moï të përvé lionëtë.

2. Oh, gather them in thy silken apron, so soft and tender,
   Too fragile the apron, spun of finest cloth, ne'er made better;
   It cannot hold the blossoms, torn, destroyed it will be.
   So be it! let all of it tear completely!

Greece

A Klephtic song expressing the deep anguish and despair at being separated from his native homeland.

Kláhpsete—Oh, Weep Mine Eyes

English version by
Charles Haywood

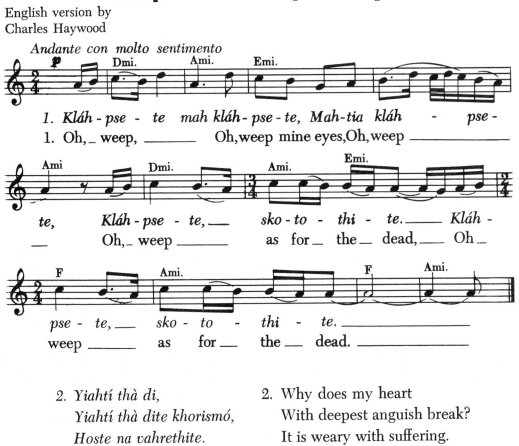

Andante con molto sentimento

1. *Kláh - pse - te mah kláh - pse - te, Mah-tia kláh — pse-*
1. Oh, _ weep, ———— Oh, weep mine eyes, Oh, weep —————

te, Kláh - pse - te, ___ sko - to - thi - te. ___ Kláh -
_ Oh, _ weep ———— as for _ the _ dead, ___ Oh _

pse - te, ___ sko - to - thi - te. ———————
weep ———— as for _ the _ dead. ———————

2. *Yiahtí thà di,*
   Yiahtí thà dite khorismó,
   Hoste na vahrethite.

2. Why does my heart
   With deepest anguish break?
   It is weary with suffering.

Cyprus

A song, filled with deep religious sentiment and warm affection, blessing the new bride for a happy and good life.

Tō Tragōthi tō Gamō—The Wedding Song

English version by
Charles Haywood

Allegretto

Hō - ra ka - lée   jō _____ ra - ba thée,   Jō
May all your life be filled _____ with joy,   E -

ra ev - lo - - ee - mé - nee.
ter - nal bless - - - - ing grace this day;

Tō - tee do - lyá par - ké - psa - men.
This ho - ly task we have just be - gun,

Na vchee ste - re - o - mé - nee;
May it be strength - ened, this we pray;

Pō ton a - phén - teen __ ton Chri - ston
For - ev - er bles - sed and pro - tect - ed,

Na ni ev - lo - ee - mé - nee.
With Christ, our Lord, _____ keep - ing __ watch.

Asia

The Middle East

Arabian Music

This is the world of the prophet Mohammed and the religious beliefs of Islam. It embraces a vast territory extending from the borders of India westward to the Mediterranean and across northern Africa. During centuries of territorial and spiritual expansion of its domain, many diversified cultures made their impact upon Islamic civilization. As a consequence, Arabian music is a product or synthesis of Persian (theoretical treatises and vocal techniques), Turkish (passionate intensity), and indigenous Arabic (Syria, Egypt and Arabia) musical systems. Moreover, the fusion of the rich musical tradition of the court and folk, existing for centuries before the rise of Islam, gave distinctive color to Arabian music: vocal, instrumental, and the dance. Of considerable significance was the influence of Persian and Greek music and lore.

The chief characteristics of Arabian music that become apparent to the Western ear are, first, the use of the *maquam*, the melodic configuration or motive, which the singer employs in molding the song. This is not to be confused with the church mode or our scale. While it includes both of these concepts, the *maquam* (possessing affinity with the Hindu *raga*) has a much wider tonal range and greater melodic flexibility. As in other Eastern countries and some Western lands, their particular use is determined by the *ethos*, the spiritual and ethical factors associated with each *maquam*. Other elements that the Western listener frequently associates with Arabian music are the use of the so-called "oriental minor," the interval of the augmented second (e.g., b flat to c sharp), the sliding of the voice from one note to another, permitting small or microtonal intervals, and the use of elaborate ornamentation and embellishment of the

197

melody, displaying ingenious artistry and remarkable virtuosity.

The vital role folk music has played in the Arab's life has been eloquently described by George Henry Farmer, the outstanding scholar in this field (*The New Oxford History of Music*, Vol. I [*Ancient and Oriental Music*], London, 1957, pp. 434-35):

"What is of greater interest is the more universal approval of music as the story-teller in *The Arabian Nights* puts it, likening the art to 'a fan [on a sultry day]'. When a child was born into Islam the opening lines of the call to prayer (*adhdhān*) was chanted in its ear, whilst the neighbouring matrons assembled with their tambourines (*dufūf*) to herald joy. At the celebrations of circumcision there was further music and entertainment. Marriage occasioned an even greater display, since the procession had its shawms (*zumūr*) and drums (*ṭubūl*) in noisy service, while hired female musicians (*mughanniyāt*) performed less strident music in the courtyard. Even at the bier, the wailing (*wilwāl*) of the mourning women (*naddābāt*) at the thud of their tambourines, was followed by the chanting of the Qur'an. Thus, between the cradle and the grave, music was ever present in Islam. All the great religious festivals encouraged public music, for the cry was 'Gladden thine heart, drum thine drum, and pipe thine pipe'. Military and processional music was cultivated on a grandiose scale in the shape of trumpets (*anfār*), horns (*būqāt*), shawms (*zumūr*), drums (*ṭūbūl*), kettledrums (*naqqārāt*), and cymbals (*kasāt*). Its performance of a divertimento (*nauba*) at certain prescribed hours of the day must have beckoned the crowd. In addition there was the attraction of the singing-girls (*qaināt*) in the taverns, against which the pious raved in wrath, and the less scandalous story-teller (*rāwī*) and violist (*rabābī*) in the coffee-houses. The household in general found the matrons indulging in singing to the rhythm of the tambourine.

"The music of the Islamic folk was little different then from what it is today. The toil song, a relic from the cradle of humanity, was practised by the boatman, the sailor, the porter, the weaver, the gleaner, and the rest, for its lilt and measure not only softened the sweat of toil but ordered it rhythmically. Then there was domestic music: the lullaby, the children's ditties, the bridal song, and the elegy. Nor was this simple homely art confined to the folk. The Caliph Hārūn delighted in listening to his minstrels repeating the songs of the people, as we know from the reception he gave Ibn Jami' when he sang the song of the Yemenite negress, and Abu Sadaqa when he chanted the ditties of sailors and masons."

Israel, Including the Yiddish Folksong

The Jewish people, lacking, until recently, a national homeland, created a folk music reflecting the various cultures where they lived, or were forced to live. The three major factors influencing the quality of its melodic and linguistic idiosyncrasies have been the Oriental (Yemen, Persia, etc.), the Mediterranean Sephardic (Spain, Tunis, the Balkans, etc.), and Ashkenazic (Eastern and Western Europe) communities. Yet, however divergent the mainstream of these ethnomusical elements were, there was always present a cohesive, binding force, giving an all-embracing unity to the Jewish folk music. And that was the use and identity of poetic paraphrases of the Holy Scriptures and the liturgical patterns of Biblical cantillation. No matter where the Diaspora scattered the Jewish people, regardless of incessant social, political, economic, and cultural pressure and ostracism imposed upon them—indeed, the more isolated they became, particularly in the Ghettos, the more closely did they maintain the ethical, spiritual, mystical, and melodic affiliation with ancient Israel. This pervading quality is as true in the gay, satirical, humorous (and how they learned to laugh!) songs and dances, as in their contemplative, mystical, plaintive melodies and declamatory exhortations.

Today, in this young nation in the old land of Israel, the folklore scholars are enthusiastically engaged in bringing together all the musical strands of their ethnomusical components, scattered all over the earth. Systematic collecting and scientific analysis are being made of the Biblical modes and psalm tunes, which have been such potent links in the continuity of the Jewish folksong. Let us mention briefly the other vital "links" in the chain of Jewish musical "continuity": the extraordinary isolation of the Yemenite Jews for the past 2,500 years that presents an important source for such study; the tender simplicity of the Yemenite social songs, particularly the lyrical wedding songs and the warm ecstasy of the spiritual tunes; the Arabic influences on the music of Iraqian Jews, with their strong rhythmic accents; the richly ornamented songs of the Persian Jews, or the simple metrical songs of the Moslem Jews; the interesting admixture in the ethnomusical elements of the Bene-Israelites of India; the fascinating musical blend from Spanish, Moorish, and Jewish ingredients and their influence on the countries of the Mediterranean basin; and the rich vitality of the Yiddish sacred (including the Hassidic) and secular folksongs of eastern Europe, particularly in Russia and Poland—perhaps the richest strain of Jewish folk music—mirroring every aspect of their inner life and difficult environment. Add to this, the zestful, spirited songs of the *Halutzim* of Israel, building a new life, depicting an inner joy, an indomitable determination, and a hopeful prayer. All these above-mentioned components shape, determine and vitalize the character of Israeli music today.

Turkey

There is little evidence to show that the European musical systems have affected the folk music of Turkey. One rarely encounters the Western major and minor scales. The predominant characteristics of Turkish folk tunes are their general downward motion, the influence of the Greek modes (Phrygian, Dorian, and Aeolian), and their dependence on the pentatonic scale. These melodies fall under two major classifications. The *Uzun hava* (long chant), or free melodies, are recitative or declamatory in nature, with extended, elaborate embellishment, extolling heroic deeds, nostalgic yearning for the homeland, or amorous adventure. The other group may be described as measured melodies, "usually of a lighter character or in the nature of dance tunes."

Various instruments, string (especially the *saz* and the *kemence*), and wind (the *zurna, kaval, argun,* and *dumbelek*), accompany, singly or in groups, the various songs, adding to the richness of color and rhythmic vitality.

Iran

The contrast between the joyful sentiment of the text (admiration for the lovely Hadjar) and the slow, plaintive melody (all within the interval of a fifth, with little motivic variation), creates the effect of a suppliant, spiritual chant.

English version by
Charles Haywood

Kouh Beh Kouh—On the Road

1. Kouh beh kouh_ mi - gar - di - dam, dom - ba - lé khar - gousch,
1. On the road_ the moun-tain side, Chas - ing rab - bit in_fast stride,

yâ - ré khod - ra man di-dam gousch-va - ré dar __ gousch,
There my sweet-heart did ap-pear Wear-ing gold ring in __ her ear,

gousch - va - ré dar _____ gousch Hoi! _ hoi! _ hoi!
Wear - ing gold ring in __ her ear. Hoi! _ hoi! _ hoi!

Ha - djar gra - schang é, mast - o ma - lang é! _____
Ha - djar so_ love - ly, Joy - ful and__ hap-py! _____

2. Kouh beh kouh migardidam,
   az peiyé âhou,
   yâré khodra man didam
   pahlou beh pahlou,
   Djân! djân! djân!
   Hadjar gaschang é,
   masto malang é!

2. On the road the mountain side,
   Hunting reindeer running wild,
   There my sweetheart did appear
   Filled my heart with boundless cheer.
   Hoi! hoi! hoi!
   Hadjar so lovely,
   Joyful and happy!

Iraq

A love song of great lyrical beauty in which the lovelorn youth avows his passion for the girl "with the soft black eyes." The repetition of the basic motif of the song, a downward progression of a fifth, adds to the structural unity of the song, and emphasizes the lover's yearning. An accompaniment producing a drone effect, by playing in open fifths, may help convey a proper mood.

Yammil Abaya—Lovely Maiden

Yam - mil_ A - ba - ya, _____ Hil - wa_ A - ba -
Love - ly_ maid - en _____ Wear - ing_ the A -

tich. Ya - sam - ra __ H - wa - ya, _____
ba. Love - ly __ is __ your face, _____

Zi - na B - si - fa - tich. Ha - la - wo - me - et Ha -
Full of glow - ing_ grace. A thou - sand wel -

la. _____ Ya - ri __ mal - fa - la.
comes _____ O girl with the soft_ black_ eyes.

Wil - kal - bin - si - la, Ya - ri ___ mal - fa -
My heart_ is burn - ing, Girl with the soft_ black_

la,   *Wil - kal - bin - si - la,*   *Wil - kal - bin - si -*
eyes.   My heart__ is burn-ing   My heart__ is __ burn-

la, _____   *Jam - min__ Gham - za - tich.*
ing, _____   For your __ re - turn - ing.

Israel

A song of exuberant enthusiasm and fearless courage of the Israeli youth and *halutzim* (pioneers) building a new and happy national homeland.

English version by
Charles Haywood

Hava L'Venim—Bring the Bricks

Ha - va l' - ve - nim,   *en pnai la - mod af re - ga!*
Bring, oh bring the bricks,   This is no time to loi - ter!

Bnu ha - ba - na - im,   *al pa - chad v' - al ye - ga!*
Hur - ry build - ers, build;   No need to fear or fal - ter!

Kir el kir na - rim   *lik - rat mich - shol va - fe - ga. Kul-*
Raise the might - y walls,   Come work - ers, build new life __ here. Let's

la - nu na - shir, him - non bin - yan ar - tze - nu. Bim -
all join in song, With hap - py hearts re - sound - ing, The

kom et - mol yesh la - nu ma - char, u - v' - ad kol
new day's near And peace is dawn - ing. Heav - y is the

kir, b' - he - nef bin - ya - ne - nu, A -
bur - den To build a new foun - da - tion, But

tid a - me - nu hu la - nu sa - char.
we're re - ward - ed In strength'- ning our na - tion.

Ha - vu, ha - vu l' - ve - nim, kfar, mo - shav va - ke - ret!
Bring, oh bring the stur - dy bricks, Towns and cit - ies grow - ing!

Shi - ru ze - mer ha - bo - nim, shir bin - yan va - me - red!
Sing the build - ers' val - iant song, Hap - py hearts o'er - flow - ing!

English version Copyright © 1966 by Charles Haywood

A courtship song. On the verge of a break-up, the despondent lover pleads with the proud maiden to forgive and forget.

English version by
Charles Haywood

Lomir Sich Iberbetn

Let Us Be Friends Again

Allegretto

1. Lo - mir sich i - ber - be - tn, i - ber - be - tn,
1. Let us be friends a - gain, friends a - gain,

Hob af mir rach - mo - nes; Hob af mir rach -
Oh! have pit - y on me; Oh, have pit - y

mo - nes; Lo - mir sich i - ber - be - tn,
on me; Let us be friends a - gain, I

C'h'ob dir lib sa - ko - nes. ko - nes.
love you ve - ry deep - ly. deep - ly.

2. *Lomir sich iberbetn, iberbetn,*
   Vos shteistu far der tir? (2)
   Lomir sich iberbetn,
   Kum arein zu mir.
   Lomir sich iberbetn,
   Kum arein zu mir.

2. Let us be friends again, friends again,
   Don't be standing outside; (2)
   Let us be friends again,
   My door is open wide.
   Let us be friends again,
   My door is open wide.

3. *Lomir sich iberbetn, iberbetn,*
   Loz di mamen vissn; (2)
   Lomir sich iberbetn,
   Fùn libe fùl genissn.
   Lomir sich iberbetn,
   Fùn libe fùl genissn.

3. Let us be friends again, friends again,
   Go and tell your mother; (2)
   Let us be friends again,
   Because we love each other.
   Let us be friends again,
   Because we love each other.

Lebanon

A tender love song of quiet and subdued expression, also very popular in Egypt.

English translation by
Baheega Sidky Rasheed
Adapted by Charles Haywood

Bintil Shalabeya
Fairest Maid

Moderato

1. Bin - til sha - la - be - ya hill - wa lo - ze - - - ya,
1. Fair - est of all pret -ty maids, Sweet as __ hon - ey _ dew,

Yih - la - li w' - sa - lik ya noor ê - nai - i - ya.
Come to me, my_ dear_ love, Star shin - ing bright_are_ you.

2. Libsitil bambi
   alaâitil bambi.
   Taàli ganbi
   ya noor ênaiya.

2. Put on your silken gown,
   Loveliest shade of rose;
   Come sit beside me, dear,
   Your eyes with starlight glows.

3. Libsitil bonni
   wialâitil bonni,
   Nawyat gannennil
   hilwal shalabeya.

3. Put on your gown of gray,
   Let all your joys depart,
   While I am pining away,
   Loving you deep in my heart.

Saudi Arabia

Walking through the streets the vendor extols the virtues of Indian muslin, which is indeed the finest and the most delicate in the world.

English version by
Baheega Sidky Rasheed

Bafti Hindi

Allegretto

1. Baf - ta hin - di, baf - ta hin - di shash __ â - reed
1. In - dian mus - lin, In - dian mus - lin, Silks and da - mask,

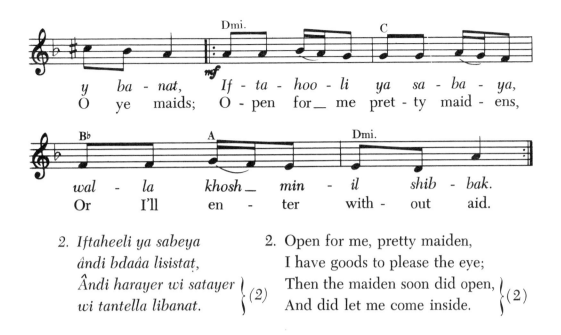

y   ba - nat,   If - ta - hoo - li   ya   sa - ba - ya,
O   ye   maids;   O - pen   for__ me   pret - ty   maid - ens,

wal - la   khosh__ min - il   shib - bak.
Or   I'll   en - ter   with - out   aid.

2. *Iftaheeli ya sabeya*
   ándi bdaâa lisistat,
   Ândi harayer wi satayer $\big\}$ (2)
   wi tantella libanat.

2. Open for me, pretty maiden,
   I have goods to please the eye;
   Then the maiden soon did open, $\big\}$ (2)
   And did let me come inside.

Syria

"Zane-il-Abedeen" is the name of her beloved; its literal meaning is "fairest of all worshippers."

English version by
Baheega Sidky Rasheed

Al Ya Zane—Oh Thou Zane

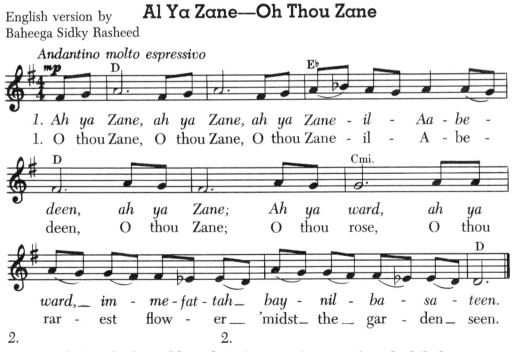

Andantino molto espressivo

1. *Ah ya Zane, ah ya Zane, ah ya Zane - il - Aa - be -*
1. O thou Zane, O thou Zane, O thou Zane - il - A - be -

deen,   ah   ya   Zane;   Ah   ya   ward,   ah   ya
deen,   O   thou   Zane;   O   thou   rose,   O   thou

ward,__ im - me - fat - tah__ bay - nil - ba - sa - teen.
rar - est   flow - er__ 'midst__ the__ gar - den__ seen.

2.   2.

Wi soon kalamak ah ya dilâzool, O sleep, O sleep, O sleep had fled my eyes,
Willi willi garaly yikfany.   As when, as when my love had forsaken me.

207

Turkey

A song of the *Uzun hava* type; with its long, expansive, embellished vocal line it conveys a feeling of loneliness and sadness.

Akhsham Oldu—Behold the Sun

English version by
Charles Haywood

Akh - sha - am - ol - du, kun ___ ka - vush - ti
Be - hold ___ the ___ sun sink - ing in ___ the West,

Kim - se ___ khal - khmaz tan - ya - rikh.
Man and ___ na - ture in ___ peace- ful ___ rest.

E - ti - shi - le, kush ___ da - vu - shi,
Thro' the still ___ night - song ___ of bird re - sound - ing,

Che - ker ___ ke - fes chokh ___ ya - nikh.
Heart full ___ of sad - ness, sor - row and ___ long - ing.

This popular folk tune, with its rapid dancelike rhythm, captures the joyful and hopeful mood of the song.

English version by
Charles Haywood

Üsküdar

Allegro moderato

1. Üs - kü - dar' a gi - der ___ i ken
1. As I walked ___ one ___ rain - y morn' The

al - di - da bir yağ mur, Ka - ti - bi - min
road to ___ Üs - kü - dar, There I saw my

se - tre - si u - zun e - te - ği ___ ça - mur.
dear ___ be - lov - ed, Com - ing ___ from ___ a - far.

e - te - gi ___ ça - mur.
Com - ing ___ from ___ a - far.

2. Üsküdar' a ğider iken
   bir mendel buldum,   } (2)
   Mendilimin içinede
   locum doldurdum.   } (2)

2. On that road I later found
   A kerchief of finest cloth, } (2)
   Cleaning it with tend'rest care,
   Surely 'twas his, I thought. }

3. Katibimi arar iken
   yanimada buldum;   } (2)
   Katip benim ben katibim,
   el ne karişir   } (2)

3. Anxiously I looked for him,
   When he appeared near me; } (2)
   Promising to wander no more,
   Mine he'll forever be.   } (2)

Afghanistan

While the dominant ethnic strains are those of Iran (Persia) and Turkey, the influence of India, Turkmenia, Tadjikistan and Arabia is of considerable importance in the musical culture of Afghanistan. The proud heritage and heroic achievements of its leaders are reflected in many ancient ballads. The sentiments that are cherished and highly praised are honor (*Nangi Pakhtana*), revenge against evil and injustice (*Badal*), and hospitality (*Mailmastai*); these are mirrored in their epics and songs. Equally respected and honored is the folk singer (*Dum*), who has kept alive and transmitted the traditional heritage; he is distinguished from the literary and learned poet, and singer (the *sha-ir*). Besides the historical songs and ballads are the religious songs and ceremonial dances, lamentations for the dead (*Voceros*), and songs of supplication. Love songs are usually set in the *misra*, a popular poetical genre that expresses one dominant idea, love. It provides the folk singer occasion for improvising new *misras*. The nursery rhymes are miniature tales and allegories, depicting all aspects of children's lives.

The various instruments used by the Afghanistan singers and players show particularly the effects of cultural contacts with Turkey, Iran and India. The string instruments, frequently heard in solo and ensemble, are the *sarinda* (three-string fiddle, short neck, without frets), the *robab* (six strings, long neck, played with plectrum), the *dotar* (two-stringed lute), *ritchak* (two-stringed fiddle, played with bow), popular in the northern part of the country. It might be interesting to note that this instrument is now generally made out of kerosene cans. Quite a change from its ancient ancestor! The *zourna* (oboe) is frequently used for vocal accompaniment. Of the percussion instruments one hears, among numerous others, the *zir-i-baghali* (large circular drum with long cylindrical resonator), the *dhoi* (two-headed drum), and the *davoul* (cymbals).

Ceylon

The dominant musical influence of Sinhalese folk music stems from India. However, more than three hundred years of European domination—the Portuguese, Dutch and English—have left their impressions. Very little is left today of the folksongs of the Veddas, the aborigines of Ceylon. Their music was based on a short motive of two or three notes, within the limited range of a second or third, repeated and expanded numerous times. The rhythmic pulse was emphasized by the bodily motion of the performers. The songs display a strong tonal feeling, always beginning on the same pitch, and frequently showing an upward direction at the cadence. Melody and text, as well as rhythm, are closely bound and interdependent.

Since Ceylon is largely an agricultural country, with rice as its main source of food, many folksongs are connected with paddy cultivation, with songs of plowmen and the harvest. These songs express both the hardships of primitive labor and the simple joys, secular and religious, of their lives. There is also an abundant number of songs reflecting other physical activities, such as boatmen songs, carter songs, a variety of characteristic animal songs, watch-hut songs, as well as love songs (*viraha*). The popular Sinhalese folk poetry (*Siupada*) consists of four long metric lines, with a "long-drawn-out melody," frequently elaborated by the singer. The songs are often accompanied by drumming on the *rabena*, "a one-faced drum."

India

The oldest Indian music is the one connected with the *Vedic* sacrifices. The chanting of the *Rigvedic* hymns is essentially a declamatory intoned or recitative style, strictly adhering to the accents and rhythms of the words, with a note to each syllable. The more elaborate *Samavedic* chants, connected with ritual and sacrifices, are more involved melodically and textually, employing greater ornamentation and melismas, and of much wider tonal range. Closely associated with the *Vedic* hymns are the instrumental accompaniment and the dance. The latter is of much greater importance.

Through various evolutionary changes Indian music has attained its highest tonal, rhythmic (*tāla*), structural flexibility and expressiveness in the *rāgas*. These are outline patterns, or "melody-molds," associated with specific emotions, and suggesting specific color and atmosphere. Each *rāga* has a definite incipient note, a melodic center, and final note. However, permutations and combinations of different *rāgas* can be made to evoke the desired mood, emotion, or moral implication (the *ethos*). The improvisatory aspect of *rāga* performance permits great inventiveness and individuality. These attributes are closely linked to folk creation and variation. Rhythmic interest is added by the accompanying instruments: the *tambura* (a four-stringed unfretted lute), the *tablā* (drum), or fretted instruments, such as the *sitār* (a long-necked four- to seven-stringed lute), and the *vinā* (a long bamboo fingerboard with movable frets and a gourd resonator at each end). The subtlety of performance is enhanced by the elaborate embellishments indulged by the voice and instruments. The *talā*, or rhythmic divisions of the beat, is independent of the melody it accompanies; it can be a simple pulse or accent or a dazzling display of virtuosity in complex patterns. But these effects, rhythmic and melodic, are always guided by tradition, taste and desired mood. Since the Hindu scale is divided into twenty-two microtonal parts (*shrutis*), the possibilities for delicate melodic inflections are quite beyond what the Occidental ear is accustomed.

The music of the North (*Hindustani*) and that of the South (*Carnatic*) differ mainly in style and in the names given to the *rāgas* and notes. Instrumental music is more highly developed in the South. Many changes were introduced in the North by Islam (Persian music, in particular).

While contemporary pressure, economic and social changes, and Western influences have tended to modify India's indigenous musical system, the rural folk still retain their traditional heritage. Rabindranath Tagore recognized this fact in seeking inspiration in the folk melodies of Bengal.

Afghanistan

A sorrowful plaint of a despairing maiden who is abandoned by her lover.

Vaj, Gulum Gitti?—Where Is My Red Rose?

English version by
Charles Haywood

Andante

DRUM
(To the end of the song)

Vai, gu-lum git - ti,___
Where is my red rose?___

___ vai gu-lum git - ti,___ Çan, çan e - lim-
___ Where is my red rose?_ Where's my night - in -

den. Bil - bil - im___ git - ti. ___ Jar, me - ni
gale? Gone__ are__ they___ from me.___ Fled is my

mej - ha - na,___ Taş - lap___ e - lim-
bold fal - con,___ Emp - ty___ stands the

den._ La - ci - nim_ git - ti. ___ Ve, ja - ra,
cage,_ Name - less,_ a - ban - doned. _ Great is my

ja - ra!___ Ja çeb - bar - a ___ e - ma-
sor - row;___ My be - lov'd chose___ a - noth - er

lin._ Ja ___ re - sul_ al - la!___
one._ How___ can _ I for- get him!___

English version Copyright © 1966 by Charles Haywood

213

Nepal

The folk music of Nepal is "a fusion of two bordering cultures: India contributing its complex scales, its melodic and rhythmic patterns, and Tibet, its pentatonic scales, the sustained notes, and the strict duple (or common) meter." (Walter Kaufmann)

English translation by
Walter Kaufmann
Adapted by Charles Haywood

Kana Ma Laune—My Husband

Allegro (♩=108)

Kana ma lau - ne kan - de fu - li, yo - o - o pa - pi
My _ hus- band has be - come _ bad, My - y-y pre - cious

ra - ja - le be- chi kha - yo; __ kana ma lau-ne kan-de fu-
ear - ring _ he _ has _ sold; _ My _ hus-band has be-come _

li, yo _____ pa-pi ra - ja - le be-chi kha-yo, yo, ___
bad, With all that mon-ey he _ bought food _ and _ drink. _

yo pa - pi ra - ja ko - a - sha ma - lai
No long - er can _ I _ love this cru - el

chhai - na; cha - li jaun - la mai - ti ko desh.
hus - band; I'll go back to my fath - er's home.

Ceylon

A harvesting song, employing the popular folk poetic structure, the *Siupada*.

214

English version by
Charles Haywood

Varga Pāvati—Nature's Splendor

Allegretto

Var - ga pā - va - ti pi - li - ve la - ku - la
Na - ture's splen - dor fills the whole earth with its

can - dra vam - sa sa - pi - ri nā - da,
won - der, mu - sic joy - ful - ly sound - ing;

Dir - gà po - rà - na a - ra - na de - ra - na
Sky's a - glow___ with sun's ra - diant light, bring - ing

ura - na ru - pun bin - de - pu vā - da.
hap - pi - ness to all ___ the peo - ple.

Gar - ga ga - ga - na ghō - ra ga - ga - na
Fields are fer - tile, har - vest rich - ly a -

gar - ja na - ka - ra me - gna___ nā - da,
bun - dant, proud - ly we la - bor to - geth er.

Svar - ga pā - da mas - ta ti - to ___
Won - drous deeds we ac - comp - lish, just like the

ra - jun si - ra - sa sa - der ___ pā - da.
he - roes, who fought for the free - dom we cher - ish.

India

The song is usually sung by women, but is also known to men. The women stand in two rows facing each other, the women in each row having their arms around each other's necks. Each row walks forward and backward two steps, alternately, in time with the song. One side sings the first line only, repeating after every line or two lines, the other side the whole song. It is thus a true dance-song. The song is sung without the slightest pause throughout, and rather quickened toward the end.

Gūri Gūri Karayō—I Will Rock Thee

English version by
Charles Haywood

(Kashmir)

216

A dance performed around a pole (similar to the Western Maypole dances), from which colored ribbons are hanging. With appropriate slow rhythmic movements, and the use of Kolattam sticks, 8 to 10 inches long and 3/4 inch thick, the ribbons are woven into plaits (*Pinnal*). In this dance, the fourth weaving dance, the movements are concerned with the unwinding of the plaits. The melody is in the *Punnagāvarālī Rāga*, used for songs of sorrow, night, and melancholy. The rhythmic grouping, or time measure, belongs to the *Ādi tāla*, one of the most common rhythms in the music of south Indian music. The text is in Tamil.

Pinnal Kolattam—Weaving Dance

English version by
Charles Haywood

(*Madras*)

Kāk - kai   ci - ra - gi - n - i - lē
In   the   spread wings   of   the   black   crow,

nan - da - lā - lā - ni - n - ran   ka - riya ni - ram
Nan - da   La - la,   fair - est   one,   Your dark im - age

tōn - ru - dai - yē   nan - da - lā - lā;
I   see   in   them,   Nan - da   La - la;

pārk - kum   ma - ra - ṅ - ga - lel - lām
In   the   splen - dor   of   the   green   trees,

nan - da - lā - lā - ninran   pac - cai   ni - ram
Nan - da   La - la,   Oh!   There your beau - ty

ton - ru - dai - ya   nan - da - lā - lā.
I   see   shimm'- ring,   Nan - da   La - la.

CLAP   (counting with fingers)   CLAP (wave motion) CLAP (wave motion)

Pakistan

"This is a pure folksong, both in words and music . . . the noble gravity and directness of the music well fit the passionate simplicity of the words. The latter need the explanation that the Kashmir court moves from Jammu to Srinagar in the summer, so that the *Jammu maa* taking service there had to go far away when summer came; and it is this separation which the woman laments." (A. K. Coomaraswamy) The tune belongs to the Rag *Chamba Pahārī*; the text is in Dogri dialect.

Áṅgan Phūlī
Jasmine Flower in Bloom

English version by
Charles Haywood

Lento con espressione

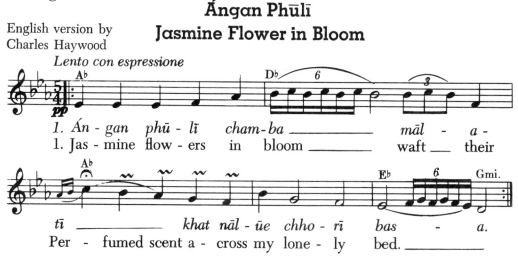

1. Án - gan   phū - lī   cham-ba _____ māl - a -
1. Jas - mine flow - ers   in   bloom _____ waft __ their

tī _____   khat nāl - ūe chho - rī   bas - a.
Per - fumed scent a - cross my lone - ly   bed. _____

2. *Jamūān dī karni pyariā*
   chākrī, Kashmīrān dīpa'ī mahīm.

2. O beloved, thou art gone to Jammu,
   Thou must stay now in Kashmir.

3. *Chittian bhejda koī nahīn,*
   āondā terā suka sānd.

3. Letters of deep longing I send thee,
   Yet no answers come to me.

218

Southeast Asia

Burma

The influence of Indian culture plays a large part in Burmese music. Its symmetrical structure and rhythmic character show the influence of Indian drumming. The Burmese instrumental ensembles bear close resemblance to those of India. Moreover, Chinese culture contacts show their effects on the tonal character of numerous folk melodies. In addition, Occidental traits left their imprints on Burmese music, particularly in the use of the diatonic scale, and cadential endings on the tonic or dominant.

Cambodia

The music of Cambodia shows close affinity with that of Thailand, in its similarity in the scale consisting of seven equidistant notes— equal to about 6/7 of the Western tempered scale—and in the frequent use of identical instruments. Cambodian rhythm is predominantly in common time (4/4), often accelerating and increasing in volume toward the end. Improvisation and variation play a vital part in musical performance, built around a definite and previously stated theme or melody. The variations occur simultaneously with each instrument and performer, producing a very elaborate and complex polyphony or counterpoint. Chinese instruments (gongs and xylophones) play a very significant part in their music for song and dance.

Laos

The Laotian musical scale, like that of most of the Southeast Asian countries, consists of seven equidistant steps, of which five tones (pentatonic) are usually employed. The pinched nasal vocal style, of Chinese origin, so common in the neighboring countries, is frequently heard. The Laotians are fond of accompanying their songs with sustained tones on the native instrument the *khen*, made of bamboo reeds, "a kind of mouth organ" from one to two yards in length.

Other instruments, for accompaniment or solo, include the *renêt* (a curved xylophone), high flute, hurdy-gurdy, and cymbals.

Thailand

The musical cultures of China and India have been the major influences in shaping the character of Thai music. Through the centuries, an indigenous and distinctive style has evolved. The Thai musical scale is based on equal temperament, in which the octave is divided into seven equal parts. This is akin to Western music, although the ratios are not the same. However, the fourth degree of the scale is never used, and the seventh infrequently; this produces a pentatonic effect. This quality is strongly emphasized by the instrumental accompaniments, which often employ microtonal intervals. These combinations produce harmonic effects, although the main body of Thai music is homophonic. Music plays a vital part in their everyday activities, religious and secular.

In spite of the comparatively small size of Thailand, four distinctive musical styles can be discerned: in the north (usually slower in tempo; strong Burmese influence); the northeast (extensive use of the *khen*—a bamboo reed mouth organ; Laotian influence); the south (syncopated rhythms; Indo-Javanese influence), and the central area (string ensembles [*mahori*], flageolets, oboes and the *ching* [cymbals], and percussion instruments: xylophones, gongs, and various drums; strong Chinese influence).

Vietnam

In the general character of the melodic contour, the type and quality of the instruments—for solo and accompaniment—Vietnamese music exhibits the unmistakable influence of China. Quite striking and indigenous are courtship songs, accompanied by the ground-zither, played by men only, and the antiphonal songs of the watermen of the Hue River. The people display a strong love for music with an inherent fondness for improvisation. According to Arthur Pritchard Moor, the music of Vietnam is "less austere than the Chinese and Japanese, less intense than the Arabic, more humorous than the Hindu, perhaps the sunniest and most genial of all Oriental Music."

Burma

A song of deep yearning of a princess who fears that her lover's affection is waning. She avows profound and unswerving love for her prince; a love that is purer than the purest gem, and that outshines the splendor of the moon. Not even a *deva* of the heavenly regions can steal her heart away.

Sein Kyu Kya Nyaung—Song of the Princess

English version by
Charles Haywood

Sein kyu kya Nyaung kya Nyaung lă lă yaung lin___ bá lo,
Pur - er light flows from my heart Than fin - est gems of Ori - ent;

Hman shwe-pyu din - yay kă may - ku-hmyaw thon-chet si daw,
Moon - light fades__ 'gainst__ light of love, Glow-ing rad-iant.

Yike - saw - hnyin day lay _____ lin lu paw naw.
Heav'n-ly de - va, power a - bove, Ne'er can win my love.

221

Cambodia

A love song. The term *Prôm kut* refers to a specific poetic verse form (iambic trimeter) and appropriate melodic line.

English version by
Charles Haywood

Prôm Kut—Love Song

1. O ___ duong bân - thé - a tès, ___ Rom - sai ké - sâr
1. Oh, ___ fair - est of all maid - ens, Hair as soft as

mé - a - li, ___ Dôch khlên du - ông chi - oi,
tend' - rest flow - er, Heav'nly frag - rance pour - ing forth,

Krâôp chéap noú mong- sa. Dôch ___ khlên du - ong ___
Bring- ing mem'-ries of love's power. Heav'n - ly frag - rance pour - ing

chi - oi, Krâ - ôp ché - ap noú mong-sa.
forth, ___ Bring - ing mem' - ries of love's pow'r.

2. *Bâng thop phéak phôr phâng,*
   Phéak trâchang trâchéas thla,
   Thop méat, méat det sla,
   Har chârcha srâs bâ pray,
   Bâ prey nho nhim prom
   Kuor thnèt thnâm kéo.

2. I embrace her lovely face,
   Rosy cheeks aglow with sunshine,
   Spicy lips like betel palm
   Open for a kiss divine;
   Smiling happy, love inviting,
   Hungry lover's heart enticing.

Laos

The song is preceded by an instrumental prelude on the *so-ou* (a small violin, similar to the Chinese, widely used in Indochina). The accompanying melody (in the c major tonality) is flowing and ornamental in sixteenth-note figurations and imitative patterns. It has a "baroque" quality, and expresses the Laotian love for the "contrapuntal" style.

Thoum—Most Adored

English version by
Charles Haywood

Oi no____ noi ____ nong oeui, ____ I ____ no an - sai __
Oh, thou most a-dored, __ with yearn-ing love _____ I look in-to __

ta ti - en gme na_____ nong oeu - i. Son - thi
thine ____ eyes. Grant me ____ thy fa - vor! I ___

pong ,a ou _____ nong; No na __
sought thee where the lo - tus grows, My ____

tha - i nan - nong____ phou diao _____ na tam.
heart __ is __ trou - bled; I die _____ for your love.

Thailand

The text of the song being unavailable, the sound "ah" was substituted.

Ah! Ah! Ah!

Ah, _____ ah, ah, Ah, _____ Ah, _____ ah, ah, Ah, __

_____ ah, _____ ah, ah, ah, ah, ah, _____

_____ ah, _____ Ah, ah, ah, ah, _____

Ah, ah, ah, ah, ah, Ah, ah, ah, ah, _____ ah, _____

_____ ah, _____ ah, _____ ah.

224

Vietnam

This song was sung by a group of young girls at Kontum, with utmost simplicity, expressive inflection, and with great rhythmic freedom—with little regard for the bar line.

English version by
Charles Haywood

Nhim Né Nhim—Lullaby

Né mé him a a o a mé - nié
Weep not my love, O weep not dear one;

min a o, Ou nin né ou ei _____ dam nia
Sleep, sleep, _ let peace-ful dreams Dis-pel all dan-gers,

ou a o, Nin go oué ko ka _ né - nié, Him ouai eu _
sleep, sleep, my dear-est child. _ Guard-ian an-gels watch o'er you,_

a né gné oum a o, Guen-né a _ o _ dam nia,
Close your eyes, sleep, sleep, sleep; You will be _ strong and hap-py,

Ou nin go oué ko ka _ nim ba o a o, _
Loved, hon-ored by all peo - ple, _ sleep, sleep, sleep. _

_ Dat nian ké tian dan moi _ ou ma. _
Stars are shin - ing, night is fall - ing, O, sleep! _

The Far East

China

To the Chinese, music embodies unalterable universal principles and reflects the cosmic harmony between heaven and earth. In common with the people of other early cultures, the musical sounds were endowed with magical and divine power, and corresponded to the orderly system of the universe. Thus, each season, autumn, spring, summer and winter, was denoted by a specific pitch and melodic configuration. Musical sound and expression, in concord with these principles, ennoble and purify, make one good and virtuous. In the words of one of its sages, Yo Ki: "He who sings becomes straight and displays his moral influence and, when he himself comes into motion, Heaven and Earth respond, the four seasons are in harmony, stars and planets are orderly, life is sustained in all beings."

The pentatonic (five-tone) scale, in varying patterns and sequences, is the basis of Chinese music, of the court and the folk. Chinese melody is to a great degree influenced by the inflectional emphasis and tonal direction of the spoken word. The aphorism of Yüeh Chi, poet of the second century B.C., states this clearly: "A song is nothing but words, yet words prolonged." Moreover, many tunes show the influence derived from bodily movement and the beat of individual and group work activity. These display strong rhythmic pulse and incisive repetitive patterns. Thus, most work songs—of the coolies, the boatmen, the farmers, soldiers, miners—wedding songs and funeral chants, as well as the old historical ballads and children's jingles, find their appropriate, characteristic melodies. The old ritual and festival songs and dances, with their antiphonal method of performance, grouped by sexes (supposed "to symbolize the alternate rhythm of the opposed and complementary principles of the Universe: *Yin* and *Yang*"), still play a prominent part in Chinese folk life. The accompanying instruments of flutes, lutes, oboes, trumpets, cymbals, and gongs add appropriate accent and color.

226

Tibet

Living on top of the world, unaffected for centuries by other cultures, the Tibetans have developed a unique musical idiom. One can still hear the shepherds calling their flocks on the ancient pastoral instrument the *glin-bu* (a whistle-flute), the priests intoning the ritual incantations to the accompaniment of the *rkan-dum* (a trumpet of human thighbone), the pulsing rhythms of the *rna-ch'un* (a hand drum made from two half-skulls in the shape of an hourglass), and the *lag-na* (frame drum). However, from the eighth to the thirteenth century Indian and Moslem influences left their imprint on Tibetan civilization. "Today this music [based on a complex musical ritual associated with Lamaism] consists of prayers and scriptures, hymns and psalms sung variously in rapid syllabic recitative and slow sustained metrical chant. The singing is in unison and deep-voiced, fully an octave lower than one would normally expect; and it is sometimes supported by a choral drone (like some Byzantine chant), no doubt based on an idea of Indian origin. The singing is supported by orchestral accompaniment and interlude."

From the thirteenth to the seventeenth century Mongolian, through Kublai Khan, and Chinese influences strongly affected the Tibetan style, religious and secular, vocal and instrumental. These elements achieved their highest expression in the religious plays and dance dramas (*achhe lhamo*) and historical scenes from the lives of kings (*rnam-t'ar*).

All these elements left their mark on the traditional folk idiom. The whole gamut of human emotion, and all kinds of work, individual and collective, are richly expressed in song, dance, and instrumental accompaniment. In contrast to religious performance, the folk use flutes and string instruments, the lute (*pi-wan*)— showing strong kinship to the Chinese *p'i-p'a* and the Japanese *biwa*. The melodies are based largely on the pentatonic scale. "Folk music flourishes everywhere. Grass-cutters, coolies, log-carriers, winnowers, and field labourers all have their songs, and the solo (leader)-and-chorus structure is not infrequently to be found in them. Short melodic phrases of restricted compass are (with endless variants) repeated over and over again; with that inherent circular quality which leads, not to a final note but inescapably back to the first, they help to carry the labourers on over long and weary stretches of time." A distinctive feature to be noted in Tibetan folk singing is the prolongation of the last note of the phrase, as the second singer begins the antiphonal response of the answering phrase.

Korea

The history of the Korean people, a long chronicle of foreign domination and internal dissension, is reflected in their folk music. In spite of a pervading sadness and melancholy, their songs and dances are frequently enlivened by lively humor and trenchant satire. This dual aspect is most characteristic in the farmers' songs, depicting their toil and hardships, and yet expressing a spirit of hope and cheer, and even thanksgiving. Although Korean culture has been, to a large extent, influenced by its powerful neighbor China, it has nevertheless been able to maintain a marked individuality of its own. Korean melody is mainly based on the pentatonic scale, and shows a strong predilection for 3/4 and 6/8 rhythms. The folksongs also deal with historic events (comparable to Western ballads), and the tender, poignant sentiments of love.

Japan

The extent to which music plays an important role in the life of the Japanese, and particularly their love for dramatic expression, in gesture and bodily movement, led one observer to remark that with the Japanese "all life seems to be lived as if it were on a stage. The very seasons can be marked by a series of songs that are sung by the goldfish man, the bamboo man, the junk man, or any one of a host of seasoned food sellers." These tendencies and characteristics reach a high level of dramatic participation in the religious folk festivals and ceremonies—Shinto and Buddhist—celebrating the seasons and fertility rites, and many other aspects of peasant life. These call for singing, instrumental accompaniment (flute and drum), and elaborate, colorful dances.

All Japanese folksongs—work songs (with a preponderant number of these connected with rice growing and fishing, the two staples in their diet), love songs, lullabies, dirges, religious songs, children's songs, and others—have one element in common: they are all in the *yo–in* scale system, with modulatory alternations and changes between them. They are both pentatonic, but the important difference lies in the position of the half steps. Thus a *yo* scale could be represented on our keyboard in the following sequence: d f g (a) c d, and the *in* scale would read: d (e♭) f g a (b♭) c d. Most of the Japanese folk melodies are in 2/4 and 4/4 meter, and in simple two-part (binary) or three-part (ternary) structure. There are, of course, exceptions to the above. A characteristic idiosyncrasy one often encounters in the singing of these folk tunes is the frequent tendency of emphasizing the note above or below the basic tone of the melody.

While the general pattern of Japanese folksongs is based on the pentatonic scale, one frequently becomes aware of the major mode in the rural songs (*Inkabushi*) and of the minor mode in the urban tunes (*Miyakobushi*). They also display distinct characteristics in the final cadence. One also notices two distinct qualities in the rhythmic character in Japanese folksongs: strict and regular rhythm in the *Yasibushi* type, and the free rhythms in the *Oiwahe* type. Polyphony in the Western sense is lacking in Japanese songs, but one finds numerous examples of heterophony.

Early Japanese folk singing made sparing use of accompanying instruments; handclapping and bodily movement were considered sufficient. Now, however, due to the influence of art and folk theatricals, the accompanying apparatus has been considerably enlarged in the percussion (drums, rattles, gongs) and melodic instruments (flutes, mouth-organ bass lute, the *shamisen*—a three-stringed instrument—and the *koto*—a board zither, consisting of thirteen silk strings). Music for the *koto* makes effective use of microtonal embellishments (fractional tonal grace notes above the principal notes), demanding remarkable technique and virtuosity from the performer. However, when accompanying the voice, it follows the latter very closely in pitch and rhythm.

Mongolia

The stylistic quality of this pentatonic melody and its configuration is very characteristic of the people of Ouliastai (or Uliassutai), who formerly resided farther west in Dzoungarie.

English version by Charles Haywood

Ouliastaï — The Waters of Ouliastaï

Moderato

1. Ou - las - ta - khn   go - li - gué   ya - gad - ji
1. Gent - ly flow the   wa - ters of   Ou - lia - sta - ï,

tou - ril - dâ   ko - mi - ñi,   Ou - r - din __
Wind - ing thro' fields and moun - tain   side;   Al - ways mov-ing,

ta - li - va - ksn   yo - rial éet - zé
nev - er ceas - ing,   splash - ing gai - ly

ya - ga - dji ____   da - bou - il - da.
With   the rhyth - mic   mo - tion   of the tide.

2. *Artztakhan goligué yagadji tourilda komiñi,*
   Amourk guin kéleksen uguigué yagadji martakhoubi.

2. Smell the fragrant air, cypress perfumed laden,
   Wafted by caressing breeze,
   Whisper lover's vows impassioned tenderly,—
   Lead me onward, I am yours always.

China

A sacred folksong—the first verse of a longer poem—expressing in joyful exaltation the spiritual travails and journeys of Buddha. The downward motion of the pentatonic tune, the chromatic changes (at best, only an approximation in Western notation), and the repetition of motivic figures convey some of the ethnic characteristics of Chinese folk music.

English version by
Charles Haywood

Wóu Liàng—Hymn to Buddha

Wóu liàng — a a Fó _____
Blest e - ter - nal Bud - dha _____ a -

yào _ tch'ōū _____ kīa ya, nai _ híng _ e
band - oned wife and _ child, _ He jour - ney'd

híng k'ou a _____ Kīn a tāo a
to a place of suff' - ring. With gold-en sword He

louèn a fa, tch'éng teng _ tsèng _ na _____ kóuei
cut His hair; Trans-formed _ then to ho - li - ness.

Hóua jéng tà _ fā: a mí t'ouo _____ Fó.
His great pro-found law: "ā mí t'ouo _____ Fó."

231

The popular entertainments connected with the Flower Drum Songs originated in Feng-Yang, in northern Anhwei, very likely by impoverished rice farmers turned vagabonds, during the reign of Emperor Chu Yüan-chang. These songs and dialogue are essentially derisive and satirical commentary on tragic and calamitous events; a way of making light of their own hunger and poverty. Since accompaniments in Chinese songs are in unison with the voice, Western instrumentalists should bear this in mind.

English version by
Shih-hsiang Chen

Hua Ku Ko—The Flower Drum

Tso __ shou __ lo, Yu __ shou __ ku,
Feng - yang __ drum, Feng - yang __ gong

Shou na cho lo __ ku __ lai __ ch'ang __ ko.
With drum, and gong __ we'll __ sing __ a __ song.

Pieh ti __ ko erh __ wo yeh pu hui ch'ang,
What shall we sing? For we know __ on - ly one;

Tan hui __ ch'ang __ ko __ Feng - yang __ ko.
We on - ly know __ the __ Feng - yang __ song.

Feng la Feng- yang ko __ lai. __ Ai - ya - ai - hu - ya.
Feng la Feng- yang flow'r __ drum. __

Drrr - lang-dang-p'iao-yi - p'iao, Drrr - lang-dang-p'iao-yi - p'iao,

Drrr - p'iao, Drrr - p'iao, Drrr - p'iao-drrr- p'iao - p'iao yu drrr -

p'iao- p'iao- p'iao-p'iao-yi - p'iao.

2. *(Nü-jén)*

   Wo ming k'u, Chen ming k'u!

   Yi sheng yi shih chia pucho hao chang fu.

   Jen chia chang fu tso kuan tso fu,

   Wo chia chang fu tan hui ta hua ku.

   Ta ta hua ku. Ai-ya-ai-hu-ya.

     Drrr-lang-dang-p'iao-yi-p'iao, etc. etc.

3. *(Nán-jén)*

   Wo ming po, Chen ming po!

   Yi sheng yi shih ch'ii pucho hao loa p'o.

   Jen chia lao p'o hsiu hua yu hsiu to,

   Wo chia lao p'o yi shuang ta hua chio.

   Liang la liang liang yi ch'ih to. Ai-ya-ai-hu-ya.

     Drrr-lang-dang-p'iao-yi-p'iao, etc. etc.

2. (Woman)

   Sad is my fate, Oh how sad!

   I married a man with a Flow'r drum.

   Stupid is he, Oh how stupid and dumb,

   All day long he beats his sing-song drum.

   Beating his sing-song drum. *Ai-ya-ai-hu-ya.*

     Drrr-lang-dang-p'iao-yi-p'iao, etc. etc.

3. (Man)

   Sad is my fate, Oh how sad!

   To spend my life with such an ugly mate.

   Of·all the women you ever did meet,

   My wife has the largest pair of feet.

   Largest pair of feet. *Ai-ya-ai-hu-ya.*

     Drrr-lang-dang-p'iao-yi-p'iao, etc. etc.

Tibet

The short melodic phrases, moving in repetitive circular motion, and the limited compass, convey the essential qualities of Tibetan folksong. The suggested accompaniment in open fifths (without the third in the chord) helps to approximate (!) the quality of the native timbre.

Seba Alaso Trodje—The Dew Is Dry at Midday

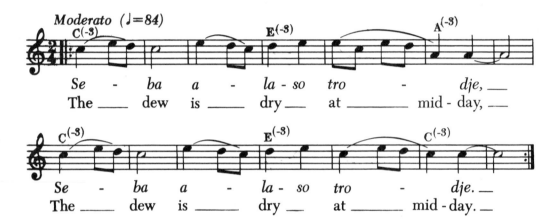

Korea

The narrow compass of the melody and the repetitive minor third interval seem to reinforce the continuous motion of the weaver's shuttle and the monotony of his labor—from evening (when "dogs are

barking") to dawn (when "sun is rising"). The refrain consists
largely of nonsense words.

English version by
Hallah Huhn
Adapted by Charles Haywood

Thul Tahryung

Moderato

1. Kai - ka chit - ne, Kai - ka chit - ne,
1. Dogs are bark - ing, Dogs are bark - ing,

Kun - nuh _____ mu - uh - si wat - kun
O'er yon - der vil - - lage bark-ing,

uhl - sa chit - ne. Kuh - ruh - ta, Num - sil - num - sil,
oh, yes, bark-ing.

Nan - da - nan - da, Chi - wa - cha jul - si - ku.

2. Taki une,
   Taki une,
   Kunnuh muuhsi watkun uhlsa une.
   Refrain:

3. Hehga dune,
   Hehga dune,
   Tongjok hanulre uhlsa dune.
   Refrain:

2. Cock is crowing,
   Cock is crowing,
   O'er yonder village crowing, oh, yes, crowing.
   Refrain:

3. Sun is rising,
   Sun is rising,
   O'er yonder village rising, oh, yes, rising.
   Refrain:

Japan

"One of a number of spiritual songs, expressing deep religious fervor at the shrine *Yoneyama Yakushi*, built by the priest Taicho, many years ago, on top of the mountain Yoneyama in the northern part of Nakakubiki County in Niigata Prefecture" (Ryutato Hattori). Great care must be taken in fitting the Japanese and, particularly, the English texts of the second verse to the melody; follow the general procedure in the first verse.

English version by
Charles Haywood

Yonlyem Jinku

2. *Hitotsua*   2. For my fair lover
   Mino tame Sasa   All the suff'ring I will gladly bear,
   Nushi no tame   Going all the way barefoot.

A famous processional song, one of the many inspired by the paintings of the *Tokai-dô* highway by Hiroshigé (1797–1858). There are many more verses describing the fifty-three stages of the journey. *Nishon-bashi* (Nippon bridge) of *Yedo* (Japan) was the starting point of the highway. The song describes the journey of a young son of a feudal lord on his way to visit for the first time his father's castle. The melody is in the *Hon-Jôshi*, or minor authentic, mode. Puccini used this tune in his opera *Madame Butterfly*.

English version by
Charles Haywood

Kochaē-Bushi
From Nippon Bridge

Andantino

O - e - do ni-hon - ba - shi, Na - na - tsu Da-
From Nip - pon Bridge of E - do slow - ly winds pro -

chi, Ha - tsu - no - bo - ri; Gyô - re - tsu
ces - sion At the break of day; Long lines of

so - ro - e - te Are - wai - sa - no - sa! Ko - cha,
peo - ple com - ing, from all sides they come march - ing;

Ta - ka - na - wa yo - a - ke no, ___ Chô -
Lamps go out at Ta - ka - na - wa ___ When the

chin ke - su; Ko - cha - é! Ko - cha - é!
sun ap - pears; Ko - cha - é! Ko - cha - é!

English version Copyright © 1966 by Charles Haywood

Africa

Africa—North of the Sahara

BERBER MUSIC: In discussing Arabian music one is obliged to include the musical culture of the Berbers, an ancient Mediterranean people, still, after centuries of Arab conquest, the dominant race occupying vast stretches of the north African littoral from Egypt to the shores of Morocco. Their cultural identity (Hamitic) is quite distinct and their ethnomusicological characteristics unique. Nevertheless, contacts with other peoples have, however subtly, affected their folk music. Thus, the Berbers from the Siwan oasis in the Libyan Desert display similar qualities to Egyptian town music. Antiphonal response is a vital feature of their songs, and in Tunisia the peasant songs show strong affinity to Arabic melody. In Algerian Sahara, where the predominant Berber population has been able to maintain greater cohesiveness as well as isolation, their folk music possesses "purer" characteristics in melodic, rhythmic, and performance aspects.

These features become apparent in the significant role music plays in the social life among the Kabyle in Algeria and the Tuareg in the desert. "Indeed, each tribe has its own particular songs and instrumental music." Quite fascinating, in their variety and rhythmic vitality, are the folksongs and dances in Morocco. Their melodies are generally diatonic, with intruding "non-Western" intervals. The highest degree of musical activity and expression, vocal and instrumental, is found very prominently among the Shilluq in the Sús. The alternating rhythms of 3/8 and 6/8 and 2/4, the reinforced melody on the *ribab* (viol) and the *lutar* (pandore), and the delicately percussive pulsations on the *bandair* (tambourine), the choreographic undulations of the dancers' subtle body movements, and the "plaintive" quality of the vocal line, all these elements contribute to the distinctive characteristics of Berber folk music.

Tunisia

Allowing for differences brought about by historical factors and indigenous ethnic aspects, Maghribí music—of the countries of the North African littoral from Morocco to Egypt—is well represented in the musical folkways of Tunisia. The determining and continuing influence is Arabic culture. To be more exact, it is the world of Islam, since that encompasses a much larger geographic distribution, with greater cultural involvement.

Originally occupied by the Berbers in prehistoric times, Tunisia has faced and been subjected to many conquests: Roman, Vandal, Byzantine, Arab, Turkish, and, more recently, French. Each wave left its imprint on the social and cultural life of the inhabitants. Tunisian folk music reflects this myriad cavalcade of its historic evolution. The highly complex musical systems devised by Islamic scholars and composers, the varied fine art instrumental and vocal compositions performed at the courts of the numerous rulers and potentates, and at religious rituals and festivals, are not within the scope of our present survey. But the influence of this learned music upon the folk, who heard and often shared in their performances, was considerable. However, the folk music is less studied, more spontaneous, less affected, simpler and more direct.

Many of the older folksongs employ the recitative-declamatory style, and these often show melodic kinship to Biblical cantillation. The melodies are syllabic, limited in range, with a rising motion and return to the starting note, in a rather free rhythm. Indeed, there is great richness and variety in Arabic musical rhythm. It is determined by the poetic meters of three, four, or five syllables grouped into patterns of five or seven units of time. Other tunes, which show urban influences, display greater sophistication, are highly melismatic with many vocal embellishments and are sung in a high-pitched voice. The songs are performed by individual singers or antiphonally, in solo-chorus pattern. Choral singing is rare, and usually in unison. While most of the folksongs are truly the property of the folk and sung by them, there are some, used for special occasions—weddings, funeral laments, religious chants, and others—that are frequently performed by "professional" singers, who also have a number of topical and contemporary songs in their repertory.

The folksongs recapture the history, character, and events of Tunisia. To mention but a few: hero songs (*darbashi*); prophet songs

240

(*yat*); the work songs, conveying the rhythms and tempi of the activity, with the accompanying bodily movements reflecting the type of labor: corn grinding and treading (*merzûgi* and *radassi*); camel songs; the highly spirited and humorous tunes sung at plucking chicken feathers (*rîsh*); wedding songs; laments, especially the *salhi* type, sung with high tensed tones, in a shaking tremolo quality, moving in a downward motion within the interval of a fifth; the *ardhâwî* type of laments that employ a more sustained vocal style and in a different tonal pattern, resembling (but not strictly in intonation) our Dorian mode.

Numerous instruments of different traditions and cultures are employed in singing, dancing, and instrumental solos and ensembles. The percussion group is headed by the popular *darabuqua* (a jug-shaped clay drum), the large Turkish *t'bal* (drum), resembling our bass drum, tambourines of varying sizes (*tar* and *bendir*). Of the woodwinds: the widely used *qasaba* (vertical flute), the *zūqra* (oboe, double reed, conical-shaped), *mezûd* (bagpipe), the *reita* and *magrûna* (clarinet family), and the *fhal* (recorder).

United Arab Republic (Egypt)

Traces of ancient traditions and practices can still be heard in present-day folk performances. Some of the tunes, according to Alfred Berner, are set in various modes (for their relations to the *maquam*, see the comments on "Arabian Music" in the section *The Middle East*), such as the *Rast, Síkáh, Bayáti, Jahárkáh, Sabá, Hijáz Nachwand*, and *Hijáz-Kar*. These are but a few of the many modal scales used in Islamic music. Each one is determined by interchanging the places of semitones and of major and minor whole tones, and various other intervallic permutations and combinations. These modes also convey spiritual and ethical principles. Thus, *Rast*, equivalent to playing the Lydian scale (f to f on the white keys transposed a tone higher to g) has the power of healing the eyes, is associated with the ram, and represents sunrise. In relation to the Western tempered scale, the Islamic tonal patterns make use of smaller intervals, such as quarter tones. Oriental influences, employing the harmonic minor, with augmented seconds and tonal ornamentation,

241

also play a significant part in Egyptian folk music.

The musical rhythm in Egyptian music is determined by the metrical structure of the poem, the natural quantity of the syllables. Repetition of musical phrases is dependent on the iterative patterns of opening and closing words of the poetic lines. The rhythm is further intensified by the accompanying instruments as well as hand-clapping. Chironomy, the corresponding expressive gestures of the right hand to convey the mood, quality and emotional content of the melody, can still be seen as an integral part of Egyptian musical performance. Folk singing is usually by solo voice; choral performance is in unison.

Many instruments, tracing their origin to ancient times and Middle Eastern and other Asiatic cultures, and with inevitable modifications, are still in use today. Of these the most popular are the *'úd* (lute), *kamanja* (violin), *quánúm* (psaltery), various lyres and harps, occasionally heard as background to the singing of ancient *muwashshah* (ballads) and heroic epics. Vertical flutes (*nay*) of varying lengths, the *zummâra* (double clarinet) and the *ma't* (oboe) are the chief wind instruments. There is a rich variety of percussion instruments (drums, tambourines, castanets, cymbals) that accompany the song, dance, the religious service and festival. Of these one may mention especially the *tabl* (kettledrum made of baked clay), *tar* (big drum), *regg* (small earthenware pot covered with a skin, and struck with a small stick), not to be confused with *riqq* (tambourine).

The repertory of Egyptian folksongs is wide and varied: the peasant (*fellāh*) plowing the field; the fisherman gathering in the net; harvesting and haymaking, occasion for great merriment in song and dance; songs for recruitment of soldiers, and the anguish of separation; love songs; songs glorifying their god and prophet, religious festivals, and military victories; lullabies, children's games and songs; wedding songs and funeral dirges; and many other categories of folk expression. The rhythm of the work songs reflects the accent and beat of the task, to which clapping of hands and stamping of feet intensifies the common effort.

242

Algeria

A caravan, after a long and arduous journey, has reached the market-place. Before unpacking their wares, this prayer and blessing is intoned.

Rana Djinak—We Have Come Here

English version by
Charles Haywood

RHYTHM ACCOMP.

Libya

This highly expressive and ornamental melody, lying within the range of a fifth, is a plaintive chant.   "Za" is the driver's call to urge the beast to keep going.

English version by
Charles Haywood

Ajjamal Wannā—Caravan Song

Morocco

This tune belongs to the rare *san'a* type, having little embellishment or prolongation of notes; usually employed for religious and didactic texts.

English version by
Charles Haywood

Wallā Zalā Mudduja
Night's Dark Shadows

Vivo (♩=170)

Wa - llā____ za - lā mu - ddu - jā,____
Night's dark____ shad - ows swift - ly fly____

____ Li - l - ga - r - bi mun - ha - zi - mu____
____ A - cross____ the rim of the West -

n wa____ Ddau____ 'u fī 'i - tri - hi____ ya, _
ern sky;____ Sun's____ bright rays ad - vance in haste,_

____ Bdū____ wa ya - n'a - li - mu____ wa. _
____ Of moon and stars they leave no____ trace._

____ Ddau____ 'u fī 'i - tri - hi____ ya____
____ Sun's____ bright rays ad - vance in haste,_

____ Bdū____ wa ya - n'a - li - mu.____
____ Of moon and stars they leave no trace.____

Tunisia

The Andalusian musical tradition is still very marked in many Tunisian folksongs; this is to be found particularly in street cries. The strong accent is played on a tambourine and the weak one on castanets.

Mahiya Illā Zalāb—Song of the Fig Vendors

English version by
Charles Haywood

United Arab Republic—Egypt

A lover's rapture expressed in spirited dance rhythm and appropriate movement and gesture.

English version by
Charles Haywood

Doos yá Lellee
Dance with Gladness

1. *Doos yá lel - lee, doos yá lel - lee, ___ Doos yá*
1. Dance with glad - ness, dance with glad - ness, ___ Dance with

lel - lee, doos yá lel - lee, ___ doos yá
glad - ness, dance with glad - ness, ___ Dance with

lel - lee, doos yá ___ lel - lee. ___ 'Esh - kë
glad - ness, dance with ___ glad - ness. ___ Filled with

mah - boo - bee ___ fe - ten - nee.
pas - sion, lov - er's ___ mad - ness.

2. *Kämil-el owsáf fetennee*
   Wa-l'-oyoon es-sood ramoonee,
   Min häwáhum sirt agahannee,
   Wa-l-häwa zowwad gunoonee.
   Chorus: *Doos ya lellee, etc.*

2. All my days are filled with anguish,
   Haunted by her eyes and form divine.
   Songs of tenderness I fashioned,
   Rapturous in maddening strain.
   Chorus: Dance with Gladness, etc.

3. *Gema'om gem'al al-'awázil,*
   'An habeebee yemna'oonee.
   Wa-lláh ana má afoot häwáhum
   Bi-s-suyoof low katta 'oonee.
   Chorus:

3. Though reproaches league together,
   Cold indifference bar my path,
   Ne'er will I my vows abandon
   Even when her eyes pour wrath.
   Chorus:

Africa—South of the Sahara

Although there are a number of racial and linguistic groups in "Black Africa," and each of these is divided into numerous tribal organizations, the *general* characteristics of their music have so many elements in common that they may be considered, with reservations, as a unit. Since the Bantu language-speaking people occupy the major portion of central and southern Africa, a discussion of their music will have vital reference to the other black Africans south of the Sahara. A. M. Jones, who has devoted many years to the study of African music, emphasized this point when he stated: "The practice of different tribes varies, and this limitation must be borne in mind, when the terms 'African' or 'Bantu' are used. At the same time there is evidence to show that underlying variety of practice there is a unity of musical principle which applies everywhere and justifies the term 'African Music.'" The characteristics of Bantu music are clearly summed up by Hugh Tracey, outstanding scholar in the field:

"Africa, from the Equator southwards, is mostly inhabited by the Bantu, a race of people who are believed to have originated somewhere in the region of the great lakes which are the sources of the White Nile.

"They migrated slowly outwards into the whole of the subcontinent, the stronger tribes claiming for themselves the richer valleys and the weaker being forced up into the hills or out onto the arid plains. When white men first arrived in the interior during the course of the nineteenth century, they found the tribes in strictly hostile isolation, each with its customs, its distinctive language and consequently its own social music.

"Today, this self-imposed separation has resulted in the evolution of a large number of folk musics, created by over 130

249

tribal groups, all of which have the common Bantu heritage but each retaining its distinctive tribal characteristics.

"Variations in the terrain, the climate and the vegetation have all tended to mould and modify the tribal styles of music-making to suit both the environment and the temperament of the local inhabitants. As a result of this historic background the folk music of Southern Africa can be recognized by their common racial basis on the one hand and their idiosyncrasies on the other.

"All Bantu languages are tone languages, and therefore, unlike European practice, musical melody must be subordinated to semantic tone by following the rise and fall of the tonal structure of the language rather than by setting the words to a fixed melodic line. African folk music therefore was developed primarily as an embellishment to the languages, so much so, that today there is a clear-cut change of musical style with every change of dialect. Secondly, the widely differing types of vegetation, from tropical forest and swamps to temperate open savannah, restricted the construction of instruments to those types for which the raw material could be found locally without having to trespass upon the territory of another tribe.

"Large drums, therefore, are found only in the forest areas, flutes where there are reeds, and unaccompanied choral singing in the open grass plains.

"All these restrictions and subordinations have combined to produce a wide variety of folk musics which in this part of Africa we are justified in calling Bantu but which are so diverse that it is unwise for us to generalize too broadly. Certain common characteristics are widely spread and may be briefly summarized under such remarks as these . . . that Bantu folk music is primarily antiphonal; that where polyphony occurs it is generally in the form of parallel melodies or in a combination of subjects and counter-subjects from which a certain form of harmony is produced as an incidental concomitant to the forward march of the music; that Bantu Africans sing in a great number of modes, none of which remotely corresponds to our Western scales, and so on.

"The majority of tribes prefer one or other of the many pentatonic modes, others adopt sexatonic, while the most musically developed usually perform on heptatonic scales in which the principal intervals are minor tones of approximately one and three-quarters of a semitone.

"The use of intervals as small as a semitone is rare and of still smaller intervals almost non-existent.

"Although a few tribes instinctively adopt the true fifth and fourth they are in the minority. On the other hand, all tribes without known exception recognize the true octave.

"Africans, it may be noted, have no altitude conception of music but rather one of magnitude, a note of *high* pitch being 'small' and one of *low* pitch 'great.'

"Bantu rhythmic music is usually built up from a clever combination of simple rhythms so interspersed that the resultant is a highly complex and lively syncopation in strict tempo. Crossed rhythms are the very essence of all drumming and of most of their more vivid music.

"Their instruments cover a wide range from simple musical bows to advanced forms of xylophone and *Mbira* (a family of small instruments whose operative element is an array of metal tongues plucked with the tips of the fingers. This may sometimes cover a wide range of three octaves and is indigenous to this continent alone). Percussion instruments are prevalent everywhere, anything that can be banged or beaten, scraped or shaken being brought into play whatever the occasion. Drums are the most widely spread of the simpler instruments [complexity and "polyphony" of drumming play a greater role in West Africa], and xylophones, mbira, lyres, lutes and several kinds of flute are common foundation of Bantu melodic music...

"Although Western influence is a comparatively recent intrusion into the continent, it has been thrust upon Africans with such evangelical fervour that there are now few if any areas in which its effects cannot be felt. Industry has broken the pattern of tribal isolation by attracting large numbers of men and women into the towns and mines. Education has been the great leveller of individuality forcing African youth into the same close-fitting mould, while foreign religion has effectively removed their faith in the past without as yet providing an adequate vision of the future in juxtaposition with economic realities and increasing populations."

It is important to note that in African music, rhythm is conceived as a total unity, a complete *gestalt*, not as separate units, and that it springs mainly from the drummer's accents. All of the African's activities, religious and "secular," his rites, rituals, dances and daily tasks are propelled and performed by rhythmic movement. Thus rhythm is for the black African as basic as walking, eating, speaking, etc. The rhythms may be simple isorhythmic and linear, as well as complex and polyphonic, comprising different patterns, with accents distributed and varied (syncopation).

According to Richard A. Waterman, who has made a very careful and scientific study of the musical characteristics of a particular African culture, namely the Guinea Coast, the essential qualities are manifested in "the metronome sense, dominance of percussion, polymeter, off-beat phrasing of melodic accents, and overlapping call-and-response pattern." On the other hand, Alan P. Merriam finds the following characteristics dominant in the music of the Congo and Ruanda Urundi: "a lack of specific emphasis on percussion, an enormous variety of musical instruments and styles, a heavy influence from the Arabic world, and a considerable amount of current change in process." He reminds and cautions the student that while drumming dominates in West Africa, this *regional* aspect has regrettably confounded and distorted the *general* role of percussion in African music.

Ethiopia

Ethiopian folk music has been affected by various cultures and musical traits. In appraising its music one must take into account the musical styles—vocal and instrumental—of the Bantu, Semitic, Coptic, Islamic, Sudanese, Nilotic, Middle Eastern, Indian, and Yemenite folk. Out of this admixture has come about what is distinctive or "national" in Ethiopian music. However, ethnic "pockets," carrying on their old traditions, in song and lore, still exist.

The Copts, the early Christians, dwelling mainly in the northern regions, display in their religious chants the continuing influence of the vocal style and religious practices of Pharaonic Egypt. The Oriental, ornamental style of the melodies shows close affinity with the Middle East. The link with early Jewish tradition and Biblical cantillation is still present in various religious folksongs, dances, and traditional instruments. Polyphonic and harmonic elements are to be found not only in liturgic music but in secular folksongs as well. The lepers, singing their plaintive *lalibaloč* at the doors of their more fortunate countrymen, perform in "a simple harmony, generally based on the third." The *zafan* songs are performed in a manner displaying great musical interest and sophistication: The leader sings the verse, the group joins him in the refrain; while they continue singing the coda, the voices drop out one by one until one singer is left—reminiscent of Haydn's "Farewell Symphony." Polyphony is also found in some of the instrumental accompaniment, through the use of the drone. Ethiopian folksongs cover a wide repertory, including war songs, songs of derision and praise, wailing songs, heroic ballads, healing songs, tender and romantic love songs, and religious festival songs and dances.

The Ethiopian folk employ a great variety of instruments, some dating from ancient times and other cultures. The percussion instruments consist of various drums, bells and rattles. The most representative are the *coboro* (two-headed drum, used in religious ceremony), the *nugarit* (kettledrum), *sitet* (war drum), *dowel* (stone gongs), *tsenasil* (brass sistrum), and *quakel* (bell rattles, tied in a leather string, and worn by the priests on their wrists during the ritual ceremony). The leading string instruments are the *massanequo* (one-stringed "fiddle," rich in Biblical tradition), the *begenna* (large lyre), and the *Trigonon* harp. The most frequently used wind instruments are the *shambukaw* (flute), the *'mbilta* (metal pipe, sounded by blowing across the open end), *nibiles* (bagpipe), and the *lemana* (bamboo flute).

Madagascar (Malagasy Republic)

Although the island of Madagascar, lying near the southeastern coast of Africa, belongs geographically to that continent, its cultural affiliations are largely Indonesian. However, various tribes on the island display strong characteristics of other culture influences. Besides the two dominant ethnic divisions, the Indonesian-Mongoloid (the Merina) and the Negroid (the Sakalava), there are also the Caucasoid, where the Arab (the Antakarana) and European settled, the Indo-Melanesian (the Bezonzano), as well as Indian and Chinese groups. The tribes (given in parentheses), which are also geographic designations, are not the only ones sharing those culture strains. The African influences are not only found in the western coastal areas, but have penetrated into parts of the interior and great portions of the east coast; Islamic traditions have vitally influenced Malagasy culture; the Merina, the most populous and most advanced of all tribes, has dominated the social and political life, and left its Indonesian imprint on the island. We find many acculturated and "assimilated" clans and tribes.

Each one of the tribes, to varying degree, retains many of its old traditions and beliefs, customs and ceremonies—religious and secular—with music playing an integral part. The songs, dances and variety of instrumental accompaniment display the remarkable musicality of the people: the expressiveness of the melodies, the vitality of the rhythm, and the virtuosity of instrumental performance. The most representative features of Indonesian musical style can be heard among the Merina in central Madagascar: in the vocal technique and musical patterns—solo and choral, extending in range from low medium to high shrill falsetto; the frequency of melodic intervals of thirds and sixths; a predominance of fast rhythmic figures and spirited tempi; in their choral style it is reminiscent of Tahitian chants. The rapid, intense sounds of the accompanying *váliha* (bamboo tube zither, with strings tied vertically, common in the Malayan Archipelago) add to the exotic quality of the performance. Their dances, with the carefully controlled, fluid bodily movements, and expressive hand gestures, bear close resemblance to those seen in

Java, and other Oceania cultures. The *hain-teni* songs, with the melodic structure determined by the poetic form, employ a variety of musical expression, involving the lyrical solo, declamation, choral participation, and spoken passages; they suggest many aspects of the lyric theatre.

Among the Sakalavas, occupying a vast portion of western Madagascar, the musical practices of their African ancestry still continue: the rich rhythmic polyphony of the drummers, the solo-chorus pattern, in which the former is sung in a rather free expressive style and the more formal repetitions of the latter, but with great rhythmic gusto and variety; the general downward movement of the melody, usually ending with greater forceful intensity. The choral singing of the Sakalava women, particularly in the north and northeast, has attained a high level of polyphonic subtlety and artistry.

The Malagasy exploit a great variety of musical instruments with a high degree of technical facility. (See Curt Sachs' monograph on this subject, and G. Rouget's perceptive comments upon which some of these observations are based.) Besides the great battery of drums, they also use rattles of different sizes, shapes and pitches; the leg xylophone (played only by women), with the bars carefully tuned, with the melody sounded by one player, while another woman, sitting at right angles, plays a drone; musical bows, with or without gourd resonators, are common. Vertical flutes, oboes, and various trumpets add nuance and harmonic color to their musical ensembles. The popularity and ritual symbolism of shell trumpets are attested by their widespread use on the island for purely artistic and functional reasons.

Basutoland

According to Aren Koole the Basutos "have made practically no cultural progress, although they have been in contact with Europeans for more than a century. However, music plays a very important part in their lives, participating in all their important religious, social and ritual activities." They have two different types of drums, the *moropa* (made of clay like a pot, covered with the hide of a goat), and the *sekupu* (small drum, fitted with small bells, like a tambourine); the latter is used exclusively in *balé*, the initiation ceremony of the Basuto girls. The ankle rattle is also common among the Basutos.

English version by
Arend Koole

Khoë Li—The Moon

etc.

Bechuanaland

This Bushman song is from the tale: "The Lizard Brought Home His Own Flesh." The Bushmen are found largely in the western part of Bechuanaland, in the Kalahari Desert and around Lake Ngami.

Kattăn, Kattăn—Run, Run

English translation by
Percival R. Kirby
Adapted by Charles Haywood

!Kat - tăn !Kat - tăn nau - ru !no, !Kha - u !kwe !kwe
Run, run, run, run, Roll, roll, up! Liz- ard's kid - ney!

!Kha - u !kwe !kwe - ta !kũ !Kat - tăn !kat - tăn,
Liz - ard's kid - ney! Oh, oh! Run run, run, run,

nau - ru !no I - bo !kwe !kwe I - bo !kwe !kwe-ta !kũ.
Roll, roll, up! Fath- er's kid - ney! Fath-er's kid - ney! Oh, oh!

HAND CLAPS

etc.

257

Burundi

A Burundi mother expresses her deep gratitude to the Supreme Being Tangishaka for having blessed her with child.

Tangishaka

English version by
Charles Haywood

2. *Shikura inkoni,*
   Twingine ibibondo.

2. Bring these children adornments rare,
   Bless them now with your loving care.

3. *Izo ni inyambo,*
   Ntizimirwa.

3. Of the royal flock are they,
   Let no trouble come their way.

4. *Iyi ningeri za Buyenzi*
   Sukiranyi z'amazi.

4. With the waters of Buyenzi,
   Fill these jugs plentifully.

(Fragment of a long poem)

Chad

A song-dance, part of a ceremony of young girls celebrating the new moon. The performance was observed in Éré, on the Logone River, in Chad.

English version by
Charles Haywood

É Lala É Liyo

1. La - ra la - ra dsoum ka ï dé, La - ra la - ra li - la - yo.
1. Moon- light shin-ing, join in the dance, Danc-ing in the moon- light.

HAND CLAP

etc.

2. *Solo—Chorus:* (as above.)
   Solo: Join in singing loud and gay,
   Chorus: Join in singing loud and gay.

3. *Solo:* Lift your feet in steps bounding high,
   Chorus: Lift your feet in steps so high.

4. *Solo:* Dawn is rising look in the sky,
   Chorus: Dawn is rising in the sky.

5. *Solo:* We must part now day has begun,
   Chorus: We must part now day's begun.

Congo Republic (Brazzaville)

The "Bikoumbi" (young maidens) are shut in the "house of Tacoul," waiting for the day when they will leave, ready for marriage. The song is in Vili dialect.

English version by
Charles Haywood

Debwangué

HAND CLAPS

etc.

2. *Solo:* To day shut indoors, to-morrow free.
   I think of my dear one Débwangué yé.

   Chorus:

3. *Solo:* I wait to be thy beloved wife,
   I think of my dear one Débwangué yé.

   Chorus:

4. *Solo:* My husband you will be Débwangué,
   I think of my dear one Débwangué yé.

   Chorus:

English version Copyright © 1966 by Charles Haywood

260

Ethiopia

A passionate courtesan song. These amorous lyrics usually contain short repetitive refrains, and abound in erotic allusions. This is only a fragment of the melody; the text is in the Galla dialect.

English version by Charles Haywood

Tole Ya Wati—Thank You, Wati

2. *Ya mucayo ati hin duftu,*
   Ani kaze galure.
   Refrain:

2. My fair beauty, most adored of all maidens,
   O do not leave me now,
   Refrain:

Ghana

We are presenting here only the clapping portion of the complex polyrhythmic percussion score accompanying the dance of the Ewe tribe. This is only the primary pattern of the song; it varies consider-

Sovu Dance

Moderato

CLAPS 1 & 2

CLAPS 3 & 4

CLAPS 5

Solo

Wlui na- do loo,   a- do-e nya

Chorus   *Solo*

hõ Ah ă - wă   vo - dua wlui na - do.   Wlui na -

ably with each repetition, ending in an accelerated tempo. The tune is pentatonic. The meaning of the text is known only to the members of the Yeve cult, associated with the God of Thunder.

Gabon

A very popular *cante fable* (a folk tale interspersed with song), a favorite of children.

Ka Tam Ma Wui—One Morning I Rose

English version by
Charles Haywood

HAND CLAPS

etc.

2. *Solo:*   The heavens above
   Chorus: Shining bright,
   Solo: A bird waking up,
   Chorus: Singing merrily a happy tune.
       É, é, this is what I heard then.

3. *Solo:*   The bird chirping loud:
   Chorus: Cui, cui, cui;
   Solo: The bird said to me:
   Chorus: Do not touch my babes in the nest.
       É, é, this is what I said then.

Kenya

There is a delightful folk tale connected with this song: "A number of villages has been made desolate by a monstrous serpent who lives in a cave at Kalungu, and threatens to attack even remote villages. The King has vainly offered prizes for valiant men. The snake has devoured them all. As terror and despair increases day by day, a clever little old man sets out alone to fight the monster with an empty waterpot!" (John Kyagambiddwa)

Ssemusota—Giant Snake

English version by
John Kyagambiddwa

Liberia

Although Liberia includes a large number of tribes, each with its own language and traditions, the largest and controlling group of the population is the English-speaking, nonindigenous settlers, who were brought from the United States to Liberia by the American Colonization Society. The spirit of this song, in rhythm and melody, shows its kinship to the folk music of the North American Negro.

I'm Goin' Chop Crab

1. I'm goin' chop crab, __ crab, __ crab, __ I'm goin' chop crab __ for me ma lov - er to eat. __

DRUM

etc.

2. I'm goin' dig gold for me ma lover to live.
3. I'm goin' to plant farm for me ma lover to eat.
4. I'm goin' to dig stone* for me ma lover to sell.
5. I'm goin' to build house for me ma lover to sleep.
6. I'm goin' to buy to car for me ma lover to ride.

* *diamond*

Madagascar

This island, formerly belonging to France, is now also known as the Malagasy Republic. The melodic contour, the rhythmic accents, and the solo-chorus pattern of this song show its African Negroid origin.

Ny O L'on Nanacy—Song of the Orphan

English version by
Charles Haywood

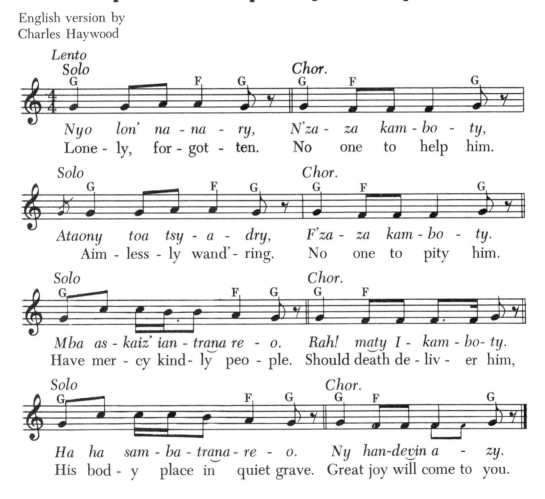

Malawi

The anguished plea of a Thonga mother whose son was snatched by this cruel beast. This song occurs in a folktale (*cante fable*), widely known and appearing in variant forms, in which a child is snatched by wild animals, monsters, ogres, or evil spirits.

Mfene Sandhleni—Cruel Baboon

English version by
Charles Haywood

Mfe - ne sa - ndhle - ni, Mfe - ne sa - ndhle - ni, A
Cru - el ba - boon,____ Cru - el ba - boon,____ Re -

u ngi dhla - yi - se - le mu - nta - na - me, Si ya ndo ndo
turn to me my dear - est son. Hear my child cry - ing for my

za! Si ngi - ya mu - ka, ngi ya mu - ka.
help! Oh, let me see him, let me see him!

I - i, In - ko - si ya mee,____ I - i.
I - i, Help me Lord and mas - ter, I - i.

DRUM BEAT

etc.

Mozambique

A dance-song performed by *Makua* women. They form a large circle around the song leader, facing each other, clapping each other's hand, and moving slowly from left to right.

É, Ie, Ie

English version by
Charles Haywood

É, ie, ie, mo tu-le-ne li no lion
É, ie, ie, let's take it off, our backs are

ku la ma mua ku mon-go. Ka la ka la
break-ing with this heav-y load. All of you who

na zin dum-ba na ba tuem-be. A a.
fear the dark and e-vil shad-ows. A a!

Non go-ro oa sham ba zan gom-be. A a.
You can see them com-ing clos-er now. A a!

HAND CLAPS

etc.

The tender and intense pleading of the mother, and the contrasting, insistent, syncopated rhythm of the accompaniment convey most effectively the inner agitation and fears of the child.

Yeke, Omo Mi—Do Not Cry, My Child

-re.
-er;
-re,
-er;

Ye - ke, o - mo mi,   o - mo mi,
O do not cry,___   my lit - tle
O - to, o - mo mi,   o - mo mi,
O hush- a - bye,___   my lit - tle

1.
ye - ke.
treas - ure.
o - to.
treas - ure.

2.
ye - ke.
treas - ure.
o - to.
treas - ure.

3. E
3. Dear

Allegro

pe bo - mi o - mo,___ Ge - ge bi - ra - wo___
child - ren yon - der strewn___ A round me come soon,___

1.   **2.**

___ Ti pe b'o - su - pa, E pa.
___ Lit-tle stars 'round the moon, Dear moon.

A tempo I°

O - to, o - mo mi,   o - mo mi,
O hush- a - bye,___   my lit - tle

o - to.
treas - ure.

271

Republic of the Congo (Léopoldville)

Song of derision upon a young lad who does not believe in the power of sorcery or witchcraft.

English version by
Charles Haywood

Tou Oua

2. *Solo:* Stop all that laughing at magic and witchcraft.
   Chor.: You must accept the truth.
   Tou, oua oya mou kouézié. ⎱
   You must accept the truth. ⎰ (2)

3. *Solo:* You will be punished for that with all his power.
   Chor.: Yes, you will know his strength.
   Tou, oua, oya mou kouézié, ⎱
   Yes, you will know his strength. ⎰ (2)

* *oya mou kouézié—the witch doctor.*

Rhodesia

One of the songs in the Ndau ceremony in which the *Zinthi'ki* (the familiar spirit), having performed its healing power, is being exorcised from the body of the *Nyamsólo* (the Diviner). The people, through song, bodily movements, and hand clapping, urge the departure of the spirit, likening its flight to a bird. On the final outcry *"Wensia,"* the spirit is expelled.

Manthi'ki—Spirit Song

273

Republic of South Africa

White influence on the melody and structure of this Zulu tune is quite apparent.

Iga'ma Lo Ta'ndo—Song of Love

Moderato espressivo   (*Zululand*)

U - da - li u - se - le 'ma - tshon,' U' ma-
My dar - ling stayed in the West, West - ward

tsho - na u - le - le 'ma - tshon.' U -
far - ing, he slept in the West. My___

da - li u - ham - ba 'ma - tshon' ka-
dar - ling walked toward the West; Slow,

ča - ne u - ne - nga - ne 'čan. U -
think - ing of his lit - tle one. My___

da - li u - se - le 'ma - tshon,'___ ye - ka mta-
dar - ling stayed in the West.___ He, my be-

kwe - tu u - se - le 'ma - tshon.' U - da - li u - le - le 'ma -
lov'd, he stayed in the West. My dar - ling slept in the

tshon,' U - ye - le - le - mam,' u - ye - le - le - mam.'
West, A - las,___ a - las, a - las,___ a - las.

"A [Bavenda] girl asked a young man, Gabara, for a pinch of snuff, which he gave her although she was a stranger. As a result of breaking the snuff tabu, he became a vicious character and worried her with indecent suggestions until, finally, he committed adultery with her. After that she composed this song, which is well known in Vendaland. It is sung very sadly." (Hugh A. Stayt) The tentative aspects of harmonization, discussed in the preface, are particularly pertinent here.

Fhola Li Na Mulanda—Snuff Is Very Guilty

English version by
Hugh A. Stayt

(*Transvaal*)

Of Western provenience, this folksong sung in Afrikaans is widely known in variant versions in many countries.

Mamma, 'Kwill 'N Man He'—Mother, I Want a Husband

(The White Population—Afrikaans)

English version by
Charles Haywood

1. Mam - ma, 'k wil n' man hê! Wat - ter man, mij
1. Moth - er, I want a hus - band! Tell me dear - est

lie - we kind? Wil jij dan 'n Frans - man hê?
child, what kind? Will a French - man please you, dear?

Nee, mam - ma, nee! 'N Fran - se man, die
No, moth - er, no! For French - man's love I

wil ek nie. Want par - lez vous ver - staan ek nie.
do not care, his *par - lez vous* gives me the scare.

Dit is mij ple - sier Met die Boer - jong - ke - rels hier.
What will give me joy Is a hand - some Bo - er boy.

276

Mamma, 'K Wil 'N Man Hê   Mother, I Want A Husband

2. *Mamma, 'k wil 'n man hê!*   2. Mother, I want a husband!
   Watter man, mij liewe kind?   Tell me dearest child, what kind?
   Wil jij dan 'n Hollander hê?   Will a Dutchman please you, dear?
   Nee, mamma, nee!   No, mother, no!
   'N Hollander, die wil ek nie,   For Dutchman's love I do not care,
   Want God vervloek dit kan ek nie.   His blasphemy I will not share.
   Dit is mij plesier   What will give me joy
   Met die Boerjongkerels hier.   Is a handsome Boer boy.

3. *Mamma, 'k wil 'n man hê!*   3. Mother, I want a hsuband!
   Watter man, mij liewe kind?   Tell me dearest child, what kind?
   Wil jij dan 'n Duister hê?   Will a German please you, dear?
   Nee, mamma, nee!   No, mother, no!
   'N Duisterman, die wil ek nie,   For German's love I do not care,
   Want schweinenfleisch dit lus ek nie.   His greasy pork I cannot bear.
   Dit is mij plesier   What will give me joy
   Met die Boerjongkerels hier.   Is a handsome Boer boy.

4. *Mamma, 'k wil 'n man hê!*   4. Mother, I want a husband!
   Watter man, mij liewe kind?   Tell me dearest child, what kind?
   Wil jij dan 'n Boersoms hê?   Will a Boerman please you, dear?
   Ja, mamma, ja!   Yes, mother, yes!
   'N Boerman, die wil ek hê,   For Boerman's love I really care,
   In 'n Boer se arme wil ek lê.   His love is best, beyond compare.
   Dit is mij plesier   What gives me joy
   Met die Boerjongkerels hier.   Is a handsome Boer boy.

277

Rwanda

A ceremonial song that is part of the elaborate ritual of the Secret Society of the Imandwa Cult among the Watusi of Rwanda.

English version by
Charles Haywood

Imandwa

Allegro (♩=120)

Solo

1. L'an-gom-be a - ti: "Ki - lum - ba"
1. L'an-gom-be had said: "O sit down!"

ay - i - kat-sin - da! Ha - ma nda - že
He's the might - y Lord! I humb - ly kneel.

DRUM BEAT

etc.

2. Solo: *Ati ikxanže ndašwandalika, ayikatsinda!*
   Chorus: *Hama ndaže.*

3. Solo: *Binego ati: "Kilumba", ayikatsinda!*
   Chorus: *Hama ndaže.*

4. Solo: *Ati ikxanže ndašwandalika, ayikatsinda!*
   Chorus: *Hama ndaže.*

2. *Solo:*   No complaint for my discomfort, He's the mighty Lord!
   Chorus: I humbly kneel.

3. *Solo:*   Binego had said: "O sit down!", He's the might Lord!
   Chorus: I humbly kneel.

4. *Solo:*   No complaint for my discomfort, He's the mighty Lord!
   Chorus: I humbly kneel.

Sierra Leone

This song (best perfomed in solo-chorus manner) has become widely popular with folksingers and youth groups. Its charm and humor lie in singing additional verses in various languages. To mention a few possibilities:

Tout le monde aime samedi soir (French)
Yeder āiner gleicht Shabes bei nacht (Yiddish)
Piace a tutti sabato sera (Italian)
Rénren dōu syĭ hwan lĭbai lyou wǎn shang (Chinese)
Vse lúbyat subótu vécherom (Russian)
Nos gústa a tódos la nóche de sábado (Spanish)
Pántes agapoúsi tin níkta tou Sábbata (Greek)
Yeder freut sich auf Samstag Abend (German)

Mofe Moni S'mo Ho Gbeke
Ev'rybody Loves Saturday Night

Somalia

A warrior's song glorifying the heroic deeds of the famous Mahdi Mullah Mohammed bin Said, who died in 1921.

Shellilà Shek—Our Great Leader

English version by
Charles Haywood

Sudan

This is a popular Azande children's singing game.

English version by
Charles Haywood

Gbodi—The Gazelle

Allegretto

Gbo - di man - gi we - re. Gbo - di man - gi we - re,
Look what the ga - zelle does. Look what the ga - zelle does,

Gbo - di o. Gbo - di wo ti turn._ Gbo - di wo ti turn,_
Do it, oh! Now she rolls her ears._ Now she rolls her ears,_

Gbo - di o. Gbo - di gu a gu. Gbo - di gu a gu,
Do it, oh! Now she shakes her tail. Now she shakes her tail,

Gbo - di o. Gbo - di sun - gun sen - de.
Do it, oh! Now she lies down to sleep.

Gbo - di sun - gun sen - de, Gbo - di o.
Now she lies down to sleep, Do it, oh!

Gbo - di gua - ri. Gbo - di gua - ri, Gbo - di o.
Now she jumps up. Now she jumps up, Do it, oh!

DRUM OR HAND CLAP

etc.

Tanzania

An ancient war chant of the Wabende tribe.

English version by
Charles Haywood

Yaya—War Song

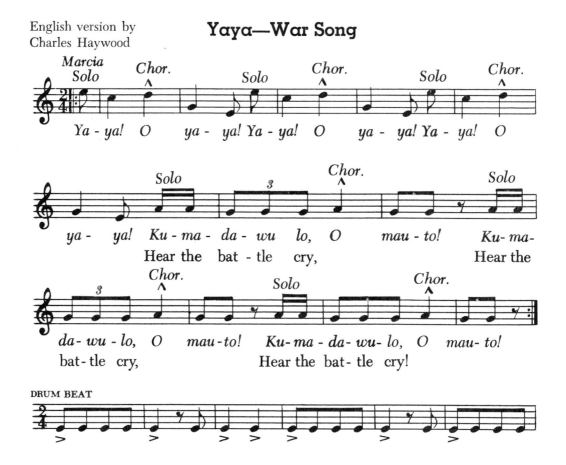

Ya - ya! O ya - ya! Ya - ya! O ya - ya! Ya - ya! O

ya - ya! Ku - ma - da - wu lo, O mau - to! Ku - ma-
Hear the bat - tle cry, Hear the

da- wu - lo, O mau - to! Ku - ma - da - wu- lo, O mau - to!
bat - tle cry, Hear the bat- tle cry!

DRUM BEAT

2. *Solo-Chorus:* Yaya! O yaya!
   Solo-Chorus: Yaya! O yaya!
   Solo-Chorus: Yaya! O yaya!
   Solo: Strike the enemy.
   Chorus: O mauto.
   Solo: Strike the enemy.
   Chorus: O mauto.
   Solo: Strike the enemy.
   Chorus: O mauto.

3. *Solo-Chorus:* Yaya! O yaya!
   Solo-Chorus: Yaya! O yaya!
   Solo-Chorus: Yaya! O yaya!
   Solo: We are powerful.
   Chorus: O mauto.
   Solo: We are powerful.
   Chorus: O mauto.
   Solo: We are powerful.
   Chorus: O mauto.

Uganda

A song of deep mourning for a high-ranking member of the tribe. There is a soft accompaniment on the *embûtu* drum.

English version by
John Kyagambiddwa
Adapted by Charles Haywood

Bwalobera Nkere
The Frogs

Ba - tu - dde mu ddy î - ro, Na - lō - se o - mu -
You who sit in the — room, I dream'd I saw

lo - ngo a - tû - se. O - bu - dde o - bu - ta - kya bu - li - nda
my be - lov - ed. But why, I ask, does bright day-light not

ki? Bwa - lo - be - ra nke - re o - kwa - nya - nga! Si - ri - mba,_
come? The frogs no long- er are heard croak- ing! I'm not ly -

_ nze nno na - lō - se, O - mu - lo - ngo mmu - la -
- ing, I tell you I saw my be - lov -

bye. O - bu - dde o - bu - ta - kya bu - ba - dde
ed. But why, I ask a - gain, doesn't day - light

ki? Bwa - lo - be - ra nke - re o - kwa - nya - nga!
come? The frogs no long - er are heard croak - ing!

DRUM
BEAT

etc.

283

Zambia

This Bantu song occurs in a folk tale (a *cante fable*), describing the adventures of a group of little girls with Miss Rabbit.

English translation by
J. Torrena
Adapted by Charles Haywood

Ozibane! Ozibane! Ozibane!
O, Dance Like That!

Oceania

Indonesia

Many influences are apparent in the musical culture of Indonesia, a vast archipelago of 3,000 islands. Here one finds contacts with the ancient Hindu epic, links with musical systems of Indochina, close relationships with the melodic and rhythmic patterning of Chinese music, imprints of Arabic and Persian in vocal and instrumental styles, Western influences of Portuguese sailor songs and Dutch folk tunes. One also becomes strongly aware, according to Jaap Kunst, of "many affinities to that of South-Eastern Asia, especially Siam [Thailand], Burma and Cambodia. There too, we find large gong-orchestras and scales related to Javanese and Balinese scales. The Indonesian vocal style, often pinched and nasal, reminds one forcibly of the way songs in China and many other parts of South-Eastern Asia are sung."

From the writings of this outstanding scholar we learn that "the most brilliant phenomena of Indonesian music may be found in Bali and Java, two equally fascinating, closely related and yet distinct tone worlds. The music of Bali is characterized by its directness, its exuberance and its irrepressible vitality, while the music of Java may be admired for its refinement and its controlled expression of sentiment. The tone systems called *sléndro* and *pélog*, both quite different from that of Western European classical music, are both characterized by the use of pentatonic scales. In *sléndro* the tones are nearly equigrade (about 4/5s of the European whole tone); *pélog* scales consist of three smaller and two larger intervals together with one or two extra tones. On Bali, the Hindu island, the *pélog* system predominates, while in Central and East Java it is the *sléndro*."

"Musical notation and a learned art of music," Professor Kunst declares, "live side by side with a popular tradition, and both . . . are played upon large orchestras, the gamelan, the most complex of musical organizations outside of the European symphony orchestra." The rich sonority of the gamelan is achieved by the different percussion instruments, predominantly xylophones and gongs, each with its own pitch and particular rhythm; the *suling* (flute), panpipes, the *rêbab* (a two-stringed violin of Arabic-Persian origin), the *gĕndér* (small marimba), *saron* and *demoeng* (metallophones), the *tjelempoeng* (14-stringed psaltery), a board zither and a tube zither (*ketoeng-ketoeng*), the *angklung* (bamboo chimes), and *kendang* (drums).

On the islands of Bali and Java there are thousands of gamelan orchestras of various types, each with "its own musical scale, its special function and a special repertoire." These orchestras, whether they belong to princely courts or to a little village, "play the same complex music in roughly the same way, varying only in strength of the ensembles and the degree of stylization and refinement. Although the Javanese have a system of musical notation, they invariably play from memory, more or less in the fashion of gypsy musicians. Each instrument has its own function, and the total ensemble creates a well-defined, and exotic polyphony." The improvisatory variations on the main theme by the different individual instruments are quite astonishing in their inventiveness and virtuosity.

Polynesia

The chief island groups of Polynesia are Hawaii, Phoenix, Samoa, Tonga, Cook, Society, Tuamotu Archipelago, Marquesas, Easter and New Zealand. The inhabitants have spread the farthest through the islands of the Pacific. "Because Polynesians are remarkably homogeneous in culture, including their mythology and Malayo-Polynesian dialect, it is believed that their ancestors, once they had arrived in an area an estimated 2000 to 2500 years ago from Indonesia by way of Micronesia, originated a pattern of culture which they carried with them when they later colonized the rest of the area and occupied certain islands in Melanesia." The attractive features of the Polynesians—whom Captain Cook characterized surpassing in fair form and regular features any other people in the world—their social

288

life, customs, traditions, song and dance have been the subject of much fact and fiction.

The Samoans display great love for colorful costumes and are very fond of singing and dancing. Their elaborate courtship rites involve many song sequences, bodily movement and drumming. The Society Islanders, considered the most attractive in the Pacific—"in their symmetry the people are unsurpassed"—of whom the inhabitants of Tahiti are the most widely known, make extensive use of the conch shell, nose flute and drums in their musical performance.

Hawaii

Hawaiian folk music finds expression in three major categories: ancient Hawaiian music, old Hawaiian music, and modern Hawaiian music. Quoting Professor Barbara B. Smith of the University of Hawaii: "Ancient Hawaiian music and poetry are almost synonymous. The language is mellifluous and lends itself easily to chanting. *Mele* means both poetry and music and may be divided into two main categories, the *mele oli* (chant) and the *mele hula* (dance).

"The *mele oli* is logogenic and is performed by a soloist. The text has no rhyme and often no regular meter, but does have repetition, balance, contrast, and sometimes alliteration. Phrases are similar but not identical in length, and they sometimes conclude in a tonal prolongation with *'i'i* (a trill-like fluctuation in pitch). Vocal style and inflection are of great significance in the performance of the ditonic or tritonic melodies. There are *mele* for prayers and prophecies, dirges, love songs, war songs, name chants (including genealogies), and for practical things that needed to be remembered, such as directions for navigation. With the change from a non-literate to a modern society and to a different religion, the *oli* no longer serve the same purposes as in ancient Hawaii...

"The *hula* is a dance which gives physical expression to the meaning of the text. Although modern adaptations of the *hula* are extremely popular—they are practically a trademark of Hawaii—very few of the ancient *hula* are known. According to Hawaiian mythology, the first *hula* was danced by the goddess Hi'i-aka. In ancient Hawaii, initiates were trained in the hula temple. The *mele hula* is performed by a soloist or in chorus with instrumental accompaniment. In rare instances stamping and body-slapping are used instead of instruments. Melodically, it has a wider range than the *mele oli*, usually five or six tones, and it has a more regular rhythmic pulse. Single melodic lines predominate, but there may have been some use of simple harmonic intervals, mostly of the bourdon type, as in other Polynesian music....

"Old Hawaiian music has short regular phrases derived from hymn tune structure; simple harmonies suitable to the ukulele or guitar; melodic outlines based mostly on scale steps, skips within the basic chords, and lower-neighbour-note inflections; simple rhythmic patterns which are languidly performed; and a vocal style which may have been retained from ancient Hawaiian music, in which the singer slides from pitch to pitch. The words are mostly sentimental, often a combination of English and Hawaiian like that of the Latin vernacular in the macaronic carols of Europe. Old Hawaiian music is widely known, loved, and performed in Hawaii today. . . .

"Modern Hawaiian music, or Hawaiian popular music, has developed from the interaction of jazz and Latin rhythms with old Hawaiian music. Some ancient chants have been used as the basis for popular compositions, and the sliding vocal line is characteristic of their performance. Ancient percussion instruments, the ukulele and guitar, and modern Western instruments compose the popular orchestras."

Maori (New Zealand)

Many of the songs and chants are historical in character and of tribal kinship. The Maori is very much concerned with accuracy in oral transmission of both text and melody. The singer "must have the ability to maintain an inflexible tempo and to enunciate in rhythmically accurate fashion." This characteristic may be described as "rhythmic unison," which the Maori call *whakaeke*. The same qualities are demanded in the matter of style. Nothing must interfere with the continuous flow of the song; even the breathing must be made imperceptibly. To avoid a break in continuity, meaningless syllables are frequently inserted between the lines of the text in the leader's part. Tempo is rigidly maintained "despite the astonishingly complex rhythms which occur in many Maori chants." Their melodies usually lie within the tonal interval of a fifth, and their scales usually correspond to the Western major mode and the Aeolian (with a lowered seventh).

Melanesia

In varying degrees—in quality, variety and complexity—music plays a significant role in the cultural life of the various tribes. Panpipes, of different sizes, played singly or in combination, are widespread. Some observers have found the pipes of the Solomon Islanders to be generally of a larger size than those found in other islands: the Admiralty, New Hebrides, the Tonga group, and New Zealand. The type of pipe used usually depends on the kind of song to be performed. The participants frequently accompany their playing with a nodding of the head and a swaying of the hips. The jew's-harp is very popular in Melanesia. The eastern islanders, those of New Hebrides and New Guinea, fashion them out of bamboo. On Treasury Island the jew's-harp is made out of a five-stringed bow about fifteen inches long; the string is gently struck with the fingers, the cavity of the mouth acting as resonator. The Melanesian drum, a portion of a trunk of a tree, eight to ten feet long, with a slit in the middle, is placed lengthwise on the ground and struck with two short sticks. A common percussion instrument used in dancing is a board placed in a pit in the ground, and struck by the dancers' feet, in varying rhythms and accents. Two large conch shells, the *triton* and *cassis*, are frequently used. They are played by blowing through a hole on the side of the spire. Some Melanesian islanders use trumpets made out of long and large bamboos, blown through a hole on one side, producing deep hollow sounds.

The Pygmies of the interior mountains of New Guinea possess elaborate rituals and ceremonies with colorful costumes and masks, and a highly complex and expressive musical idiom closely related to their kinsmen in Africa. "The remarkable vocal music of the pygmoid tribes of the Central Mountains moves in rapidly sung triads with flourishes. Melodies of this type also occur in the interior of New Britain, New Ireland, Bougainville and Keresan—all similar in the triad structure of the music of the Pygmies of Central Africa. Perhaps one may say therefore, that this music of triads with flourishes is the cultural possession of a primitive pygmoid population pushed back by later migrants." (Jaap Kunst) They also have a great variety of musical instruments, including flutes, panpipes, and drums. The Fiji Islanders, renowned for their skill as handcraftsmen, carpenters and canoe makers, are fond of singing, dancing, and possess a poetry of considerable advance.

Professor Douglas L. Oliver, who has made an intensive study of the Siuai of Bougainville, Solomon Islands, presents illuminating observations on the importance of music in their culture: "The *Siuai* devote more time to music than to graphic and plastic art. Every clubhouse contains several wooden slit gongs ranging in size from fifteen feet long by five feet in diameter to three feet long by one foot in diameter. These gongs are sounded with vertically held wooden beaters struck against the lip of the slit, and they are used both for signaling and for making music. The gong played by women consists of a single wooden board laid in a waist-deep hole dug in the ground. Two or three females stand in the hole and jump on the board in unison to mark the tempo for their companions' dancing and singing around the hole.

"Flute-playing in concert by large numbers of men and boys accompanies many feasts and ceremonies, but individuals also play on the flute by themselves for their diversion. Flutes are made of many sizes and are made of bamboo; they vary in number of units from one to ten. The *Siuai* also play large trumpets made by attaching a half coconut-shell mouthpiece to one end of a hollow wooden cylinder. Children sometimes amuse themselves by playing on small musical bows, but young men prefer the trade-store jew's-harp.

"Singing is highly popular and accompanies many kinds of occasions." Parents sing lullabies to their children and use songs to teach them new words. Lovers compose boastful songs about their adventures, and relatives express their grief in moving laments. Even wailing follows a conventional musical pattern. Most dramatic of all, however, is harmonized singing of large numbers of men and boys, which takes place at feasts. The melodies, consisting of short reiterative motives, with occasional variations, and pentatonic in character, are chiefly based on intervals of fourths and fifths, with smaller intervals of seconds and thirds interspersed.

Micronesia

Micronesia, "little islands," is made up of four archipelagoes— Marianas, Carolines, Marshalls, and Gilberts. The close proximity of these inhabitants to the Asia coast is evident in the more pronounced traces of Mongoloid characteristics in their racial composition. They are, however, closely related to the Polynesians.

Although they all belong to the same culture area, they display great variety in musical expression. Katherine Luomala speaks of the great charm of the sea lyrics of the Marshall Islanders, "with the direct simplicity of their description of weather at sea and the mariner's exultation in defying the elements and death." She also comments on the strong element of "comic relief" found in Micronesian dances, notably among the Tabiteueans. Her further impressions of Micronesian music are quite illuminating: "Neither new nor modern chants and songs have terminal rhymes. In the Marshalls and Carolines, many songs and dances have European melodies and native words. . . . In the Gilberts, the more melodic tunes and less visualized dances of the Polynesian Ellice Islands have been given native words to which young people dance, with the additional rhythm of a mercilessly beaten bottom of an upended box or a 44-gallon kerosene tin. A certain mode of behavior, solemnly cultivated by the younger set among the intense-spirited Tabiteueans, goes along with these dances, which are merry in contrast to the highly stylized, set-expressioned old dances (*ruoia*), still important for ritual and entertainment."

Although the music of Ifaluk, according to Edwin Grant Burrows, is essentially vocal– accompanied by dancing—much use is made of two instruments: the conch shell trumpet and a conical roll of coconut leaf with double reed, sounding like an oboe. The latter is widely distributed in Micronesia and other Pacific areas.

Republic of Indonesia

A popular children's Solonese *dongèng* song. The *dongèng* songs are of ancient origin and are usually sung during the telling of fairy tales (*dongèng*). It occurs in a story closely resembling "Hop o' Me Thumb."

Man Paman Goejang Djarang
Little Father Horse-Washer

English version by
J. Kunst and Emile Van Loo

(Java)

Man pa - man goe - jang_ dja - ran, Ngri-koe ware
Lit- tle fa - ther _ horse - wash-er, Did you per-

won - ten po - poh be - roek kè -
chance see my co - co - nut and nap - kins

li, Po - poh goem bal loe - rih _ ke - pioer, Koe-
float a - way? The nap-kins are rags of lu - rih ke - pyur*, Been

là loe - roe se - ki - sock bo - ten ke - te - moe.
look-ing for them all the morn-ing with- out find - ing them.

294

Malaysia

This tune belongs to the *Baram Kdayan,* or healing songs. The *day-ang* (medicine man) compares the curative effect of the betel nut to the strength of love and the power of money. Characteristic of Sarawak melodies is the prevalence of the downward movement within the interval of a fourth. Their chief musical instruments are the *keluric,* consisting of six pipes inserted into a gourd, a two-stringed guitar, a bamboo harp, a nose flute, and a variety of gongs and drums.

English version by
Charles Haywood

Aroi Toyong—Oh, Beloved

(Sarawak)

A - roi, a - roi, a - roi, a - roi di, a - roi___ di
Your gift, your gift, your gift, your gift of be - tel nut

ka - sih si - ri li i - nan; A - roi, a - roi di,
a - wakes my strong-est love,___ Your gift, your gift___

si - ri li,___ si - ri li_____ i - nan
stirs my heart,___ stirs my heart,_____

di ra - sa me - no - yong, Wang da -
fills me with___ great love, As if I

lam_____ tan - - gan.
had mon - ey_____ in___ my hand.

Philippines

In contrast, this song shows the influence of Western music—more strongly, perhaps, of the nineteenth-century sentimental salon pieces.

Lulay—Serenade

English version by
E. S. Reyso-Cruz

A - nong la - king hi - rap kung pa - ka - i - i - si - pin,_
Noth- ing you at- tempt in the world is so hard to do, _

_ Ang ga wang u - mi - big sa ba - ba - ing
_ As to win the love of a maid - en who's

ma - hi - hin; ___ Lu - mu - lu - hod ka na'y di
mod - est and true; ___ Kneel- ing at her feet, not a

ka - pa man - din pan - sin, ___ Sa hi - rap i -
glance will she cast on you, ___ Ere she tests your

kao kan - yang _ su - su - bu - kin. ____ Li - ga -
love to prove _ that it is true. ____ 'Tis the

ya - - - ng bu - hay,____ Ba - ba - eng ____

great ____ joy of life, ____ Such a girl ____

____ sak - dal i - nam. Ang ha - la - ga ni - ya'y di

____ at last to win. Oh, she's of wond - rous worth, ____

ma - tu - tum - ba - san, Ka - hin - hin - an ni - ya'y ta -

pre - cious be - yond com - pare, Her mod - est - y and grace are

nging ka - ya - ma - nan.____ Li - ga - nan.____

treas - ures rich and rare. ____ 'Tis the rare. ____

"After a wedding celebration this ceremonial prayer [from Sagada Mountain Province] is sung, in which the appearance of seasonal foods (like mushrooms and edible beetles) and the blessing of children are requested. All those who attend the wedding ceremony that precedes the *sob-oy* must send their adult and young males to the villages of Geday and Demang with pieces of meat as offerings. These are placed in a big vat, and while the meat is being cooked, the *sob-oy* is sung." (José Maceda)

Nan Sob-oy—We Pray

English version by
Jose Maceda

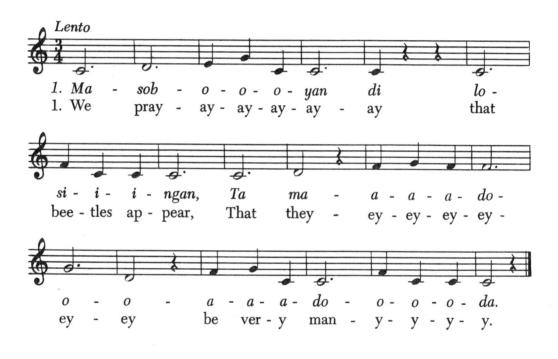

Lento

1. Ma - sob - o - o - o - yan   di   lo -
1. We   pray - ay - ay - ay - ay - ay   that

si - i - i - ngan,   Ta   ma -   a - a - a - do -
bee - tles ap - pear, That they - ey - ey - ey - ey -

o   -   o   -   a - a - a - do - o - o - o - da.
ey - ey   be ver - y   man - y - y - y - y.

2. *Masob-oyan di damayan,*
   Ta ma-ado-ado da.

3. *Masob-oyan di o-ngong-a,*
   Ta ma-ado-ado-da.

2. We pray for mushrooms,
   That they be very many.

3. We pray for children,
   That they be very many.

Hawaii (United States)

A lyric song of tender sentiment, showing strong influence of European nineteenth-century romantic musical idiom. Melodies of this style—in moderately slow tempo, expressing "deep longing" for person or place, and usually in ternary form—are known as *himeni*. These have evolved from the missionary hymns.

Like No A Like—Remembrance

English version by
Charles Haywood

U - a li - ke___ no a li - ke Me ka
When the rain on ___ leaves falls gent - ly In my

u - a ka - ni - le - hu - a Me he la e ___ i mai
heart a - wak - ens deep long- ing; I hear voic - es ___ whisp'-ring

a - na, A - ia i - lai - la ke a - lo - ha.___
soft- ly — Be - hold, your love to you is com- ing.___

Chorus

O - o - e no ka'u i u - pu ai,_____ Ku' - u
I long for you ev' - ry wak - ing mo - ment, For the

le - i hi - ki a - hi - a - hi, O ke ka - ni a na
pleas-ures and___ joys of the eve- ning; When I hear the cock crowing

ma - nu, ___ I na ho - ra o ke a - u - mo - e.
gai - ly, ___ Then I know, a - las, new day is dawn-ing.

Tuamotu Archipelago

"The *Mereu* is a love song of a more elaborate kind than the *teki* (little ditties, chiefly love songs, to which words are readily improvised, sung, generally, on one pitch with a quavering voice). *Mereu* are characterized by a distinct introductory section before the main theme is sung, and by a prolonged final note. . . . European influence appears particularly strong in the *mereu*, but, the above example, from Falgatau Island, is of a purely native character. . . . This song is the plaint of a woman who has no lover but the post in her house." (E. G. Burrows)

Mereu—Love Song

English version by
Kenneth P. Emory
Adapted by Charles Haywood

Allegro (♩=144)

O - vai e? _____ O - vai ta - ku ho - a io e?
Tell me who? ____ tell me, please, what friend I have there?

Te tu - ru i ta - ku fa - re ta - ku ha - a e.
My one friend _ is that wood-en post in our big house.

E _____ pi - ko va - u ki - te ru - ki
I sleep _ at the post, my lone-ly nights are

ne - i, E moe - moe a - tu va -
spent _____ there, And I dream and hope for

u a, Fa - re i hu - a. _ Ki - a te
some - one; No one hears my _ cry. _ The house lifts

ta - pe i ta - ku ka - re - u. _____
up the edge of _ my pa - re - u. _____

300

New Zealand

A plaintive chant whose poignancy is strongly emphasized by the chromaticism, particularly, in measures six to eight. Although the range of the tune is a minor sixth (g to e flat), conveying a feeling of the Aeolian mode, the chief melodic activity lies in the interval of a fourth (g to c).

English version by
Charles Haywood

Waiata Aroha—Love Song
(Maori)

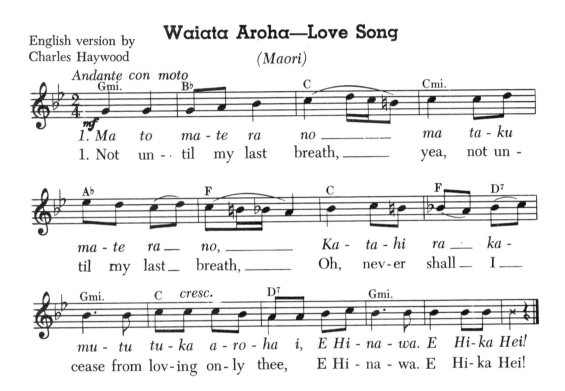

1. Ma to ma - te ra no _____ ma ta - ku
1. Not un - til my last breath, _____ yea, not un -

ma - te ra ___ no, _____ Ka - ta - hi ra ___ ka -
til my last ___ breath, _____ Oh, nev - er shall ___ I ___

mu - tu tu - ka a - ro - ha i, E Hi - na - wa. E Hi - ka Hei!
cease from lov - ing on - ly thee, E Hi - na - wa. E Hi - ka Hei!

2. *Kaore he wahine hei rite ki a Hinemoa,*
   Tae ana tonu hiahia ki te mutangs, E Hinawa. E Hika Hei!

3. *Tirohia Mokoia ka ngaro i te rehutai,*
   Kihai rawa i meneti ngarirau, E Hinawa. E Hika Hei!

2. Dost thou know, my love, the wondrous splendor of Hinemoa?
   Her yearning love and deep desire were fulfilled, E Hinawa. E Hika Hei!

3. See'st thou glorious Mokoia, mists hide its beauty from sight,
   All mists of doubt will be dispelled by my love, E Hinawa. E Hika Hei!

A popular folksong among the English-speaking population of New Zealand. The link with the culture and tradition of the mother country is strongly maintained.

Keel Row

1. As I came to Sand- gate, to Sand- gate, to Sand - gate,

As I came to Sand - gate, I heard a lark to sing.

Oh, well— may the keel row, the keel row, the keel— row,

Well— may the keel row that my — lad - die's in.

2. He wears a blue ribbon, blue ribbon, blue ribbon,
   He wears a blue ribbon, a dimple in his chin.
   Chorus:

Trobriand Sunset Isles

The songs of the Kiriwinians are contemporaneous and are of immediate and personal interest. *Kaduguwai* is a very long song (of which only the first tune and first verse are given here). It consists of a kind of suite of five tunes. It is a spirit song, composed by Igali, one of the wives of Uweilasi, one of the leading chiefs. It was inspired by the death of her child Kolaleu. Indeed, "all Trobriand island songs are inspired by the wailings for the dead and the common lamentations that are heard every day." (B. Baldwin)

English version by
B. Baldwin
Adapted by Charles Haywood

Kaduguwai—The Gathering

Ka va-du-du ka gu-ya-we ___
It was a roy-al ___ gath-er-ing,

du-de-gu o me, ___ ta ___ ba si-po-lu
Gath-er-ing on the ___ straits, When ___ I re-hearsed this

ma-do-wi-si. Ka va-du-du ka gu-ya-we,
song of ours. For U-wei-la-si we gath-ered there;

du-de gwe wa me-e-ta, ba si-po-lu ma-
With pre-cious belts and strings of wealth on the breast, When

da-wo-si. ___ (Hm) ___
I re-hearsed this song.

Papua

A war song—sung by the Mambule and Sivu communities of the Mafulu tribe in their joint hostilities against another community. The tune is first whistled, and then sung with great energy, softening toward the end.

English version by
Charles Haywood

E! E! E!

2. E! E! E!
   Noul e nul em u jeka la
   E! bulu juju le.

2. E! e! e!
   My village is the same as yours,
   Yes, we are equal now!

Solomon Islands

A dirge sung by a distant sib-mother at the cremation of a young boy. The singer belongs to the Siuai of Bougainville.

English translation by
Douglas L. Oliver
Adapted by Charles Haywood

Nuri—My Son

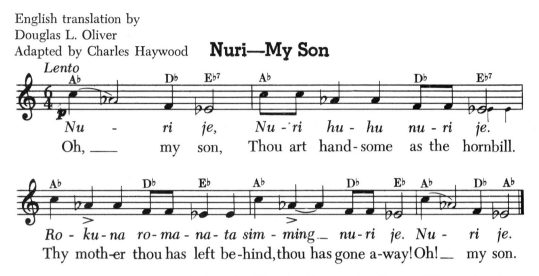

Nu - ri je, Nu - ri hu - hu nu - ri je.
Oh, ___ my son, Thou art hand-some as the hornbill.

Ro - ku-na ro-ma-na-ta sim - ming _ nu-ri je. Nu - ri je.
Thy moth-er thou has left be-hind, thou has gone a-way! Oh! _ my son.

Caroline Islands

Seated about the medicinal caldron, the Ifaluk Atoll islanders invoke the blessing of the gods and intone a supplication to ward off disease. This is a fragment of a long hymn; the first line consists of nonsense syllables.

English version by
Charles Haywood

Ngai I Tanga I

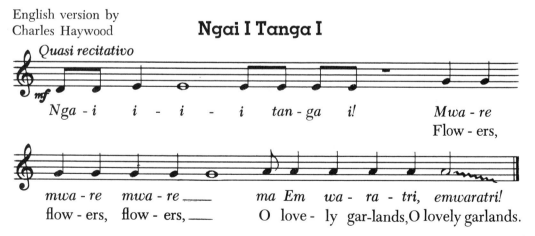

Nga - i i - i - i tan - ga i! Mwa - re
Flow - ers,

mwa - re mwa - re ___ ma Em wa - ra - tri, emwaratri!
flow - ers, flow - ers, ___ O love - ly gar-lands, O lovely garlands.

Australia

ABORIGINAL MUSIC: The aboriginal of Australia is "a brown-skinned, wide-nosed person of medium height, with black wavy hair, often with prominent bony ridges above the eyes. Though dark-skinned, he is not a member of the Negro race." The aborigines are mainly hunters or fishermen.

Although there are distinct differences in the type of melodies, rhythmic structure, manner of performance and use of instruments among the various tribes, one may, nevertheless, find general characteristics common to most of the aborigines: a predominant downward motion of the melody, usually pentatonic; the initial attack on the highest pitch, gradually moving to the lowest note as a point of rest; and the use of syncopation and sequential repetition of motives. The inhabitants of Arnhem Land, whose musical habits have been carefully studied, show a preference for the heptatonic scale, isometric structure, polyphony, instrumental interludes, and a quiet unaccented style of performance.

The music of the Central Australian aboriginal has been clearly described by Dr. T. G. H. Strehlow: "Australian songs are ancient and traditional poems, intoned according to old and customary modes . . . they are a composite form of art, namely intoned verse; and their most striking feature is the element common to both music and poetry, namely rhythm. Rhythm is also an important element of the dance; and many of the verses in the Australian songs were intended to regulate the movements of ceremonial dances.

"The original Australian poets combined difficult rhythmic forms in an amazing series of variations. When a song was being chanted, it was not unusual for the singers to bring out its strong musical stresses in their chanting while tapping out simultaneously a different rhythm with their boomerangs. Slurring is one of the dominant characteristics of the music of the Central Australian aboriginal songs. Numerous repetitions of the verses and key words are essential in their performance."

MUSIC OF THE WHITE POPULATION: The English settlers of this vast continent portray in their folksongs the same tribulations, adventures, hope, as well as lusty humor, as do their fellow countrymen who settled the wide stretches of the North American continent. The Australian bushman sings, dances and makes merry much as the American frontiersman does. "The vigor and inventiveness of Australian expression is revealed in the bush ballads and yarns, passed down from generation to generation." Their language and idiom, the bombast and boldness, are quite different from those of their brethren in the British Isles. But their tunes and rhythms, like those of the American frontier, come from similar sources, namely the Irish, English, and Scotch folksongs, as well as those of other European immigrants. Many songs were brought by English convicts, who expressed their loneliness and hardships by singing of their homeland, as well as in songs of protest. Their chief occupations in sheepshearing, bushwhacking and, later, mining are richly revealed in numerous songs and ballads.

The marked characteristics discussed above—the downward motion of the melody, the pentatonic quality, the repetition of short motives and the last notes of the song—are quite apparent in this chant.

Măkérēnbĕn
Honey-Ant Song of Ljába

English version by
T. G. H. Strehlow

Allegretto

Ma - kē - rēn - - bĕn - nēl - a - nōu - pā - jā -nōu,
The ant - work - ers yon - der dwell, ev - er dwell;

Ma - kā - mā - rin - kā - la - nōu - pā - jā - nōu, Ma -
In ring - tier - ed homes they dwell, ev - er dwell, In

kā - mā - rin - kā - la - nōu - pā - jā - nou, Ma -
ring - tier - ed homes they dwell, ev - er dwell. The

kē - rēn - bĕn - nēl - a nōu - pā - jā - nōu, Ma -
ant - work - ers yon - der dwell, ev - er dwell; The

kē - rēn - bĕn - nēl - a nōu - pā - jā - nōu. Ma -
ant - work - ers yon - der dwell, ev - er dwell; In

kā - mā - rin - kā - la - nōu - pā - jā -nou. Ma - kā - mā - rin -
ring - tier - ed homes they dwell, ev - er dwell, In ring - tier - ed

kā - la - nōu - pā - jā - nōu. (Tones fade out—
homes they dwell, ev - er dwell. all notes are slurred)

309

Like the American cowboy, the Australian overlander sang to keep his restless cattle in line and to help ease the monotony and fatigue of a long ride in the saddle. He too dreams of "pretty girls in Brisbane" (as the American cowpuncher often envisioned them in Dodge City) and plenty of drinks to go around.

The Overlander

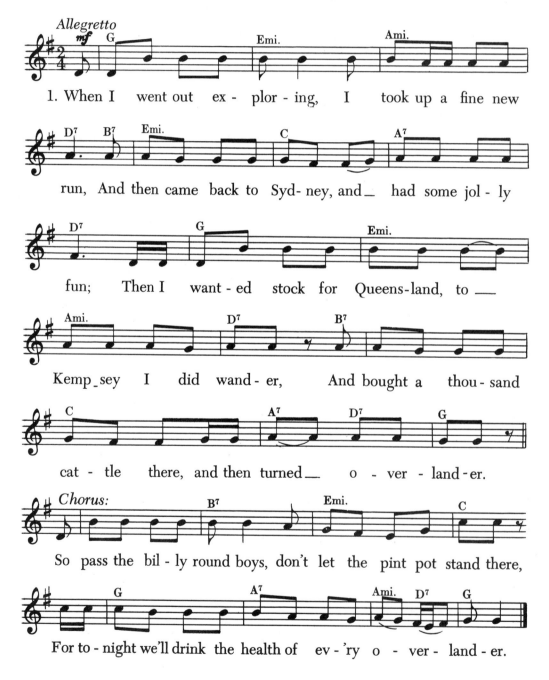

1. When I went out ex - plor - ing, I took up a fine new run, And then came back to Syd- ney, and_ had some jol - ly fun; Then I want - ed stock for Queens-land, to __ Kemp_sey I did wand - er, And bought a thou - sand cat - tle there, and then turned_ o - ver - land - er.

Chorus: So pass the bil - ly round boys, don't let the pint pot stand there, For to - night we'll drink the health of ev - 'ry o - ver - land - er.

The Overlander

2. When the cattle were all mustered, and the outfit ready to start,
    I saw the boys all mounted, with their swags left in the cart;
    All sorts of men I had, from France, Germany and Flanders,
    Lawyers, doctors, good and bad, in my mob of overlanders.
    Chorus:

3. From the road I then fed out, where the grass was green and long,
    When a squatter with a curse and shout, told me to move along;
    Said I, "Come draw it mild—take care don't rise my dander,
    For I'm a regular growing child, a Victorian overlander."
    Chorus:

4. He swore he'd pound my cattle, but I bullied him that time,
    They very seldom saw me out, and then never got the fine;
    They think we lived on poor beef, but no, I'm not a gander,
    When a straggler joined the mob, he'll do, says the overlander.
    Chorus:

5. The pretty girls in Brisbane were hanging out their duds,
    I wished to have a chat with them, so steered straight for the tubs,
    Some dirty urchins saw me, and soon they raised my dander,
    Crying, "Mammy, quick, take in your clothes, here comes an overlander."
    Chorus:

6. In town we drain the wine cup, and go to see the play,
    We never think of being hard up, but how to spend the day;
    We steer up to the girls, that ring themselves with grandeur,
    And while they sweat our checques—they swear, they love the overlander.
    Chorus:

Bibliography

This is a highly selective, and, of necessity, limited bibliography. In preparation of this volume hundreds of folksong collections and critical studies were examined. Merely to list them would be a sizable book in itself. Most of these titles can be found in the general bibliographies suggested. Here we present only those items which were most directly involved in shaping the general contents of this anthology: in the selection of the melodies and the character of the descriptive commentary.

General Collections and Studies

Ancient and Oriental Music. Wellesz, Egon, ed, Vol. 1, *The New Oxford History of Music.* London, 1957.

Bantock, Granville, *One Hundred Folk Songs of All Nations.* Oliver Ditson Co., 1911.

Bose, Fritz, *Musikalische Völkerkunde.* Freiburg i/Br., 1953.

Botsford, Florence, *Botsford Collection of Folk Songs.* New York: G. Schirmer, 1930. 3 Vols.

Colliers Encyclopedia. New York, 1962. Various articles on folksongs, Vols. 10, 17.

Cooperative Recreation Service. Delaware, Ohio. A series of folksong booklets of worldwide coverage.

Deutsch, Leonhard, *A Treasury of the World's Finest Folk Songs.* New York, 1942.

Encyclopédie de la Musique et Dictionnaire du Conservatoire, Paris, 1920. Vols. 4, 5.

Ethnic Folkways Library, New York. Descriptive notes with the recordings; comments by leading specialists in the various fields of primitive and folk music; most invaluable for student and scholar.

Ethnomusicology. Journal of the American Ethnomusicological Society. Wesleyan University Press, Middletown, Conn.

Funk & Wagnalls Dictionary of Folklore, Mythology and Legend. Maria Leach, ed., New York, 1950. 2 Vols.

Grove's Dictionary of Music and Musicians. Eric Blom, ed., New York, 1954. "Folk Music," Vol. 3, 10; country and subject headings in other volumes. Excellent bibliographies.

Herzog, George, "General Characteristics of Primitive Music." *Bull. Amer. Musicol. Soc.* 7(1943), 23–26.

———, "Song. Folk Song and the Music of Folk Song." *Funk & Wagnalls Dictionary of Folklore.* Vol. 2, pp. 1032–1050.

International Cyclopedia of Music and Musicians. Oscar Thompson, ed., 6th rev. edition by Nicolas Slonimsky. New York, 1952. "Folk Music," by various authors, Vol. 1, pp. 559–606.

Journal of the International Folk Music Council. London, 1949—.

Kunst, Jaap, *Ethnomusicology.* The Hague, 1959; *Supplement,* 1960. Most useful bibliography.

Martinengo-Cesaresco, E. *Essays in the Study of Folk Songs.* London, 1936.

Merriam, Alan P., *The Anthropology of Music.* Evanston, Ill., 1964.

Möller, Heinrich, *Das Lied der Völker.* Mainz: B. Schott's Sohne. 13 Vols.

Musical Quarterly. New York, 1915—.

Die Musik in Geschichte und Gegenwart. Friedrich Blume, ed. Articles on the folk music of various countries, and subject entries; good bibliographies.

Nettl, Bruno, *Music in Primitive Culture.* Cambridge, Mass., 1959.

———, *Theory and Method in Ethnomusicology.* New York, 1964.

Reimann, Heinrich, *Internationales Volksliederbuch.* Berlin, 1893. 3 Vols.

Sachs, Curt, *World History of the Dance.* New York, 1937.

———, *The History of Musical Instruments.* New York, 1940.

———, *The Rise of Music in the Ancient World.* N.Y., 1943.

———, *The Wellsprings of Music.* The Hague, 1962.

———, *Real-Lexicon der Musikinstrumente.* N. Y., 1964.

North America

CANADA and GREENLAND

Barbeau, Marius; Lismer, Arthur; and Bourinot, Arthur, *Come A' Singing!.* Ottawa, 1947.

———, and Sapir, Edward. *Folksongs of French Canada.* New Haven, Conn., 1925.

Creighton, Helen, *Songs and Ballads from Nova Scotia.* Toronto, 1933.

Fowke, E. W. and Johnston R., *Folk Songs of Canada.* Waterloo, Ont., 1954.

Gagnon, Ernest, *Chansons Populaires du Canada.* Montreal, 1941.

Greenleaf, Elisabeth B., *Ballads and Sea Songs of Newfoundland.* Cambridge, Mass., 1933.

Thuren, Hjalmar, *La Musique chez les Eskimo.* Paris, 1912.

UNITED STATES

Arnold, Byron, *Folksongs of Alabama.* University, Ala., 1950.

Botkin, B. A., *A Treasury of American Folklore.* New York, 1944.

Bronson, Bertrand H., *The Traditional Tunes of the Child Ballads.* Princeton, N.J., Vol. 1, 1959; Vol. 2, 1962. *See* his various articles explaining his theories and methodology.

Frank C. Brown Collection of North Carolina Folklore. Vols. 2 and 3. Durham, N.C., 1952, 1962.

Chase, Gilbert, *America's Music.* New York, 1955.

Child, Francis James, *The English and Scottish Popular Ballads.* Boston, 1882–94. 5 vols.

Coffin, Tristram P., *The British Traditional Ballad in North America.* Philadelphia, 1950.

Curtis, Natalie, *The Indians' Book.* New York, 1907.

Densmore, Frances, *Chippewa Music. II.* Bureau Amer. Ethnol. Bull. 53. Washington, D.C., 1913.

———, *Pawnee Music.* Bureau Amer. Ethnol. Bull. 93. Washington, D.C., 1929. *See* her other Indian studies.

Dobie, J. Frank, *Texas and Southwestern Lore.* Publ. Texas Folklore Soc. No. 6. Austin, Tex., 1927.

Eddy, Mary O., *Ballads and Songs from Ohio.* New York, 1939.

Flanders, Helen H., *Ballad Migrants in New England.* New York, 1953. 3 vols.

Haywood, Charles, *A Bibliography of North American Folklore and Folksong.* New York, 1961. 2 vols. Vol. 1: *The American People North of Mexico, Including Canada.* Vol. 2: *The American Indian, Including the Eskimo.*

Jackson, George P., *White Spirituals in the Southern Uplands.* Chapel Hill, North Carolina, 1933.

Johnson, James W. and Rosamund, *The Book of Negro Spirituals.* New York, 1926. 2 vols.

Journal of American Folklore, Philadelphia, Pa., 1888—

Larkin, Margaret, *Singing Cowboy.* New York, 1931.

Laws, G. Malcolm, Jr., *Native American Balladry.* Philadelphia, 1950.

Lomax, Alan, *The Folk Songs of North America.* New York, 1960.

Lomax, John, and Lomax, Alan, *Cowboy Songs.* Rev. & enl'g'd. ed. New York, 1938. *See* their other publications.

Monroe, Mina, *Bayou Ballads.* New York, 1921.

Nettl, Bruno, *An Introduction to Folk Music in the United States.* Detroit, 1962.

————, *North American Indian Musical Styles.* (Memoirs Amer. Folklore Soc. No. 45), Philadelphia, 1954.

Oak Publications, New York.

Publications of the Texas Folklore Society. Austin, Tex.

Randolph, Vance, *Ozark Folksongs.* Columbia, Mo., 1948. 4 Vols.

Sharp, Cecil, and Campbell, Olive Dame, *English Folk Songs from the Southern Appalachians.* New ed., New York, 1960.

Sing Out! New York.

White, Newman I., *American Negro Folk-Songs.* Cambridge, Mass., 1928.

Latin America

THE CARIBBEAN

Attaway, William, *Calypso Song Book.* New York, 1952.

Beckwith, Martha W., *Jamaica Folklore.* (Memoir Amer. Folklore Soc. No. 31). New York, 1928.

Blanco-Barzaga, Margarita, *La Musica de Haiti.* Habana, 1953.

Carpentier, Alejo, *La Musica en Cuba.* Mexico, D. F., 1946.

Chase, Gilbert, *Guide to the Music of Latin America.* New ed. Washington, D.C., 1962.

Ceron, Jose D., *Canciones Dominicanas Antiguas.* Ciudad Trujillo, 1947.

Coopersmith, J. M., *Music and Musicians in the Dominican Republic.* Pan American Union Publ. Washington, D.C., 1949.

Courlander, Harold, *Haiti Singing.* Chapel Hill, North Carolina, 1939.

Crowley, Daniel J., "Toward a Definition of 'Calypso.'" *Ethnomusicology.* 3(May 1959), (Sept. 1959).

Deliz, Monserate, *Renadió. Del Cantar Folklorico de Puerto Rico.* Madrid, 1952.

Edwards, Charles L., *Bahama Songs and Stories.* (Memoir of Amer. Folklore Soc. No. 3). New York, 1895.

Espinet, Charles S., and Pitts, Harry, *Land of the Calypso: the Origin and Development of Trinidad Folk Song.* Port of Spain, 1944.

Grenet, Emilio, *Popular Cuban Music.* Havana, 1939.

Hague, Eleanor, *Spanish American Folk Songs.* (Memoir Amer. Folklore Soc. No. 10). New York, 1917.

Herskovits, Melville J. and Frances, *Trinidad Village.* New York, 1947.

Morse, Jim, *Folk Songs of the Caribbean.* New York, 1958.

Ortíz, Fernando, *La Africanía de la Música Folklórica de Cuba.* Habana, 1950.

Parsons, Elsie Clews, *Folklore of the Antilles, French and English.* (Memoir Amer. Folklore Soc. No. 26, Part I). New York, 1933.

Slonimsky, Nicholas, *Music of Latin America.* New York, 1933.

Waterman, Richard A., *African Patterns in Trinidad Negro Music.* Unpubl. Ph.D. Thesis. Northwestern Univ., Evanston, Ill.

SOUTH AMERICA, MEXICO, and CENTRAL AMERICA

Alvarenga, Oneyda, *Música Popular Brasileira.* Porte Allegre, 1950.

Andrade, Mario de, *Popular Music and Dance in Brazil.* Rio de Janeiro, 1943.

Aretz-Thiele, Isabel, *Música Tradicional Argentina.* Buenos Aires, 1946.

Ayestarán, Lauro, *La musica en el Uruguay.* Montevideo, 1955.

Boletín Latino-Americano de Música. Curt Lange, ed., Montevideo.

Cancionero Popular Americano. Pan Amer. Union. Washington, D.C., 1950.

Chase, Gilbert, *A Guide to the Music of Latin America.* Pan Amer. Union. Washington, D.C., 1962.

Delgadillo, Luis A., "La Música Indigena de Nicaragua." *Revista de Estudios Musicales.* 1, No. 3(1950).

Garay, Narciso, *Tradiciones y Cantares de Panama.* Panama, 1930.

Handbook of the South American Indians. Julian H. Steward, ed. (Bureau Amer. Ethnol. Bull. 143). Washington, D.C., 1948. 6 Vols.

Harcourt, Raoul and Marguerite d', *La Musique des Incas et ses Survivances.* Paris, 1925. 2 Vols.

Herskovits, Melville and Frances, *Suriname Folk-Lore.* New York, 1936.

Houston-Peret, Elsie, *Chants Populaires du Brésil.* Paris, 1930.

Labastille, Irma, *Canciones Tipicas.* New York, 1941.

————, *Recuerdo Latino-Americano.* New York, 1943.

Mayer-Serra, Otto, *Música y Músicos de Latino-America.* Mexico, D.F., 1947. 2 Vols.

Mendoza, Vicente T., *El Romance Español y el Corrido Mexicano.* Mexico, D.F., 1939.

————, *Canciones Mexicanas.* New York, 1948.

Sargent, Winthrop, "Types of Quechua Melody." *Mus. Quart.* 20(1934).

Slonimsky, Nicolas, *Music of Latin America.* New York, 1945.

Stevenson, Robert, *Music in Mexico.* New York, 1952.

————, *The Music of Peru.* Washington, D.C., 1960.

Toor, Frances, *A Treasury of Mexican Folkways.* New York, 1956.

Vega, Carlos, *Danzas y Canciones Argentinas.* Buenos Aires, 1936.

————, *Panorama de la Música Popular Argentina.* Buenos Aires, 1944.

Europe

GENERAL COLLECTIONS

Gregor, Josef; Klausmeier, Friedrich; and Kraus, Egon, *Europäische Lieder in den Ursprachen.* Berlin, 1956. 2 Vols.

Handbooks of European National Dances. Alford, Violet, ed. New York. Chanticleer Press.

Karpeles, Maud, *Folk Songs of Europe.* London, 1956.

Lawson, J., *European Folk Dances, Its national and Musical Characteristics.* London, 1955.

Wiora, W., *Europäischer Volksgesang.* (Das Musikwerk). Koeln, n.d. An excellent comparative study; very good bibliography.

UNITED KINGDOM—ENGLAND, SCOTLAND, WALES

Britten, Benjamin, *Folk Songs of the British Isles.* London, 1943.

Child, Francis James, *The English and Scottish Popular Ballads.* Boston, 1882–1894. 5 Vols.

Duncan, Edmonstoune, *Minstrelsy of England.* London, 1905.

Graham, George Farquar, *The Songs of Scotland.* London, n.d. 3 Vols.

Graves, Alfred P., *The Celtic Song Book.* London, 1928.

Journal of the English Folk Song and Dance Society. London, 1932– (see the earlier publications).

Journal of the Welsh Folk Song Society. Wrexham and Llangollen, 1909–

Sharp, Cecil, *English Folk Songs.* Centenary Edition. London, 1959. 2 Vols.

————, *English Folk Songs, Some Conclusions.* London, 1907.

Shaw, Margaret Fay, *Folksongs and Folklore of South Uist.* London, 1955.

Williams, W. S. Gwynn, *Old Welsh Folk Songs.* London, 1927.

————, *Welsh National Music and Dance.* London, 1952.

IRELAND

Colum, Padraic, *A Treasury of Irish Folklore.* New York, 1954.

Hughes, Herbert, *Irish Country Songs.* London, 1936. 3 Vols.

Journal of the Irish Folk Song Society, London, 1904—

Joyce, P. W., *Old Irish Folk Music and Songs.* London, 1909.

Moffat, Alfred, *The Minstrelsy of Ireland.* London, 1897.

O'Sullivan, Donal, *Songs of the Irish.* Dublin, 1960.

NETHERLANDS

Bos, Conraad V., *Dutch Folk Songs*. New York, 1930.

Kunst, Jaap, *Het levende Lied Nederland*. Amsterdam, 1948.

Lange, Daniel de, *Nederlandsch Volksliederenboek*. Amsterdam, 1913. 3 Vols.

BELGIUM

Closson, Ernest, *Volksliedern van de Belgische Provincien*. Brussels, 1912.

————, *Notes sur la chanson populaire en Belgique*. Brussels, 1931.

GERMANY

Erk, Ludwig, and Böhme, Franz M., *Deutscher Liederhort*. Leipzig, 1893–94. 3 Vols.

Friedlaender, Max, *Volkslieder für die Jugend*. Leipzig, 1930. 3 Vols.

Kneip, Gustav, *Deutschland im Volkslied*. Frankfurt, 1959.

Meier, John, *Deutsche Volkslieder. Balladen*. Berlin, 1935, 1939, 1954, 1957. 4 Vols. This important series has been continued by Erich Seemann, in Freiburg im Breisgau.

Wiora, Walter, *Das echte Volkslied*. Heidelberg, 1950.

AUSTRIA

Graf, Walter, *Oesterreichs Beitrag zur Musikethnologie*. Wien, 1958.

Kotek, Georg, and Zoder, Raimund, *Ein Oesterreichisches Volksliederbuch*. Wien, 1950. 3 Vols.

Kraus, Friedrich S., *Oesterreichische Volkslieder*. Leipzig, 1906.

Zoder, Raimund, *Volkslied, Volkstanz, Volksbrauch in Oesterreich*. Wien, 1950. The Bundesverlag has published an excellent series of regional folksong collections.

FRANCE

André, Alexandre, *Chansons populaires d'Alsace*. Nancy-Paris, 1920

Barbier, Pierre, and Vernillat, France, *Histoire de France par les Chansons*. Paris, 1956. 8 Vols.

Canteloube, Joseph, *Anthologie des Chants populaires Français*. Paris, 1951. 19 Vols.

Tiersot, Julien, *Mélodies populaires des Provinces de France*. Paris, 1887. 4 Vols.

SWITZERLAND

Duesel Jakob, "Der Jodel und das Jodellied in der Schweitz." *Heimatsleben* 28, No. 2(1955).

Keller, Paul, *Unsere Schweitzerlieder*. Lausanne-Vevey, 1931.

ITALY

Cocchiara, Giuseppe, *L'Anima del Popolo Italiano nei suoi Canti*. Milano, 1929.

Croze, Austin de, *La Chanson populaire de L'Isle de Corse*. Paris, 1911.

Elia, Piero, *La Canzona Napolitana*. Roma, 1950.

Marzo, Eduardo, *Songs of Italy*. New York, 1904.

Nataletti, G., and Petrassi, G., *Canti della Campagna Romana*. Milano, 1930.

SPAIN

Anuario Musical (Barcelona), Journal, No. 1, 1946—

Falla, Manuel de, *El Canto jondo: canto primitivo Andaluz*. Granada, 1922.

Hernandez, Antonio Martinez, *Antología musical de Cantos Populares Españolas y Portugueses*. Barcelona, 1930.

Pedrell, Felipe, *Cancionero Musical Popular Español*. Barcelona, n.d.

Pol, A., *Collecíon de Canciones Populares Mallorquinas*. Barcelona, 1926.

Schindler, Kurt, *Folk Music and Poetry of Spain and Portugal*. New York, 1941.

Schneider, Marius, *Cancionero de la Provincia de Madrid*. Barcelona, 1951–52. 2 Vols.

PORTUGAL

Gallop, Rodney, "The Folk Music of Portugal." *Music & Letters* 14(1933).

Lacerda, Francisco de, *Cancionero Musical Portugues*. Lisbon, 1935.

NORWAY

Gaukstad, Ostein, *Norsk Folkemusik*. (A Bibliography), Oslo, 1951.

Lund, Engel, *Engel Lund's Book of Folksongs*. London, 1936.

Onkel, Georg, *Sanglekene Vare*. Trondheim, 1946.

DENMARK

Berggren, A. P., *Danske Folkesange og Melodier*. Copenhagen, 1869.

Thuren, Hjalmar, *Folkesangen Foeroerne*. Copenhagen, 1951.

ICELAND

Hammerich, Angul, "Studien über islandische Musik." *Sammelb. Inter. Musik Gesellschaft* 1(1899–1900), 341–371.

Selden, Margery Stomme, "The Music of Old Iceland." *Amer. Scandinavian Review* 45(1957)

FINLAND

Krohn, Ilmari, "Die finnische Volksmusik." *Bericht a.d. Institut fur Finnlandkunde*, (Greifswald), 1935.

Launis, Arman, *Estnisch-finnische Runnemelodien*. Helsinki, 1913.

Väisänen, A. O., "Finnische Volksmusik." *Der Norden* 20 (1943).

THE SOVIET UNION

Balakirev, Mily, *Sbornik Russkikh Narodnikh Pesen'*, Leipzig, 1895.

Liadov, Anatol, *Pyat' Russkikh Pesen'*. Moscow, n.d.

Lobachov, G., *Melodi Narodov*. Moscow, 1928.

Rimski-Korsakov, Nicolai, *100 Chants Nationaux Russes*. Paris, 1887.

Swan, Alfred J., "The Nature of the Russian Folk-Song." *Mus. Quart.* 29 (October 1943).

201 Ukrainian Folk Songs. New York. 1931.

Zdanovich, I. K., *Narodni Pesn'i zapadnoi Byelorussii*. Moscow, 1931.

ARMENIA (U.S.S.R.)

Komitas, Wardapet, *Armenische Dorflieder*. Leipzig, 1913. 2 Vols.

————, *Armenian Lyre*. Paris, n.d.

Poladian, Sirvart, *Armenian Folk Songs*. Berkeley. Los Angeles, 1942.

POLAND

Harasowski, Adam, *Zlota Ksiega Piésni Polskiej*. (The Golden Book of Polish Songs). London, 1955.

Polish Cultural Institute, *Folk Songs of Poland*. London, 1954.

Sobieski, Marian, *Wybor Polskich Piesni Ludowych*. Krakow, 1955. 2 Vols.

LATVIA–LITHUANIA–ESTONIA

Balys, Jonas, Articles in the *Funk & Wagnalls Dictionary of Folklore . . .*

Bielenstein, J., *Lettische Volkslieder*. Riga, 1918.

Graf, Walter, *Das esthnische Volkslied*. Vienna, 1933.

Katzenellenbogen, U., *Anthology of Lithuanian and Latvian Folksongs*. Chicago, 1935.

Paterson, A., *Old Lithuanian Songs*. Kaunas, 1939.

CZECHOSLOVAKIA

Dolauská, Vera, *Volkslieder aus der Tschechoslowakei*. Prague, 1955.

Polácek, Jan, *Slovácke Pesnicky*. Prague, 1952. 2 Vols.

Schimmerling, H. A., *Memories of Czechosovakia*. New York, 1945.

Seidel, J., *Zpevy Domova*. Prague, 1943.

HUNGARY

Bartók, Béla. *Hungarian Folk Music*. London, 1931.

————, *Fifteen Hungarian Peasant Songs*. New York, 1939.

Kodály, Zoltán, *The Music of Hungary*. New York, 1960.

YUGOSLAVIA

Closson, Ernest, *Chansons et Danses Serbes*. Zurich, 1917.

Goetz, L. K., *Volkslied und Volksleben der Kroaten ind Serben*. Heidelberg, 1937. 2 Vols.

Gojkovic, Andrijana, "The Main Characteristics of Folk Music in Jugoslavia." *The Folklorist* 4, Nos. 3, 4 (1957)

Kuba, Ludvík, *Slovantsvo ve svych zpevech*. (The Slavs and their Songs). Prague, 1884–1929. 16 Vols.

Zganec, Vinko, "The Tonal and Modal Structure of Yugoslav Folk Music." *Jour. Inter. Folk Music Council* 10(1958).

BULGARIA

Christov, Dobri, *66 Chants populaires des Bulgares macedoniens.* Sofia, 1931.

Djoudjeff, Stoyan, *Melodies Bulgares de l'Albanie du sud.* Beograd, 1936.

Kremenliev, Boris A., *Bulgarian—Macedonian Folk Music.* Los Angeles: University of Calif., 1952.

RUMANIA

Alexandru, Tiberiu, *Muzika populara.* Bucarest, 1942.

Bartók, Béla, *Volksmusik der Rumänen von Maramures.* Munchen, 1923.

Ziehm, Elsa, and Bose, Fritz, *Rumänische Volksmusik.* Berlin, 1939.

ALBANIA

Sokoli, Ramadan, *Les Danses populaires et les Instruments musiceaux Albanais.* Tirana, 1958.

GREECE (and Cyprus)

Baud-Bovy, Samuel, *Etudes sur la Chanson Clèftique.* Athens, 1958.

Bourgault-Ducoudray, L. A., *Mélodies populaires de Grece et D'Orient.* Paris, 1885.

Gallop, Rodney, "Folksongs of Modern Greece." *Mus. Quart.* 21(1935).

Kallinicos, Th., *Cyprus Folk Songs.* Nicosia, 1951.

Pachtikos, George, *260 Greek Folk Songs.* Athens, 1905.

Asia

General Studies and Collections

Ancient and Oriental Music. Wellesz, Egon, ed. Vol 1. *The New Oxford History of Music.* London, 1957.

Encyclopédie de la Musique et Dictionnaire du Conservatoire. A. Lavignac, ed. Vol. 5

Farmer, Henry George, *Oriental Studies, Mainly Musical.* London, 1953.

———, *Studies in Oriental Musical Instruments.* Glasgow, 1939.

Kunst, Jaap, *Ethnomusicology.* The Hague, 1959. *Supplement,* 1960.

Lichtenwager, William; Waterman, Richard A., and others, "Bibliography of Asiatic Musics." *Notes* 5–8 (1947–51).

Reinhard, Kurt, *Die Musik exotischer Völker.* Berlin, 1951.

THE MIDDLE EAST

Adville, V., *La Musique chez les Persanes.* Paris, 1885.

D'Erlanger, Baron Rodolphe, *La musique Arabe.* Paris, 1930–49. 5 Vols.

Enright, D. J., "Arab Music." *Music & Letters* 33 (1952).

Farmer, Henry George, *A History of Arabian Music.* London, 1929.

Foley, Rolla, *Song of the Arab.* New York, 1953.

Idelsohn, A. Z., "Die Maquamen der arabischen Musik." *Sammelb. Inter. Musikgesell.* 15(1913).

Salvador-Daniel, Francesco, *The Music and Musical Instruments of the Arab.* Ed. by H. G. Farmer. London, 1915.

———, *La musique Arabe.* Algiers, 1863.

ISRAEL (and the Yiddish Folksong)

Gerson-Kiwi, Edith, "Musical Characteristics of the East European Jewish Folk Song." *Mus. Quart.* 18(1932).

Idelsohn, A. Z., *Phonographierte Gesänge und Aussprachproben des hebraischen, jemenischen, persischen und syrischen Juden.* Wien, 1917.

———, *Jewish Music and Its Historical Development.* New York, 1929.

Kipnis, M., *80 Folkslider.* Warsaw, n.d. 2 Vols.

Rubin, Ruth, *A Treasury of Jewish Folksongs.* New York, 1950.

———, *Voices of the People.* New York, 1964.

Vinaver, Chemjo, *Anthology of Jewish Music.* New York, 1955.

Werner, Eric, *Geschichte der jüdischen Volksmusic.* Breslau, 1938.

LEBANON

Stephan, S. H., "The Smell of Lebanon: 24 Syrian Folk Songs." *Jour. Palestine Oriental Soc.* 1921.

TURKEY

Belayev, Viktor, "Turkish Music." *Mus. Quart.* 19(1933).

Picken, Laurence, "Instrumental Polyphonic Folk Music in Asia Minor." *Proc. Royal Musical Assoc.* 80 (1954).

Reinhard, Kurt, "Types of Turkmenian Songs in Turkey." *Jour. Inter. Folk Music Council* 9 (1957).

Saygun, Ahmed A., "Des danses d'Anatolis et de leur caratcere rituel." *Jour. Inter. Folk Music Council* 2(1950).

INDIA

Bake, Arnold A., "Indian Folk Music." *Proc. Musical Assoc.* 63(1936–37).

———, *Indian Music.* London, 1932.

Clements, E., *Introduction to the Study of Indian Music.* London, 1913.

Coomaraswamy, Ananda K., *Thirty Songs of Panjab and Kashmir.* London, 1913.

Daniélou, Alain., *Northern Indian Music.* London, Calcutta, 1950, 1953. 2 Vols.

Fox Strangways, A. H., *The Music of Hindostan.* Oxford, 1914.

Gesvami, O., *The Story of Indian Music.* Bombay, 1958.

Kaufmann, Walter, "The Folksongs of Nepal." *Ethnomusicology* 6, No. 2 (May 1962).

Kuppuswami, S. R., *Short Survey into the Music of North and South India.* Coimbatore, 1948.

Popley, Herbert, *The Music of India.* Calcutta, 1921.

PAKISTAN

Jasim, Uddin, "Folk Music of East Pakistan." *Jour. Inter. Folk Music Council* 3(1951).

Mansoor, Uddin M., *Folksongs. Their Uses in Pakistan.* Dacca, 1952.

CEYLON

Sena, Devar Surya, "Folk Songs of Ceylon." *Jour. Inter. Folk Music Council* 6(1952).

Wertheimer, Max, "Music der Wedda." *Sammelb. Inter. Music. Gesell.* 11 (1909–10).

SOUTHEAST ASIA

BURMA, CAMBODIA, LAOS, THAILAND, AND VIETNAM

Daniélou, Alain, *La Musique du Cambodge et du Laos.* (Publ. Institut Français d'Indologie, No. 9), Pondichery, 1957.

Draws-Tychsen, Hellmut, *Siamsänge.* Leyden, 1955.

Dumoutier, G., *Les Chants et les Traditions populaires des Annamites.* Paris, 1890.

Phillipines Unesco National Commission, "Music in Southeast Asia." *Proc. First Regional Music Conf. Southeast Asia, Manila, 1955.* Manila, 1956.

Pringsheim, Klaus, "Music of Thailand." *Contemporary Japan* 13(1944).

Stumpf, Carl, "Tonsystem und Musik der Siamesen." *Abhandlungen zur Vergl. Musikwissenschaft* (1885–1908). München, 1922.

Zin, U Than, "The Music in Burma." *The Guardian* 3, No. 14 (1956).

CHINA

Aalst, J. A. van, *Chinese Music.* Shanghai, 1884.

Chen, C. H., and Chen, S. H., *The Flower Drum and Other Chinese Songs.* New York, 1943.

Granet, Marcel, *Festivals and Songs of Ancient China.* New York, 1932.

Lachmann, Robert, *Music des Orients.* Breslau, 1929.

Laloy, Louis, *La Musique Chinoise.* Paris, n.d.

Reinhard, Kurt, *Chinesische Musik.* Eisenach & Kassel, 1956.

MONGOLIA

Nirgidma de Torhout, Princesse, *Dix-huit Chants et Poèmes Mongols.* Paris, 1937.

Oost, P. J. van, "Réceuil de chansons Mongols." *Anthropos* 3(1908).
Takeda, Chuichivo, "Songs of the Mongols, Notations, and Explanations." *Jour. Soc. for Research in Asiatic Music* 10/11(1952).

TIBET

Francke, A. H., La Musique au Thibet. In: Lavignac, *Histoire de la Musique*, Vol 5. Paris, 1922.

KOREA

Keh, Chung S., *Die Koreanische Musik*. Strassburg, 1934.
Kimm, Joh Mary C., *Folk Songs of Korea*. Dubuque, Iowa. 1950.

Lee, Kang Nyum, *Korean Folk Songs*. Seoul, 1957.

JAPAN

Embree, John, *The Japanese Peasant Songs*. (Memoirs Amer. Folklore Soc. No. 38). Philadelphia, 1943.
Hattori, Ryutaro, *Thirty-One Japanese Folk Songs*. Tokyo, 1950.
Malm, William, *Japanese Music and Musical Instruments*. Rutland, Vt., 1959.
Piggot, Francis T., *The Music and Musical Instruments of Japan*. London, 1909.
Uchida, Rurko, "Japanische Volkslieder." *Jour. Inter. Folk Music Council* 13(1961).

Africa

AFRICA—North of the Sahara

Amrouche, J., *Chants berbères de Kabylie*. Paris, 1946.
Berner, Alfred, *Studien zur arabischen Musik* . . . Leipzig. 1937(Egypt).
Chottin, Aléxis, "Airs populaires Marocains." *Le Ménestrel* 94(1932).
———, "Chants et danses berbères au Maroc." *Le Ménestrel* 95 (1933).
———, *Corpus de Musique Marocains*. Paris, 1931. 2 Vols.
D'Erlanger, Baron Rodolphe, *Mélodies Tunisiennes*. Paris, 1937.
Hemsi, A., *La Musique orientale en Egypte*. Alexandria, 1930.
Rasheed, Baheega Sidky, *Egyptian Folk Songs*. Cairo, 1958.
Rouanet, Jules, "La Chanson populaire en Algère." *Revue Musicale* 5 (1905).

AFRICA—South of the Sahara

African Music, Journal of the African Music Society, Johannesburg, I, 1954.
Arnoux, P. Aléxandre, "La Culte de la Société secrète des Imandwa au Ruanda." *Anthropos* 8 (1913).
Barat-Pepper, Elaine, *Choeurs de l'Afrique équatoriale*. Paris, 1950.
Basile, Frère, *Rythmes des Tambours. La Musique chez les Noirs d'Afrique.* Montréal, Canada, 1951.
Bowra, C. M., *Primitive Song*. London, 1962.
Brandel, Rose, *The Music of Central Africa*. The Hague, 1961.
Carrington, J. F., *Talking Drums of Africa*. London, 1949.
Curtis, Natalie, *Songs and Tales from the Dark Continent*. New York, 1920.
Heinitz, Wilhelm, *Struktur Probleme in primitive musik*. Hamburg, 1931.
Herscher-Clement, J., "Chants d'Abyssine." *Zeit. für Vergl. Musik*. 2, Nos. 2–3 (1934).
Hornbostel, Erich M. von, *African Negro Music*. Inter. Institute African Languages and Cultures, Memo. 4, 1928.

Hullebroeck, Emiel, *Skoon Suid Afrika*. Zuid-Afrikaansche Liedern. Antwerpen, 1940.
John, J. T., "Village Music of Sierra Leone." *West African Review* 23 (1952).
Jones, Arthur M., *Studies in African Music*. London, 1959. 2 Vols.
Junod, Henri A., *Moeurs et coutumes des Bantous*. Paris, 1936. 2 Vols.
Kirby, Percival R., "A Study of Bushmen Music." *Bantu Studies* 10, No. 2 (1936).
Koole, Arend, "Report on an Inquiry into the Music and Instruments of the Basutos in Basutoland." *Kongress Bericht Inter. Gesell. für Musikwissen.* (1952), 263–270.
Kyagambiddwa, John, *African Music from the Source of the Nile*. New York, 1955.
Merriam, Alan P., "The African Idiom in Music." *Jour. Amer. Folklore* 75 (1962), 120–130.
———, "An Annotated Bibliography of African-Derived Music Since 1936." *Africa* 21 (1951). Extension of Varley's bibl.
Molitor, P. H., "La Musique chez les Nègres du Tanganyika." *Anthropos* 8 (1913).
Phillips, Ekundayo, *Yoruba Music*. Johannesburg, 1953.
Schebesta, Paul, *Die Bambuti-Pygmäen von Ituri*. Brussels, 1941, 1948, 1950. 3 Vols.
Stayt, Hugh A., *The Bavenda*. London, 1931.
Tracey, Hugh, "Short Survey of Southern African Folk Music for the International Catalogue of Folk Music Records." *African Music Soc. Newsletter* 1, No. 6 (1953).
Tucker, A. N., *Tribal Music and Dancing in the Southern Sudan*. London, 1933.
Varley, D. H., *African Native Music: An Annotated Bibliography*. London, 1936.
Wachsmann, Klaus P., *Folk Musicians in Uganda*. Kampala, 1956.

Oceania-Australia

INDONESIA–POLYNESIA–MELANESIA–MICRONESIA

Anderson, Johannes C., *Maori Music, With its Polynesian Background*. New Plymouth, 1934.
Baldwin, B., "Kodaguwai. Songs of the Trobriand Sunset Isles." *Oceania* 20, No. 4 (June 1950).
Bukofzer, Manfred, "The Evolution of Javanese Tonesystems." *Inter. Congress of Musicol.* (New York), 1944.
Burrows, Edwin Grant, *Native Music of the Taumotus*. (Bernice P. Bishop Museum Bull. 109). Honolulu, 1933.
———, "Polynesian Music and Dancing." *Jour. Polynesian Soc.* 49 (1940).
Caughie, Catherine, "The Scales of some Central Australian Songs." *Jour. Inter. Folk Music Council* 10(1958).
Edwards, R. G., *The Overlander Songbook*. Ferntree Gully, Victoria, 1956.
Elkin, A. P., and Jones, Trevor A., *Arnhemland Music*. (Oceania Monograph No. 9) Sydney, 1957.

Grattan, C. Hartley, "The Australian Bushsongs." *Mus. Quart.* 15(1929).
Hagen, Karl, *Ueber die Musik einiger Naturvölker (Australier, Melanesier, Polynesier)*. Hamburg, 1892.
Handy, E. S. Craighill, and Winnie, J. L., *Music in the Marquesas Islands*. (Berenice P. Bishop Museum Bull. 17) Honolulu, 1925.
Herzog, George, "Die Musik der Karolinen Inseln." In: *Ergebnisse der Südsee-Expedition 1908–10*. Pt. IIB, Vol. 9. Hamburg, 1936.
Hood, Mantle, *The Nuclear Theme as a Determinant Patet in Javanese Music*. Groningen, 1954.
Hornbostel, Erich M. von, "Die Musik auf den nordwestlichen Salomo-Inseln." In: R. Thurnwald, *Forschungen auf den Salomo-Inseln und Bismarck-Archipel*. Vol. II. 1912.
Hubner, Herbert, *Die Musik im Bismarck-Archipel*. Berlin, 1938.
Kelly, John M., Jr., *Folk Songs Hawaii Sings*. Rutland, Vt., 1962.
Kunst, Jaap, *The Cultural Background of Indonesian Music*. Amsterdam, 1949.

———, *Music in Java*. The Hague, 1949. 2 Vols.

———, *A Study of Papua Music*. Bandung, 1930.

———, *De Toonkunst van Bali*. Weltevreden, 1925.

Maceda, José, "Chants from Sagada Mountain Province." *Ethnomusicol.* 2 (1958).

Myers, Charles S., "A Study of Sarawak Music." *Sammelb. Inter. Musikgesell.* 15(1913–14).

Oceania, Journal, I, 1932—. University of Sydney, N. S. Wales, Australia.

Oliver, Douglas L., *A Solomon Island Society*. Kinship and Leadership Among the Siuai of Bougainville. Cambridge, Mass., 1955.

Rason, Marie-Robert, "Etude sur la musique Malgache." *La Revue de Madagascar* I (1933), 41–91.

Reysio-Cruz, Emilia S., *Filipino Folk Songs*. Manila, 1950.

Roberts, Helen H., *Ancient Hawaiian Music*. (Berenice P. Bishop Mus. Bull. 29). Honolulu, 1925.

Sachs, Curt, *Les instruments de musique de Madagascar*. Paris, 1938.

Schelling, O., "Musik und Tanz der Papuas." *Globus* 56(1889).

Smith, Barbara B., "Folk Music in Hawaii." *Jour. Inter. Folk Music Council* 11 (1959), 50–55.

Strehlow, T. G. H., "Australian Aboriginal Music." *Jour. Inter. Folk Music Council* 7(1955).

Williams, F. E., *Papuans of the Trans-Fly*. Oxford, 1936.

Williamson, Robert W., *The Mafulu. Mountain People of British New Guinea*. London, 1912.

Recordings

We can only suggest a few of the major folksong recording companies and collections. No attempt is made to list the numerous phonographic archives located in various cities and ethnomusicological centers of the world. (For a detailed survey, see: Jaap Kunst, *Ethnomusicology*, 3rd Edition. The Hague, 1959. pp. 16–37; *Supplement*, 1960. pp. 5–7). Anyone desiring a particular recording can easily consult the current issue of the *Schwann Catalogue* (Boston, Mass.), *Gramophone* (Middlesex, England), *The American Record Guide* (P.O. 319, New York), *The World Encyclopedia of Recorded Music* by Francis P. Clough and G. J. Cuming (London, 1952; 2nd *Supplement*, 1953; 3rd *Supplement*, 1955), and the catalogues issued by the different recording companies, such as *Ethnic Folkways, Angel, Riverside, Decca*, etc.

Selected List

Boîte à Musique (Paris). Series of Central African music.

Catalogue of Recorded Classical and Traditional Indian Music. With an introduction on Indian musical theory and insurtments by Daniel Daniélou. Paris: Unesco, 1950.

Chant du Monde (Paris). Mongolia, Kazaks, Vietnam.

Collection Phonotèque Nationale (Paris). Archives of recorded music, Ser.C, Vol. I. Paris: Unesco, 1952.

Columbia World Library of Folk and Primitive Music. Alan Lomax, ed. Excellent series.

Contrepoint (Paris). West Africa, Borneo, Bali, Brazil, Iran.

English Decca. East Africa, Congo, Basutoland.

Ethnic Folkways Library (New York). Most extensive world coverage of folk and primitive music.

International Catalogue of Recorded Music. Archives of recorded music, Ser. C, Vol. 4. Edited by Norman Fraser. London, 1954. Africa, America (North, South, and Caribbean), Asia, Europe and Oceania.

International Library of African Music. Hugh Tracey, director. Johannesburg, South Africa. Excellent.

Library of Congress, Folklore Section. Washington, D.C. Excellent series covering every phase of American (from the Arctic through South America) folk-life.

Folksongs on Records by Ben G. Lumpkin. Boulder, Colorado. 1950.

Musée de l'Homme. (Paris). Wide coverage—Africa, Middle East, Asia, India, and Oceania.

Pacific Islands Music Recordings. Box 5254, G.P.O. Sydney, N.S.W., Australia.

Period. (New York). Armenia, Borneo, Bali.

Riverside Records. (New York). West Africa, Congo, United States.

UNESCO Series. Anthology of the Orient — Laos, Cambodia, Afghanistan, Iran I & II.

Vogue. (Paris). Spain, Afghanistan.

Waterman, Richard A., and Lichtenwanger, William, and others, "Survey of Recordings of Asiatic Music in the United States, 1950–51." *Notes* 8 (1951).

Wattle Recordings (Sydney, Australia). New Guinea.

Westminster (New York). India, Spain, Bali, etc.

Index of First Lines

*To locate a song by title,
see table of contents in front of book.*

DATE